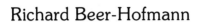

Richard Beer-Hofmann

Richard Beer-Hofmann
His Life and Work

Esther N. Elstun

The Pennsylvania State University Press
University Park and London

Library of Congress Cataloging in Publication Data

Elstun, Esther N.
Richard Beer-Hofmann, his life and work.

Includes bibliography and index.
1. Beer-Hofmann, Richard, 1866-1945. 2. Authors, Austrian—20th century—Biography.
I. Title. PT2603.E27Z63   838′.91209[B]   82-14990
ISBN 0-271-00335-9

Contents

Preface

The works of Richard Beer-Hofmann have received relatively scant attention from scholars, only three major studies having appeared over the years: the late Theodor Reik analyzed Beer-Hofmann's work on the basis of Freudian psychology in *Das Werk Richard Beer-Hofmanns* (1919); Sol Liptzin's book, *Richard Beer-Hofmann* (1936), examined the poet's work in the light of his *Lebensethos;* and Otto Oberholzer, in *Richard Beer-Hofmann* (1947), explored such specific aspects of Beer-Hofmann's work as its mythological symbolism.

The present volume is primarily a literary study, but it is not meant for specialists in German literature alone. The biographical first chapter, therefore, includes a brief summary of the historical situation in imperial, turn-of-the-century Austria. For detailed cultural, intellectual, and political histories of the period, readers are referred to several excellent works: William Johnston's *The Austrian Mind; Wittgenstein's Vienna* by Allen Janik and Stephen Toulmin; and Carl Schorske's *Fin-de-Siècle Vienna.*

My decision not to include a chapter on Beer-Hofmann's lyric poetry was a difficult one. In the end, these considerations prevailed: first, Beer-Hofmann wrote no more than two dozen poems in the course of his life, and certainly did not regard lyric poetry as his principal genre. Moreover, only a few of the poems exist in English translation, and I ruled out the possibility of translating the others, being convinced that Gottfried Benn was right to define lyric poetry as "das Unübersetzbare schlechthin" ["the absolutely untranslatable"]. At the same time, it seemed unthinkable to omit a discussion of the "Schlaflied für Mirjam" ["Lullaby for Miriam"], a poem probably known to more people than anything else Beer-Hofmann wrote. Accordingly, chapter 1 includes the text of the "Schlaflied" and an analysis of it.

The desire to write a Beer-Hofmann study not just for Germanists also influenced the system of quotations I decided to adopt. Quotations from Beer-Hofmann's works of fiction are given in the original German, with English translations. For the convenience of the reader, these immediately follow the original German in the text. All other material (including Beer-Hofmann's non-fiction) is quoted only in English translation. Unless otherwise indicated, all of the translations are mine. In translating passages from Beer-Hofmann's verse dramas, I did not attempt to reproduce such elusive elements as rhythm, metre, alliteration, assonance, etc. Stage directions are included only to the extent that they contribute significantly to the reader's understanding of the quoted lines. Nor was it possible to duplicate in translation the Viennese dialect and the Jewish-German dialect which occur in two quoted passages. The translations simply attempt to convey content as faithfully as possible, providing an aid to readers whose command of German is slight.

Unless otherwise indicated, all quotations from Beer-Hofmann's works are taken from *Gesammelte Werke* [*Collected Works*] (Frankfurt: S. Fischer Verlag, 1963; hereinafter referred to as *GW*). Most of the biographical data derives from *Daten* [*Dates*], an unpublished notebook Beer-Hofmann began keeping in 1911, in which he recorded his travels and other events important to him and his family. The notebook contains a page for each year, beginning with 1866, the year of Beer-Hofmann's birth. The original is in the Houghton Library of Harvard University with the rest of Beer-Hofmann's literary estate.

In both the research and the writing stages I received valuable advice and assistance from many colleagues and friends, and I am deeply grateful to all of them. Those who deserve the warmest thanks, however, are Helmut Kreuzer, who first stimulated my interest in the work of Richard Beer-Hofmann; Heinz W. Puppe, who guided my initial Beer-Hofmann studies at Rice University with unforgettable skill, tact, and good humor; Mirjam Beer-Hofmann Lens, for her extraordinary kindness and generosity in answering questions and placing unpublished material at my disposal; and Joseph P. Strelka, Harry Zohn, and Richard M. Sheirich, for their critical reading of the manuscript and valuable editorial suggestions.

I am also indebted to William H. Bond, Director of the Houghton Library, Harvard University, for permission to examine Beer-

Hofmann's literary estate and to quote from some of the material; Max Gruenewald, President of the Leo Baeck Institute (New York), for permission to examine and quote from the Institute's collection of Beer-Hofmann's family papers and personal correspondence; the late Helene Thimig-Reinhardt, for permission to quote from her and Max Reinhardt's correspondence with Beer-Hofmann; and Eloise Segal, former archivist of the American Academy of Arts and Letters, for her kind assistance.

   With much gratitude I also acknowledge the support of my own university. My research in Cambridge and New York was financed by a grant from the George Mason University Foundation, and publication was made possible by a subvention from combined sources within the university: the Department of Foreign Languages and Literatures (Martha Paley Francescato, Chair); the College of Arts and Sciences (F. Donald Eckelmann, Dean); and the Graduate School (Averett S. Tombes, Dean).

George Mason University
Fairfax, Virginia
May, 1982

1

The Life of
Richard Beer-Hofmann

Quantitatively, the literary production of Richard Beer-Hofmann was sparse indeed: two novellas (*Camelias* and *Das Kind*); a novel (*Der Tod Georgs*); a five-act play (*Der Graf von Charolais*); a pantomime (*Das goldene Pferd*); a cycle of Biblical dramas (*Die Historie von König David*), of which only *Jaákobs Traum, Der junge David*, and the "Vorspiel auf dem Theater zu *König David*" were completed before Beer-Hofmann's death; some twenty lyric poems, among them the well-known "Schlaflied für Mirjam"; a commemorative piece (*Gedenkrede auf Wolfgang Amadé Mozart*); and *Paula, ein Fragment*, a book of memoirs named for his wife. Still, as an arbiter of artistic taste and a friend, confidant, and advisor to others (especially Hugo von Hofmannsthal and Arthur Schnitzler), Beer-Hofmann was unquestionably the most influential member of that circle of Viennese writers known in world literature as "Young Vienna." A study of his early work suggests why that was so: *Der Tod Georgs* is probably the most representative *art nouveau* novel in the German language and, moreover, employs narrative techniques (most notably, stream-of-consciousness) that were still decidedly innovative at the turn of the century. Beer-Hofmann's influence upon his contemporaries and upon the literary tastes of his time also derived from his extraordinary efforts to revitalize the theatre and free it from what he regarded as the cul-de-sac of Naturalism.

Richard Beer-Hofmann was born into imperial Austria in the period of its decline. This decline was not readily apparent as early as the 1860's; on the contrary, the Habsburg monarchy—firmly and faithfully supported by the church, the aristocracy, the bureaucracy, and the military—seemed impervious to all threats.[1] Moreover, enlightened liberalism seemed to have triumphed. The liberals, who came to power in the 1860's, implemented some significant social, economic, and educational reforms, but did not seek to abolish the monarchy; indeed, they sometimes had occasion to be grateful for its protection. This was the case in 1895, for example, when "Emperor Francis Joseph, with the support of the Catholic hierarchy, refused to sanction the election of Karl Lueger, the anti-Semitic Catholic mayor [of Vienna]."[2] As Carl Schorske has shown, however, the triumph of liberalism was short-lived: under liberal leadership, constitutional government lasted no more than four decades (1860 to 1900).[3] By 1897 Francis Joseph, forced to bow to the will of the electorate, "ratified Lueger as mayor. The Christian Social demagogues began a decade of rule in Vienna which combined all that was anathema to classical liberalism: anti-Semitism, clericalism, and municipal socialism."[4] In the end, reason and civility were no match for the charismatic leadership and dema-goguery of the liberals' multi-faceted opposition (the proletarian Social-ists, the Pan-Germans, and the Christian Socialists, to say nothing of the various national or ethnic minorities of the Empire that were struggling for recognition and a measure of self-governance, if not outright independence). Nor were the losses limited to Vienna, for-merly a bastion of liberalism: "On the national level as well, the liberals were broken as a parliamentary political power by 1900, never to revive. They had been crushed by modern mass movements, Christian, anti-Semitic, socialist, and nationalist."[5]

It was, to use Frederic Morton's phrase, a time of "nervous splen-dor."[6] Only the most perceptive could see clear signs of decline and decay; for the most part, the nervous uneasiness that lay beneath the surface was dispelled (or papered over) by that peculiarly Austrian form of hedonism known as *Phäakentum* [phaeacianism], the "love of festivity, food, and leisure," and the "light-hearted enjoyment of the arts."[7] In this climate the *Ringstrasse* was constructed and splendid ceremonial displays abounded, as though monumental architecture and glittering pomp and pageantry could somehow restore wholeness and inner meaning to a social order that was in fact coming apart.

No one had more to lose from the defeat of liberalism than the Austrian Jews, who enjoyed a somewhat easier life than their counter-parts in other countries. They had received the right to vote and to own land in 1849,[8] and full emancipation by 1867. Some avenues, particularly in the fields of commerce and finance, had long been open to them, and there was an "increasingly prosperous stratum of Jews who, entering the modern entrepreneurial class, adopted German culture and the German language."[9] The foregoing must, of course, be understood in relative terms; the absence of aggressive persecution is not synonymous with full equality and acceptance. Some doors remained closed altogether, or were opened only by dint of great effort and perseverance.[10]

In any case, if Western Jews enjoyed a relatively easier life than the Jews of Eastern Europe and the Russias, it was largely because they seemed more willing to assimilate. In the older generation, assimilation had occurred primarily through "economic activity and religious secularization."[11] In Beer-Hofmann's generation, assimilation took a different form: the fathers, who now enjoyed a measure of economic well-being, were glad to finance their sons' university educations, which promised to provide increased social mobility and entry into the so-called higher professions. Many of these sons, however, did not feel drawn to the "respectable" professions at all, but rather to the arts. The fact that other fields offered only limited prospects for recognition and advancement may account in part for their desire to seek an outlet for their creative energies in art, but this explanation is not really sufficient. These young men were motivated just as strongly by their own aesthetic sensibilities. Reared in comfortable circumstances by genteel families, they were, in a sense, groomed for art. Some, whose talent did not match their aestheticism, had to settle for living artistically, but a striking number of them actually became practicing or performing artists, and it was they who influenced, indeed shaped, the arts and culture of the Empire around the turn of the century. It is not an exaggeration to say, for example, that without its Jewish members the literary circle known as "Young Vienna" would not have existed at all.

The difference in values between the generations seldom led to total alienation, but it certainly generated a good deal of tension within families: "The status that the fathers had purchased by their business labors meant little to the sons. . . . To the fathers, it seemed immoral that the sons should reject the values of the society in which they themselves had struggled to obtain an identity."[12] As we shall see, Beer-Hofmann's family felt this kind of concern about his own unwillingness to practice law.

As the nineteenth century neared its close, there were essentially three ways in which Austrian Jews reacted to the virulent anti-Semitism of the time. Most attempted to ignore it as the crude and ill-mannered behavior of the lower classes; a few, like Otto Weininger and his pupil, Arthur Trebitsch, became anti-Semites themselves; and others, like Theodor Herzl and Martin Buber, were galvanized by anti-Semitism to a strong commitment to Judaism and the Jewish heritage.[13] Though he never became a Zionist in the formal sense, Beer-Hofmann, in his own way, belongs to this third group.

The son of Hermann Beer, an affluent Viennese attorney, and his wife Rosa, Beer-Hofmann was born in Vienna on July 11, 1866. His mother died within a week of his birth and he was reared by an aunt and uncle, Berta and Alois Hofmann. (The couple legally adopted Beer-Hofmann in 1884, hence the hyphenated surname.) Beer-Hofmann's early childhood was spent in the Moravian city of Brünn (Brno), where Alois Hofmann owned a textile factory. In 1880 the family moved to Vienna, and there Beer-Hofmann completed his schooling at the Akademisches Gymnasium. He then studied law at the University of Vienna, receiving his law degree in 1890.

That year was a milestone in another respect that was to prove much more important to the future course of Beer-Hofmann's life: it marked the beginning of his lifelong friendship with Arthur Schnitzler. As Kurt Bergel has noted, "The friendship with Richard Beer-Hofmann was undoubtedly the warmest and least troubled in Schnitzler's life."[14] The friends saw each other often, especially in the early years when they undertook many hiking and cycling trips together; after 1910 they lived in close proximity in Vienna's "Cottage Quarter." "Der einsame Weg" ["The Lonely Path"], one of Beer-Hofmann's few lyric poems, is dedicated to Schnitzler,[15] and in his will Schnitzler named Beer-Hofmann as an advisor to his son Heinrich in matters pertaining to his literary estate. Bergel describes the two friends' relationship as "a mixture, characteristic for both men, of intimacy and genteel reserve,"[16] a description corroborated by Olga Schnitzler's book of reminiscences.[17]

When the two met, Schnitzler was twenty-nine, Beer-Hofmann twenty-four. The accounts of friends and acquaintances describe the Beer-Hofmann of this period as a dynamic, handsome, proud, indeed rather defiant son of refined and affluent origins, to whom the good things in life had always come easily; something of a dandy, famed in Viennese circles for the splendor of his dress; a young man of impeccable taste and refinement, whose judgment in artistic matters was not only highly respected, but even feared by some—and this before he himself had ever written, let alone published, a line.[18] Alfred Gold later referred to Beer-Hofmann as "the advisory conscience, the personified measuring stick" of young Viennese writers;[19] the young Hugo von Hofmannsthal, corresponding with Stefan George's secretary about the publication of "Der Tod des Tizian" ["The Death of Titian"] in the

Blätter für die Kunst [*Leaves for Art*], names Beer-Hofmann as one of four persons with whom he wishes to discuss the arrangements;[20] and in later years Hofmannsthal called Beer-Hofmann "the sternest and most incorruptible critic that I have."[21] According to those who knew him, Beer-Hofmann possessed great personal charm and made friends very easily. This evidently continued to be the case throughout his lifetime; Erich Kahler notes that "he was surrounded by friends wherever he went, and even in exile they prepared his way without any effort on his own part."[22]

In the fall of 1890, and largely through his friendship with Schnitzler, Beer-Hofmann rapidly became known in literary circles, though he had not yet begun to write. In a letter written in the spring of 1891, Schnitzler urged him to do so, outlining an idea he had had for a jointly edited anthology. He hoped that Beer-Hofmann would contribute: "You will very soon have to write something; that is certain. I have broached the idea of editing a book together. Title: From the Coffeehouse Corner. A collection of sketches, novellettes, impressions, aphorisms— each contributor to be as individual as possible. . . . I shall talk further with you about this; you have much to do with it, according to my idea. It's interesting how some, when your name was mentioned, said with a certain melancholy: 'Yes, if one could only get something from him—!' Indeed, the poetry in you has to be accepted on faith. I call your attention especially to this comment."[23] In response to Schnitzler's urgings, Beer-Hofmann did set to work, and by December, 1891 had finished his first story, *Camelias*. Schnitzler called it "for a start, a surprisingly good, utterly witty, stylistically brilliant sketch . . ."[24] Hofmannsthal, whom Beer-Hofmann had also met by this time, spoke of it as a study in "Maupassant-psychology."[25]

In 1891 Beer-Hofmann also met the volatile Hermann Bahr. Bahr's influence upon the young Viennese writers of the *fin-de-siècle* has been greatly exaggerated; indeed, he himself perpetuated many of the existing misconceptions.[26] Contrary to the impression Bahr fostered, a literary "school" did not exist. Olga Schnitzler reports a conversation with the elderly Beer-Hofmann in which he said: "One asks me here [in the United States] again and again about the nature of the Viennese School. . . . I know nothing of a Viennese School, I only know of several persons whom I liked, who interested me, and so what they produced interested me, too. There was no talk of a 'school.' "[27] An influential and widely known figure of the day, Bahr certainly must be credited with publicizing the works of young Viennese writers and thereby helping to establish their literary reputations. He saw them frequently (Vienna's Cafe Griensteidl was a favorite meeting place of the group, which, in addition to Beer-Hofmann, Schnitzler, and Hofmannsthal, included Jakob Wassermann, Felix Salten [Siegmund Salzmann], Peter Altenberg [Richard Engländer], and on the periphery, Paul Goldmann and Alfred Kerr), and continued his association with them in later years.[28] As far as Bahr's literary influence upon them is concerned, however, Rainer Maria Rilke's unflattering appraisal comes closer to the truth:

> Hermann Bahr . . . is only a kind of echo of the young Viennese [writers]. Like a shadow he repeats their essence in broader, darker dimensions and enlarges and coarsens the light and delicate movements of these refined aesthetes. . . . He does not know much at all about their art, but for much in it that is unspoken and nameless he invents a smooth, glittering name and hurls that at the gaping crowd. In doing so he considers himself the giver, and often goes so far as to play this role toward those whose sounding instrument he became. That confuses the public; people then often behave like children, who take the coachman in gold braid for the king, because behind his false splendor they do not even notice the pale, earnest man in the carriage.[29]

The affinity between Beer-Hofmann and the young Hofmannsthal, by contrast, soon led to a close friendship. In a letter to his brother-in-law, the painter Hans Schlesinger, Hofmannsthal says of Beer-Hofmann: "He is the one person in whose company I find the strongest and most certain joy . . ." (July 22, 1900, *Briefe 1890–1901*, p. 312). Three years earlier Hofmannsthal had acknowledged Beer-Hofmann's profound influence upon him in a letter dated September 5, 1897: "I shall never be in a position nor ever require myself to withdraw from the fabric of my being the threads that are your gift: the whole cloth would fall apart. I know exactly that there is no other person to whom I owe so much as I do to you; it has happened quite unpretentiously in the hundreds of talks we have had with each other in these five years."[30] Hofmannsthal clearly felt that the friendship meant more to him than to Beer-Hofmann, for in the same letter he says: "My dear Richard, you are so much more mature and complete than I and have so much more goodness and insight into what is right, that I know very well my friendship for you cannot have the value yours has for me, but only a much lesser one."[31] Although Hofmannsthal undoubtedly underestimates his own value to Beer-Hofmann here, the latter was indeed the more self-sufficient of the two and less in need of constant communication with his friends. Nevertheless, the two were together frequently, especially in the early years, often meeting in Beer-Hofmann's private apartment in the family home on the *Wollzeile* to discuss literary topics and to read aloud from their works-in-progress.

Having finished *Camelias*, Beer-Hofmann set to work on a four-act pantomime, *Pierrot Hypnotiseur*. Though never published, it remains as proof that his lively and abiding interest in everything theatrical dated from this early period. Further evidence is provided by the prologue to Hofmannsthal's early drama, *Der Tor und der Tod* [*The Fool and Death*], in which he depicts his friendship with Beer-Hofmann, Schnitzler, and Felix Salten. The central fact related about Beer-Hofmann ("Galeotto") is his passion for the theatre, and the prologue also refers by name to the principal characters in Beer-Hofmann's pantomime.[32]

By July, 1893 Beer-Hofmann had completed a second, considerably longer story, *Das Kind*. Together with *Camelias,* it was published in 1893 by Freund & Jaeckel (Berlin) under the title *Novellen*. The book was very well received and a second printing appeared in 1894.

After 1890, when Beer-Hofmann had received his law degree, tension mounted between him and his family because of his unwillingness to practice the "respectable" profession of law. The family clearly expected him to join Hermann Beer's Viennese law firm; this is explicitly stated in a letter that Alois Hofmann wrote to him on July 21, 1890: "I want you to remain in P[örtschach] no longer than the end of August and begin your practice in Papa Hermann's office on Sept. 1. Borrow money from *no one* in order to extend your stay there; 3½ months of vacation are more than enough!"[33] A later letter from Hofmann (undated, but written in 1894) reflects the foster-father's mounting concern, as well as his deep reservations about Beer-Hofmann's efforts to become a writer: "If someone wantonly squanders his fortune . . . then he must either be counting on a new fortune or thinking of suicide. Are the reddest neckties and the most Chinese embroideries of all worth a suicide? And in which of the above two alternatives does the healthier logic lie? That is just what irritates me: that your way of life and behavior are unhealthy. With such views, how do you intend to provide descriptions of man and nature that are *not* unhealthy?"[34] The matter reached a climax, in Beer-Hofmann's mind at least, in December, 1895. He recalls this period in *Paula, ein Fragment*:

Am Morgen, nach schlafloser Nacht, Entschluss, mir den 31. Dezember als letzten Termin zu setzen, bis zu dem ich Papa gesagt haben muss, dass ich es nicht ertrage, das Leben so weiter zu führen, wie bis jetzt. Ich muss für ein bis zwei Jahre fort von zu Haus, um die Welt reisen, in ganz fremde Länder, unter ganz fremde Menschen—und wenn ich dann zurückkomme, erfüllt von dem, was ich gesehen, und wenn dann doch in mir ein starker nicht niederzuhaltender Trieb ist, es zu tun, dann erst wieder versuchen zu schreiben. (*GW*, 748)

[In the morning, after a sleepless night, the decision to make December 31 my final deadline for telling Papa that I cannot bear to continue living as up to now. I must leave home for a year or two, travel about the world in entirely strange countries, among entirely strange people—and when I return, filled with what I have seen, and if there is still in me a strong, irrepressible urge to do so, only then try again to write.]

As the last lines indicate, Beer-Hofmann had considerable doubt of his own about his future as a writer, and he was not at all certain that he could pursue a literary career. One must keep in mind, of course, that these lines were written almost fifty years after the period to which they refer; but some of Schnitzler's and Hofmannsthal's early letters confirm that Beer-Hofmann was very nervous and depressed and that his work was not progressing well.[35]

The two friends believed that Beer-Hofmann's difficulties stemmed from a lack of self-discipline, a failure to apply himself steadily and regularly to his writing. In a letter of July 20, 1894 Hofmannsthal urges Beer-Hofmann in the strongest terms to force himself to work (*Briefe 1890–1901*, p. 109).[36] Writing to the Danish critic, Georg Brandes, Schnitzler says of their mutual friend, "To be sure, he is enormously lazy" (*Brandes–Schnitzler Briefwechsel*, p. 72).[37] This was also Alois Hofmann's view of the problem. He wrote to Beer-Hofmann on January 20, 1896: "If I often offended you by my speeches and letters, it happened only in the good intention to move you by drastic measures to an orderly way of life and to greater activity. . . ."[38]

The problem, however, was more than one of laziness or a lack of orderly habits. Beer-Hofmann felt called to be a writer (indeed, he later spoke of himself as "a born poet"[39]), but periodically he was also tormented by profound self-doubt and inner anguish.[40] It has been suggested that he experienced in himself "the fateful effects of decadence. . . . The external freedom [from financial worries] was counteracted to an unusual degree by an at times total incapacity, a paralysis that grasped deeply into the nature of this poet."[41]

The problem was intensified by Beer-Hofmann's uncompromising concept of the word, which frequently caused him agonizing dissatisfaction with his own efforts. His obsession with polishing and refining each work to absolute perfection, a trait which Schnitzler called his "perfectomania," has been widely noted. Most critics mention it with varying degrees of praise; Karl Kraus speaks of it with biting sarcasm in "Die demolirte Literatur."[42] Throughout his life, moreover, Beer-Hofmann had an ambivalent attitude toward the poet, regarding him on the one hand as among the elect and uniquely blessed, and on the other as a deceiver, almost in the criminal sense. In the mid–1890's he was already torn by these mixed feelings: "When I was writing my first work, I suddenly remained stuck in the middle. Like [Hofmannsthal's] Lord Chandos. I kept having to ask myself: 'Who will ever believe anything I say, if I excite myself here in words with imaginary situations?' . . . Then the other side occurred to me: 'But how wonderful that really is!' These are the two extremes. To pass between them was always like a sword dance for me."[43] In 1944 Beer-Hofmann expressed the same ambivalence in even stronger terms in a conversation with Werner Vordtriede:

> BEER-HOFMANN: The poet always comes close to committing an outrage. . . . And the greater a poet is, the more deeply he is affected by his own invention, and therefore also the more outrageous. . . . The poet is for the most part an actor.
> VORDTRIEDE: But there is nevertheless a great difference between the two. . . . When the poet invents something, then it is no longer just invented, but exists and becomes real.
> BEER-HOFMANN: Yes, while he is inventing it. But in the moment in which he forms it, the outrage is added. That's where it lies, in the forming.

Later in the conversation, Beer-Hofmann expressed his conviction that the poet is relieved of his guilt and that his activity is justified only by two things: ". . . first because he must [create] and cannot do otherwise . . . and then because he helps others by providing them with beauty. . . . But only in these two respects is he innocent. Not in anything else. His creation is not from God, but rather the other, that comes from the Devil."[44]

All of these factors had an inhibiting effect upon Beer-Hofmann and accounted for the sparseness of his literary production. The intention to stop writing, however, and to leave Vienna and travel widely for a year or more was never carried out, for on the same day that Beer-Hofmann reached that decision (December 5, 1895), he also met Paula Lissy for the first time. The encounter completely altered his plans and, indeed, the future course of his life.

Paula Lissy was of Italian and Alsatian Catholic extraction. (She converted to Judaism after her marriage to Beer-Hofmann.) When Beer-Hofmann first saw her, she was working as a clerk in a Viennese confectioner's shop.[45] Paula's mother had died a short time before, leaving the girl in the care of two older brothers. Beer-Hofmann was twenty-nine years old; Paula, a sixteen-year-old of delicate health. Their love for each other was by all accounts remarkable, indeed legendary. Though Beer-Hofmann's own description of the moment when he first saw Paula was written fifty years after the event, it nevertheless conveys the overwhelming sense of destiny he felt: ". . . Vorher war alles ein wirr verschlungener Knäuel, den ich nicht verstand—wo war der Sinn? Von Tag zu Tag hatte ich gelebt—nun war alles sinnvoll der Weg gewesen zu diesem Augenblick" (*Paula, ein Fragment, GW*, 766–67). ["Everything before was a chaotically tangled skein—where was its meaning? I had lived from day to day—now it all made sense as the path to this moment."]

The ensuing months of courtship, described with moving tenderness in *Paula*, included a trip in the late spring of 1896 to Fürberg on the Lake of St. Wolfgang, and that summer a trip to Scandinavia. Schnitzler and Paul Goldmann joined Beer-Hofmann and Paula there for excursions to Skodsborg, Copenhagen, and the Isle of Hveen.[46]

Paula's brothers strongly objected to Beer-Hofmann as a suitable husband for her, but she surprised them with a stubborn independence they had not known she possessed. The young couple spent the summer of 1897 in Bad Ischl, near Salzburg. Paula was pregnant with their first child, Mirjam. Two weeks after her birth in September, 1897, Beer-Hofmann wrote the "Schlaflied für Mirjam." First printed in the *art nouveau* journal, *Pan*, in 1898, the poem was widely acclaimed for its lyrical beauty.[47] Rilke expressed his profound admiration for the "Schlaflied" in a letter of April 25, 1922 to Ilse Blumenthal-Weiss, recalling that when he lived in Sweden, people from neighboring estates would send a carriage for him, the way one fetches a doctor, "so that I might recite the verses to people who were otherwise strangers to me, and who had heard of the extraordinary beauty of this poem."[48] The "Schlaflied" richly deserves the fame it achieved (a fame that has not diminished with time):

> Schlaf mein Kind—schlaf, es ist spät!
> Sieh wie die Sonne zur Ruhe dort geht,
> Hinter den Bergen stirbt sie im Rot.
> Du—du weisst nichts von Sonne und Tod,
> Wendest die Augen zum Licht und zum Schein—
> Schlaf, es sind soviel Sonnen noch dein,
> Schlaf mein Kind—mein Kind, schlaf ein!
>
> Schlaf mein Kind—der Abendwind weht.
> Weiss man, woher er kommt, wohin er geht?

Dunkel, verborgen die Wege hier sind,
Dir, und auch mir, und uns allen, mein Kind!
Blinde—so gehn wir und gehen allein,
Keiner kann Keinem Gefährte hier sein—
Schlaf mein Kind—mein Kind, schlaf ein!

Schlaf mein Kind und horch nicht auf mich!
Sinn hats für mich nur, und Schall ists für dich.
Schall nur, wie Windeswehn, Wassergerinn,
Worte—vielleicht eines Lebens Gewinn!
W a s ich gewonnen gräbt m i t mir man ein,
Keiner kann Keinem ein Erbe hier sein—
Schlaf mein Kind—mein Kind, schlaf ein!

Schläfst du, Mirjam?—Mirjam, mein Kind,
Ufer nur sind wir, und tief in uns rinnt
Blut von Gewesenen—zu Kommenden rollts,
Blut unsrer Väter, voll Unruh und Stolz.
I n uns sind A l l e. Wer fühlt sich allein?
Du bist ihr Leben—ihr Leben ist dein—
Mirjam, mein Leben, mein Kind—schlaf ein!   (*GW,* 654)

[Sleep, my child, it's late, go to rest.
Look how the sun sets in the west,
Over the mountains its last dying breath.
You—you know nothing of sun and of death,
Turning your eyes to light and to shine—
Sleep, so many more suns are thine.
Sleep, my child—my child, go to sleep.

Sleep, my child, the evening wind blows.
Nobody knows whence it comes, where it goes.
Dark and hidden the ways are here
For you, and for me—and for all of us, dear!
Blindly we wander and wander alone,
No companion for you—or for me here below.
Sleep, my child—my child, go to sleep.

Sleep, my child, and don't listen to me,
Meaning for me is but sounds for thee,
Sounds like the wind, like the falling of rain,
Words—but maybe a lifetime's gain.
All that I've reaped will be buried *with* me,
None can to none an heir here be.
Sleep, my child—my child, go to sleep.

Mirjam—my child, are you asleep?
We are but shores, and blood in us deep

Flows from those passed to those yet to be,
Blood of our Fathers, restless and proud.
All are within us, who feels alone?
You are their life—their life is your own.
Mirjam, my life, my child—go to sleep.][49]

The title of this remarkable poem invites, indeed encourages, us to make certain assumptions. It leads us to feel well-oriented, to assume that we know at least the nature of the text that will follow. (Before defining an elegy or an eclogue, we might need to consult a reference work, but a lullabye? *Everybody* knows what *that* is . . .) The first two, quite conventional lines of the poem foster our initial assumptions. The third and fourth lines, with their unexpected references to death, are then all the more disquieting. Our sense of assurance gives way to uncertainty.

With the second strophe, uncertainty is superseded by something approaching dismay. It, too, begins with a conventional lullabye line, but it is followed immediately by a question that suggests the mysterious, unfathomable workings of nature, which "remains mute to all of our questions," as Beer-Hofmann had said several years earlier in the novella, *Das Kind*. The lines that follow are not rhetorical questions, but statements about life and the human condition: first, the melancholy observation that we travel through life blindly, and then, the poet's devastating acknowledgment of the ultimate loneliness and isolation of the individual: "Keiner kann Keinem Gefährte hier sein." The conventional last line of the strophe returns us to familiar lullabye terrain, but it does not console us; the impact of the preceding lines is too powerful to be dispelled.

The third strophe—should we have any lingering doubts—confirms that this is not a lullabye in the traditional manner. Extending the themes introduced in the second strophe, the poet focuses here on the transitoriness and the finality of individual human existence, with the penultimate line ("Keiner kann Keinem ein Erbe hier sein") serving as the most pronounced link between the two strophes. Only in retrospect, i.e., only after reading the rest of the poem, do we recognize that the first line of the third strophe (". . . und horch nicht auf mich!") is perhaps a signal that a turning point is in the offing.

Beer-Hofmann leads us in a particular direction, intensifying the effect of his somber message from one strophe to the next. The turning point appears in the last strophe, which expresses his answer to death and the transitoriness of life. It must be emphasized that this final strophe does not repudiate or rescind the conclusions expressed in the preceding verses; it is an affirmation of life *in spite of* those conclusions. Like the poet himself, however, we are comforted by the concept of continuity (as perhaps the only sure form of immortality) that emerges in these closing lines. Beer-Hofmann's further development of this concept will be examined in subsequent chapters.

The transitoriness of life and the loneliness of the individual as dominant elements of the human condition unquestionably constitute a major theme of the "Schlaflied." The poem, however, has an unnamed but unmistakable second theme, which runs like a central thread through the entire work: the father's love for his child. The theme is sounded in the opening and closing lines of every strophe—particularly through the repetition of the words, "mein Kind, mein Kind"—and in the final verse through the tender repetition of the child's name. Largely because of this second theme, the "Schlaflied" is widely regarded as a quintessentially Jewish poem.[50] It is undoubtedly an expression of the traditionally strong bond between Jewish parents and their children; in the final analysis, however, the theme is a universal one.

Admirers of the "Schlaflied" usually emphasize its extraordinary lyrical beauty, and they are right to do so, but the poem's masterful construction is sometimes neglected in the process. An analysis of that construction reveals flawless symmetry and perfect correspondence between content and form. In each of the poem's four stanzas, the poet's somber (but ultimately affirmative) reflections on the nature of life are framed by the opening and closing lullabye lines; this structure produces an alternation of the themes discussed above, with a final focus on the theme of parental love. The trochaic metre corresponds to and enhances the contemplative content of the poem throughout; in nearly all of the lullabye lines, the trochees are intensified by caesuras. The regularity of the stanzas (each consists of seven lines) and of the unvarying rhyme scheme (aa, bb, ccc) likewise contributes to the graceful symmetry of the whole. The poem's lyrical beauty derives from its musicality. Every lullabye is meant to be sung; though the "Schlaflied" has not, to my knowledge, been set to music, it is eminently "singable." Its musicality lies in its rhyme and rhythm, of course, and in the lulling quality of its vowel sounds, but also in the poet's marked use of alliteration: the k-sounds in the important penultimate lines that link the second and third stanzas, but especially the alliterative s-, sh-, and w-sounds to be found throughout the poem.

In writing the "Schlaflied," Beer-Hofmann does not seem to have been plagued by the problems that affected so much of his literary production and account for its sparseness; the poem was cast "as a whole" from the beginning, and did not undergo the extensive, painstaking revision otherwise so characteristic of Beer-Hofmann. Work on *Der Tod Georgs*, however (begun in 1893, soon after the completion of *Das Kind*), continued only fitfully. Despite the happiness he had found with Paula, Beer-Hofmann was still beset by nervousness and periods of moodiness and depression, during which he found writing impossible. Better progress was made on the novel in 1898. Beer-Hofmann was already considering a Biblical work at this time, too; the earliest notes on *Die Historie von König David* are dated 1898. That year Beer-Hofmann also wrote the poem, "Strom vom Berge" ["Stream From the Mountains"], and the "Prolog-Entwurf zu einer 'Ariadne auf Kreta' " ["Draft-Prologue for 'Ariadne in Crete"].[51]

On May 14, 1898 Beer-Hofmann and Paula were married in a Jewish ceremony in Vienna, with Arthur Schnitzler and Leo Van Jung serving as witnesses.[52] The Beer-Hofmanns' second daughter, Naemah, was born on December 20 of that year.

Der Tod Georgs was finished in 1899, but only by dint of the greatest self-discipline. Schnitzler's and Hofmannsthal's letters to each other reflect profound concern for their friend's mental and emotional state during much of this period.[53] This points up a rather paradoxical fact about existing descriptions of Beer-Hofmann's personality and temperament. Much of the material already quoted and discussed here indicates that he often suffered deep depression, moodiness, and agonizing self-doubt; yet many who knew him well name happiness, serenity, and self-assurance as his most striking characteristics. Thus Alfred Kerr wrote: "I learned to know Beer-Hofmann as a person from whom something charmingly joyous emanated."[54] Hermann Bahr remembers him as "warm and kind,"[55] and Erich Kahler recalls: "Happiness emanated from him, the blessing of happiness and the security in himself that happiness bestows."[56] Thomas Mann is said to have remarked about him: "He has the radiance and cleverness and strength of King Solomon; his whole nature is related to him."[57] Olga Schnitzler reports, however, that "he was not so serene as Kerr saw him. This . . . posture, as genuine as it was, gave no hint of the events beyond and behind it. For long periods he was overshadowed by existential sadness, burdened by the sense of his mission, which he sometimes felt as a 'slavery' that he tried again and again to evade, whenever doubt overcame him. . . . "[58] In Beer-Hofmann's early adulthood, these two sides of his nature—the joyous serenity that derived from his strong sense of *Auserwähltsein* [election, i.e., being one of the chosen, in the Biblical sense] and the despair of profound and recurring self-doubt—clearly asserted themselves with equal force. In time he overcame the dark side of his nature, or at least subdued it; and this was undoubtedly the result of his growing appreciation of and identification with his Jewish heritage.

After the completion of *Der Tod Georgs*, Beer-Hofmann's spirits improved visibly. In August, 1899 he joined Schnitzler and Jakob Wassermann on a hiking trip in the Dolomites, and spent most of September with Hofmannsthal in Vahren. Hofmannsthal's letter of October 2, 1899 to Schnitzler indicates that during this period Beer-Hofmann had already set to work on his five-act drama, *Der Graf von Charolais* (*Hofmannsthal–Schnitzler Briefwechsel*, p. 132).

Der Tod Georgs was published by S. Fischer in 1900. The Beer-Hofmanns spent the spring of that year on the Italian Riviera. Despite the change of scene, Beer-Hofmann was again unable to overcome the moodiness and depression that assailed him so frequently in these early years. On April 2, 1900 Hofmannsthal wrote to him from Paris:

> I am preoccupied by the fact that you have not been working again, and that the mean and so dangerous sense of irritation, of an inner lack of freedom stemming from petty causes, continues to occupy such a place in your life. After all that I've said, and even more, according to all that I feel, it is strange and almost stupid to give you advice. But I really believe I am right: you are too fearful of the idea of decisive changes. . . . It is both painful and contrary to reason that you cannot find the necessary inner harmony for the continuation of your work on a trip to Italy in the company of persons like your wife and child. You must reach the point of working *from* your mood, not after it has faded. There is a deep danger in the disintegration of unrealized fantasies. (*Hofmannsthal/ Beer-Hofmann Briefwechsel*, pp. 98–99)

Late July and early August were spent in Salzburg with Hofmannsthal, and during part of the period, the latter's parents, wife, and brother-in-law, Hans Schlesinger. On August 14 Beer-Hofmann set out with Arthur Schnitzler and Leo Van Jung on a trip to the Tyrol. They were joined by Paul Goldmann and Alfred Kerr in Innsbruck, continuing from there to Bludenz, Schlappinajoch, Chur, and Pontresina.[59]

The Beer-Hofmanns' third child and only son, Gabriel, was born in 1901. That fall Beer-Hofmann made plans to move with his family to Rodaun, but at the last moment some difficulties arose. Hofmannsthal was in Varese at the time; his letter of October 10 to Beer-Hofmann indicates how happy he had been at the prospect of having his friend as a neighbor, and how distressed he now was by the news that the impending move might not take place after all:

> I hear from Papa that some difficulties have arisen in the contract settlement with your landlord, and so I am suddenly startled out of my pleasant sense of security in this matter. I cannot tell you how dreadful it would be for me, if this now came to naught. For I know full well . . . that it is a turning-point in our relationship: for years I have always had the feeling that we are not together enough, that our exchange of thoughts and feelings lacks continuity, and that it lacks only this, in order to be sufficiently beneficial and in a certain sense nourishing to both of us. . . . But I still am not completely without hope. Please do not be hot-tempered and obstinate during the negotiations, don't *throw* it away. I am hastening my trip and will be in Rodaun on Monday morning. (*Hofmannsthal/Beer-Hofmann Briefwechsel*, pp. 112–13)

Exactly what sort of difficulties had arisen is not clear, but they were surmounted and the Beer-Hofmanns moved to Rodaun. What Hofmannsthal had anticipated did indeed become the case: as neighbors, the two friends enjoyed a closer association than ever, with more frequent opportunities for working together and exchanging ideas and suggestions. Many years later Beer-Hofmann recalled an amusing detail in his reminiscences of this period, telling how he and Hofmannsthal, reluctant to end a conversation, kept walking each other home until far into the night.[60]

Rudolf Kassner, whose friendship with Hofmannsthal began in 1902, has provided some interesting impressions of Beer-Hofmann during the years he and his family lived in Rodaun:

> I usually went to Rodaun for tea and stayed through supper, for which Beer-Hofmann often appeared with his wife. "Are the bears coming?" Hofmannsthal always asked before he withdrew for an hour before supper. Compared to Hofmannsthal, Beer-Hofmann possessed a lesser knowledge . . . but what he knew, he knew exactly and understood through and through, not only where the theatre was concerned, but also persons of his acquaintance. For him the sense of life lay in his Jewishness, in his wife and in the theatre . . . in stage scenery, in the costume for a role. For a whole year he ran about with ideas for a production and staging of "Macbeth," and attempted to make plausible to everyone willing to follow him, where the ruby brooch should best be placed on Lady Macbeth's white robe. . . . [61]

According to *Daten*, Beer-Hofmann suffered appendicitis in early 1902, but recovered without having to undergo surgery. Returning to Vienna in July from a trip to Bozen and Seis, he learned of the critical illness of his natural father, Hermann Beer. The doctors gave no hope of his recovery, and he died on October 3. Though the two were not particularly close, his father's death no doubt contributed to Beer-Hofmann's depression during this period. A letter from Hofmannsthal urges him to overcome "the terrible, futile net in which a merely internal hypochondrial tendency entangles you" (*Hofmannsthal/Beer-Hofmann Briefwechsel*, p. 115). It is unlikely that Hofmannsthal uses the word "hypochondrial" here as it is usually applied today. He is probably instead referring to a more general mental and spiritual depression, an acute nervous sensibility that afflicted Beer-Hofmann and many of his contemporaries, and which is commonly named as one of the symptoms of *fin-de-siècle* decadence. Several of Alois Hofmann's letters corroborate this assumption. On July 14, 1896, for example, he wrote to Beer-Hofmann: "Despite the assurances of love which were very pleasing to me, your long letter alarmed more than pleased me; for what it does not want to be and should not be, it nevertheless is, in its entire content: an expression of unhealthy *Weltschmerz*."[62] It is clear that Beer-Hofmann suffered profoundly and often from such depression in his young years, but he did not succumb to it. His suffering instead became a sort of crucible, from which a stronger, wiser man emerged; in this sense the early decadence represents not an end, but a beginning. As will be shown in subsequent chapters, suffering, particularly the artist's, was to become a dominant theme in Beer-Hofmann's mature works.

In the spring of 1903 Arthur Schnitzler wrote to Beer-Hofmann and Hofmannsthal, asking whether they believed he should attempt to publish the recently completed *Reigen*. Their reply is a humorous ("Dear Pornographer . . ."), jointly-written letter which, despite its levity, reveals a facet of Beer-Hofmann otherwise not often seen: that of the practical man of affairs with sound business instincts. After both friends have assured Schnitzler that he ought to publish the work, Beer-Hofmann urges him to be guided by three considerations: "Seriously: decide 1. the sum; 2. the publisher; 3. the appearance. 1.) very large; 2.) very serious . . . ; 3.) dignified, i.e., 'strong' paper—like your talent—simple format, preferably large, not pocketbook size or delicate" (*Hofmannsthal–Schnitzler Briefwechsel*, pp. 167–68).

The summer of 1903 found Beer-Hofmann on a cycling trip in the South Tyrol with Arthur Schnitzler. That year he also took Paula and the children to Italy. Recollections of their stay in Venice form part of *Paula, ein Fragment* (*GW*, 784–88).

The five-act play, *Der Graf von Charolais*, was completed in 1904. In May Beer-Hofmann travelled to Budapest to negotiate a contract with Max Reinhardt for the production of the play. The premiere took place on December 23 in Reinhardt's Neues Theater in Berlin, with Friedrich Kaysler as "Charolais"; Lucie Höflich as "Desirée"; Josef Klein as "Romont"; and Hans Wassmann as the "Innkeeper." Reinhardt himself played "Red Ike," which he later called one of his favorite character roles.[63] For the role of "Philipp," Beer-Hofmann hand-picked a young unknown who was to achieve world fame as a distinguished actor: Alexander Moissi.

Beer-Hofmann spent much of that fall in Berlin, attending the rehearsals and personally supervising many of the other preparations for the premiere. He had extremely firm ideas of how the play should be produced; indeed, all of Beer-Hofmann's dramatic works contain painstaking instructions for stage settings, costumes, gestures, tone of voice, etc. This period was a trying one for him—as it must also have been for the others involved: "He has nearly killed Höflich and Sorma already," Hofmannsthal wrote to Schnitzler on December 16.[64]

Beer-Hofmann had great personal regard for Max Reinhardt and the highest respect for his professional abilities, paying him the following tribute after many years of working closely with him in the theatre: ". . . the real poets owe him a great deal. For here they have . . . an administrator who is determined to carry out . . . the poet's . . . wishes from first to last, and to translate the poetic vision into stage vision so that not only none of the spiritual effect is lost, but gains a new and surprising illumination."[65]

Reinhardt's regard for Beer-Hofmann was equally high, and nowhere more warmly expressed than in a telegram he sent him from Brussels in 1910: "Sometimes I fear that you do not know how much I love you, how much I regard your arrival, your presence, as rich and quiet gifts in my unsettled life. . . ."[66] In later years, during Reinhardt's difficult divorce and subsequent marriage to the actress, Helene Thimig, Beer-Hofmann's staunch friendship was a great comfort to him, and when Beer-Hofmann's son Gabriel went to New York in 1926 to pursue a film career, Reinhardt did everything he could to help him.

In addition to completing *Charolais*, Beer-Hofmann wrote the poem, "Mit einem kleinen silbernen Spiegel" ["With a Little Silver Mirror"], in 1904. It is dedicated to the actress, Lucie Höflich. The earliest dated notes on *Davids Tod*, which was to be the last drama in the Biblical cycle, were also written that year.[67]

Der Graf von Charolais was published by S. Fischer in 1905. In May of that year Beer-Hofmann received the Schiller Prize for the drama, sharing the award with Gerhart and Carl Hauptmann. Although the manuscripts of the *Historie von König David* show that Beer-Hofmann had begun to think of writing a series of Biblical dramas as early as 1898, plans for the trilogy did not begin to take definite shape until

1905. His notes reveal that he then intended to entitle the plays *Scha-ül*, *David*, and *Salomon*. "Der einsame Weg," the poem dedicated to Arthur Schnitzler, was also written in 1905.

The 150th anniversary of Mozart's birth was celebrated in 1906, and Beer-Hofmann agreed to write a short commemorative piece for the festival year. Despite—or perhaps because of—his boundless admiration for Mozart's music, he found the assignment so difficult that he nearly reneged on his signed agreement within days of the date on which the piece was due. Appealing to his conscience, Paula urged him to keep his promise, and in the short time that remained he wrote the *Gedenkrede auf Wolfgang Amadé Mozart*.[68] More similar to fiction than to commemorative pieces in the traditional mode, it was published by S. Fischer in 1906.

"Chor der Engel" ["Choir of Angels"], later part of *Jaákobs Traum*, and "Maáchas Lied" ["Maacha's Song"] from *Der junge David* were also written in 1906, as was "Altern" ["Aging"]. This last poem was first printed in *Die Neue Rundschau* in January, 1907; an English translation of it by Naemah Beer-Hofmann appeared in the October, 1964 issue of the *Jewish Spectator*. The summer of 1907 brought the death of Alois Hofmann, Beer-Hofmann's father by adoption. Hofmannsthal expressed his sympathy in a compassionate letter written on July 15. The rest of the letter indicates that the author was deeply troubled by a growing rift between himself and Beer-Hofmann (*Hofmannsthal/Beer-Hofmann Briefwechsel*, p. 129). A letter Hofmannsthal wrote several weeks later to Felix Salten provides a clue to the cause of the breach: "You must not misunderstand, if in ever heartier and constant sympathy I always seem to jump from the person to the poet. But for me the poet is precisely the most personal, intrinsic thing about the person I love, and I am not able to separate the two—but I seem, with this same attitude, to have alienated so old and good a friend as Richard" (*Briefe 1900–1909*, p. 286). The relationship had obviously suffered a strain, but it did not lead to dissolution of the friendship, as Hofmannsthal's sad and resigned letter seems to suggest. There were, to be sure, fewer opportunities for long conversations and the direct exchange of ideas after Beer-Hofmann and his family moved (November, 1906) into the splendid new villa in Vienna's "Cottage Quarter" that he had commissioned the renowned *Jugendstil* architect, Josef Hoffmann, to build for him. Still, the bond between the two writers remained strong, literally to the day of Hofmannsthal's death: his last note to Beer-Hofmann was written that morning.

While living in Rodaun, Beer-Hofmann had met the young poet, Rudolf Borchardt, at Hofmannsthal's house. In the spring of 1908, when Borchardt and Beer-Hofmann were both in Berlin, Beer-Hofmann urged Max Reinhardt to offer to produce Borchardt's *LaSalle*. On March 18 Borchardt wrote to Hofmannsthal from Berlin: "I had a splendid half-day of the old phantasmagoria with Beer-Hofmann. Incidentally, at the mere news of my plays he forced my hand at once and mobilized Reinhardt; I have reached an agreement with Kahane [Reinhardt's producer] and will send two plays immediately."[69] One of Borchardt's *Jugendliche Gedichte* [*Youthful Poems*] is entitled "To Richard Beer-Hofmann"; it is both a highly lyrical description of the older writer and a tribute to him.[70]

In May, 1909 Beer-Hofmann began work on *Jaákobs Traum*. By this time he had expanded the *David* cycle from a trilogy to a pentalogy consisting of *Jaákobs Traum, Ruth und Boas, Der junge David, König David,* and *Davids Tod*. What had originally been planned as a drama about King Saul became *Der junge David* (and some critics still maintain that Saul is the real protagonist of the play); plans for a drama about King Solomon had evidently been abandoned. Beer-Hofmann later returned to his original conception of a trilogy, incorporating parts of *Ruth und Boas* into *Der junge David*. *Jaákobs Traum* became the dramatic prologue to the trilogy.

During the next few years, work on the *David* cycle was often interrupted by Beer-Hofmann's growing involvement in theatrical staging and production, and also by the frequent travel that was part of his and Paula's pleasant life style. Thus, the spring of 1910 was devoted to preparations for a Reinhardt production of *Der Graf von Charolais* in Vienna, and in May Beer-Hofmann and Paula took a trip through the South Tyrol. As in many previous years, most of the summer was spent in Bad Ischl, and in September Beer-Hofmann travelled to Munich for the Reinhardt festival plays. Other travels during these years included trips to Switzerland and to Italy. Venice and the Lido were favorite vacation spots, where Arthur and Olga Schnitzler, S. Fischer, Alexander Moissi, and other friends often joined the Beer-Hofmanns.[71]

Jaákobs Traum was finished in 1915. Though Beer-Hofmann had decided to make it the prologue of his trilogy, it is a complete drama in its own right and the only part of the *David* cycle to be performed. Olga Schnitzler recalls Paula's description of Beer-Hofmann's last period of work on *Jaákobs Traum*;[72] one gains the impression from this account that the words flowed from his pen with unaccustomed ease and none of the tortuous revision so characteristic of his work. Hofmannsthal later expressed strong reservations about what he called the drama's "chauvinistic aspect," its elements of "national pride," which—in the wake of World War I—he saw as "the root of all evil" (*Hofmannsthal/Beer-Hofmann Briefwechsel*, p. 145). His artistic reactions to *Jaákobs Traum*, recorded in his letter of June 18, 1918 to Rudolf Borchardt, are much more positive: "Beer-Hofmann read me his play. It is beautiful, very beautiful, the whole man is in it, worthy of love, more authentic than in any earlier work. It is a youthful work in a certain sense, but also a mature one; in a certain breath of post-Goethean spirituality it reminds one of Immermann. Lovely, that he could give this" (*Hofmannsthal–Borchardt Briefwechsel*, p. 137).

Though completed three years earlier, *Jaákobs Traum* was not published until 1918. Clearly, Beer-Hofmann's original intention had not been to publish it separately; in a foreword to the 1918 edition he wrote: " 'The History of King David' is the title of a cycle of three plays . . . that represent the life of David. 'Jacob's Dream'—the election of David's ancestor, Jacob—is intended as a prologue to them. I would have wished to leave 'Jacob's Dream,' which has been locked away since July, 1915, unpublished until the completion of my work. Events cause me to renounce my wish. So, then, is 'Jacob's Dream' relinquished to the public" (*GW*, 879). Exactly what led Beer-Hofmann to change his mind and publish the prologue separately is not entirely clear, but the "events" he mentions may well refer to the alarming rise of anti-Semitism in Europe at the time. One certainly gains that impression from two letters of Gustav Landauer's dating from this period. The first, written December 13, 1918, is to Beer-Hofmann himself: "Yes, events. I know. And I thank you for giving us human beings, us Jews, this work now. . . ."[73] The next day Landauer wrote to the director, Gustav Lindemann, advising him that, as producer of the Düsseldorf Schauspielhaus, he had already written to Beer-Hofmann, requesting permission to produce *Jaákobs Traum* there: "Deeply moved, enraptured by 'Jacob's Dream.' Beer-Hofmann has had it completed for years and has published it now, because it must speak to people. And nothing calls more for your direction than this work. . . . That would be wonderful in this land of collapse and rise, of 'hostile' occupation and renewal."[74] Georg Brandes clearly believed that Beer-Hofmann had been prompted by political events to publish *Jaákobs Traum*; on June 13, 1920 he wrote to Schnitzler: "I understand Beer-Hofmann's strange mystery play as his answer to the ever-increasing movement of hatred of the Jews in Europe."[75]

The Berlin premiere of *Jaákobs Traum*, under Reinhardt's direction, had been scheduled for the fall of 1918, but Beer-Hofmann insisted upon a postponement because of the chaotic political situation at the end of World War I. The play premiered instead at Vienna's Burgtheater on April 5, 1919, with Alfred Gerasch playing "Jacob" and Franz Höbling in the role of "Esau." In September of that year, Beer-Hofmann travelled to Berlin for rehearsals of the play, again directed by Reinhardt; the Berlin premiere was held on November 7 at the Deutsches Theater.[76] Conditions in Germany were still very unsettled; because of the disrupted train schedules and barriers at many points, it took Paula three days to reach Berlin from Vienna, as Beer-Hofmann noted in *Daten*.

Beer-Hofmann's attitude toward Judaism and his own Jewishness now needs to be examined more closely. Those who knew him well confirm that he had always felt an intense personal pride in his own forebears, as in his Jewish heritage and ancestry generally. After reading Theodor Herzl's *The Jewish State*, Beer-Hofmann wrote to him in February, 1896: "What appealed to me even more than anything in your book was what stood behind it. At last a person who does not bear his Jewishness resignedly, like a burden or a calamity, but on the contrary is proud to be the legitimate heir of an ancient culture."[77] Like Herzl, Beer-Hofmann regarded his Jewishness as anything but a burden or a personal catastrophe. At a time when many Jews felt obliged to seek assimilation, he acknowledged his Jewishness with pride. Rilke said of him: "To me Beer-Hofmann was always an example of the greatness and dignity of the fate of the Jews."[78] He gave his children Old Testament names. Werner Vordtriede relates a story that is also characteristic of Beer-Hofmann's humor: "Someone took offense at his wanting to give his daughter the name Mirjam.'Well, what should I call her then?' 'Why not [Elsa], for example?' 'Oh, no,' Beer-Hofmann replied, 'that's too Jewish for my taste!' "[79]

Whether Beer-Hofmann viewed his Jewishness primarily as a secular matter or one of religion is a more difficult question. Probably no categorical answer can be given that would apply with equal accuracy to the young author of *Der Tod Georgs* and the older poet of the *David* cycle. Beer-Hofmann seems rather to have undergone a gradual development. In the letter of 1896 to Theodor Herzl, he speaks of the Jews not in terms of religion, but as the legitimate heirs of an ancient, venerable culture. This is also the attitude and tone which prevail in *Der Tod Georgs*, completed in 1899. Still, we know that Beer-Hofmann was drawn as early as 1898 to the idea of writing a cycle of Biblical dramas, and it is doubtful that he was motivated even then by cultural and historical interest alone. Erich Kahler mentions the possibility that in the beginning it may have been "simply defiant bravado that moved him to concentrate on the Jewish destiny—the defiance of a proud man who wishes to acknowledge . . . an affiliation that in the social circles of that generation, Christian and Jewish alike, was passed over in embarrassed silence, where it was not entirely suppressed."[80] This seems to have been Georg Brandes's impression as late as 1922, when he wrote to Arthur Schnitzler: "Can you understand that our friend Beer-Hofmann attaches himself with such passion to Judaism? It strikes me as so *deliberate* on his part."[81] The fact that Beer-Hofmann placed a very large Star of David above the entrance to his villa in the "Cottage Quarter" might also be interpreted as a gesture of defiance. Whatever the initial motivation, his subsequent treatment of the problem of Jewish destiny—the covenant with God—has religious implications too strong to be ignored.[82]

Beer-Hofmann was always very sympathetic toward the Zionist movement, but literary historians who speak of him as a strong and active Zionist overstate the case.[83] Beer-Hofmann considered himself too completely a child of Europe and European culture ever to transplant himself elsewhere voluntarily. Olga Schnitzler recalls an amusing exchange between Theodor Herzl and Beer-Hofmann, in which Herzl, anxious to persuade his friend that the new state would be a thoroughly "European" Palestine, assured him: "We shall have a university and an opera and you will go to the opera in a tuxedo with a white gardenia in your lapel." Beer-Hofmann replied, "Oh, no! If it ever comes to that, then I'll want to appear in a silk caftan, bedecked with many necklaces and a turban with a clasp of brilliants!"[84] There is no evidence that Beer-Hofmann ever seriously considered emigration to Palestine. He sympathized with Zionism for the same reasons he admired Herzl's book: the movement represented the proud acknowledgment of a venerable legacy at a time when social and political circumstances led many Jews to regard that legacy as a burden.

In 1920 Beer-Hofmann wrote an introduction to Ariel Bension's book, *Die Hochzeit des Todes* [*The Wedding of Death*], published that year by the E.P. Tal-Verlag (Vienna). (The introduction, in the form of a letter to Dr. Bension, is included in "Aufsätze und Aphorismen," *GW*, 643–44.) At Max Reinhardt's urging, Beer-Hofmann in 1921 began to write the pantomime, *Das goldene Pferd*, thus returning to a genre that had interested him as early as 1892, when he wrote *Pierrot Hypnotiseur*. Parts of *Das goldene Pferd* appeared in the Sunday supplement of Vienna's *Neue Freie Presse* on October 12, 1930; the complete pantomime was first published in 1955 in *Die Neue Rundschau*, ten years after Beer-Hofmann's death.

During the 1920's, Beer-Hofmann's work on the *Historie von König David* was interrupted repeatedly by his increased involvement in theatrical production. In 1921 he received Austria's Nestroy Prize for his theatrical work, and in March, 1922 he went to Berlin to advise Karl Grune, who directed the filming of *Der Graf von Charolais* for the Stern Film Company. He returned to Berlin in November to work with Max Reinhardt on another theatrical production of *Charolais*; it had to be postponed, however, because of the serious illness of Alexander Moissi, who this time was to play the title role. The delayed production opened in May, 1923 at the Deutsches Theater, with a cast that included Moissi as "Charolais"; Maria Fein as "Desirée"; and Walter Janssen as "Philipp."

The following year Beer-Hofmann revised and staged a production of Sutton Vane's play, *Outward Bound* [*Überfahrt*]. It opened at Max Reinhardt's Theater in der Josefstadt in Vienna on November 14, 1924, with Helene Thimig in the starring role.[85] A letter she wrote to Beer-Hofmann on October 18 conveys the enthusiasm and admiration that she and the rest of the cast felt for him as a director: "The actors . . . are so captivated by the stimulating hours you give them. . . . My impression is also a beautiful one—and I think [the production] cannot go other than well. . . . With genuine bliss I observe how deftly you cause the merely sentimental to become lyrical, how unconventional rather conventional 'love scenes' can become—in short, how convincing and powerful everything is that you say."[86] The play was indeed a great success and received excellent reviews.

The Beer-Hofmanns' children were now grown and beginning to establish themselves. Their older daughter, Mirjam, had married in 1924, and their son Gabriel left in October of 1926 for New York to pursue a film career.[87] Later that year Beer-Hofmann attended a performance of *Jaákobs Traum* in Vienna by the visiting Jewish theatrical troupe, Habima. The play was performed in Hebrew, and Beer-Hofmann later described his reactions in an interview:

> During the performance . . . I at first sat there astonished and estranged, as I noticed how a ruthless and unhesitating, yet somehow gentle, almost loving hand attempted, according to its own innermost feeling, to re-shape my work. . . . I myself had the strange feeling of experiencing, while still alive, what otherwise is only the fate of the dead: that a work detaches itself, lives its own life, goes its own way, unconcerned about him who created it. . . . When in the third scene music set in . . . I too forgot that I was the creator of this play. What resounded with such singular strangeness from above, in a language I did not understand, but in music that seemed familiar to me from ages past, was, in its totality, well known indeed to me and my blood.[88]

In 1927 Beer-Hofmann resumed work on the *Historie von König David*. He also contributed to the book, *Moissi: Der Mensch und der*

Künstler in Worten und Bildern [*Moissi: The Man and the Artist in Words and Pictures*].[89] The spring of 1928 again found Beer-Hofmann directing a theatrical production, Goethe's *Iphigenie*, for Reinhardt's Theater in der Josefstadt, with Helene Thimig in the leading role. Later that year he staged performances of *Iphigenie* at the Salzburg *Festspiele*. He also wrote the "Chorus für 'Romeo und Julia,' " which was used in Reinhardt productions of the play in 1928. The poem "Der Dichter" ["The Poet"] was Beer-Hofmann's contribution to a *Festschrift zum 50. Geburtstag von Martin Buber* [*Festschrift for the Fiftieth Birthday of Martin Buber*] published in 1928.

One of the *Daten* entries for 1929 records the death of Hugo von Hofmannsthal and notes the receipt of a card from him, written on the morning of his death and ending simply, "One has to understand everything." Hofmannsthal's son Franz had committed suicide two days earlier.

In 1930 Beer-Hofmann staged Goethe's *Iphigenie* for Max Reinhardt's Berlin *Festspiele*. He and Paula spent most of the summer in Mariazell and Bad Gastein; Gabriel visited his parents in the fall when they came home to Vienna, and then returned to New York.

The year 1932 marked the centennial of Goethe's death, and on January 1 Beer-Hofmann gave a speech, "An der Schwelle des Goethe-Jahres" ["On the Threshold of the Goethe-Year"], over Radio-Vienna. As early as 1928 Beer-Hofmann had been approached by Anton Wildgans, director of the Burgtheater, about a production of Goethe's *Faust* during the centennial year. Beer-Hofmann had revised both parts of the play, so that the entire work could be performed in one evening. He directed rehearsals from December, 1931 to February, 1932, and on February 27 the Burgtheater presented his festival production of *Faust*, which was to remain part of the theatre's standard repertory until 1938. Beer-Hofmann also wrote a number of short prose pieces in 1932, among them "Form-Chaos," which later served as his contribution to the special issue of the *Neue Rundschau* in honor of Thomas Mann's seventieth birthday.[90]

Now working steadily on the *Historie von König David*, Beer-Hofmann completed the final draft of *Der junge David* in the early months of 1933. The second scene of the play, "Königszelt in Gibea" ["Royal Tent in Gibea"], appeared in *Corona* in 1933, and the entire drama was published later that year by S. Fischer. The *Daten* entries for 1933 include the terse notation: "Ill. At home. In bed from May to June (heart)." One cannot help but suspect a connection between this illness and the appearance in the press a week earlier (April 23, 1933) of the first "Black List of Literature," banning the works of forty-four German-language writers, among them Richard Beer-Hofmann.[91]

The *Daten* entries of 1934 include for the first time some reference to political events: "12–15 February, soc[ialist] Putsch in Vienna and Linz." The following entry notes the murder of Dollfuss on July 25. Since the *Daten* notebook recorded almost exclusively events of a personal or family nature, these entries are evidence of Beer-Hofmann's deepening concern about the political developments of the time.

By now he had finished the first scene of *König David*, the second drama in the Biblical trilogy, and it appeared in *Die Neue Rundschau* in 1934. Beer-Hofmann's friend and publisher, S. Fischer, died on October 15; the poem "Vom guten Hirten" ["The Good Shepherd"], which begins scene 1 of *König David*, is dedicated to his memory.

Beer-Hofmann completed the "Vorspiel auf dem Theater zu *König David*" in 1935. The prologue bridges the twenty-five year period between *Der junge David* and *König David*, the first and second plays in the cycle. Beer-Hofmann then began revising the last scene of *Davids Tod*.[92]

In February of 1935 he travelled to Berlin for a performance of *Jaákobs Traum* in the Jewish *Kulturbund*. The political situation was already fraught with ominous implications: proof of at least one "non-Aryan" grandparent was required of all those who wished to attend the performance.[93] In the fall of 1935 the Beer-Hofmanns journeyed to Switzerland, where Beer-Hofmann had lecture engagements in Lucerne and Zurich.

At the invitation of Zionist organizations, he and Paula embarked on a four-week trip to Palestine in the spring of 1936, visiting Haifa, Jerusalem, Tel-Aviv, and Caesarea. The summer was spent in Aussee, where Beer-Hofmann celebrated his seventieth birthday on July 11. Later that year the "Vorspiel auf dem Theater zu *König David*" was published by the Johannespresse (Vienna).

The last dated item among the manuscripts of the *Historie von König David* was written on April 4, 1937.[94] Beer-Hofmann and Paula spent much of the following summer in Maria Schutz am Semmering with his cousin, Antoinette Kahler, her son Erich, and Herbert Steiner, all of whom were to become benefactors in the difficult years ahead.

By the spring of 1938 the situation in Austria had become so dangerous that Beer-Hofmann and Paula left their villa in the "Cottage Quarter" and moved into rooms at the Pension Bettina in the Haardtgasse of Vienna. The move is recorded in *Daten*; the immediately preceding notation says simply: "March–Hitler." Paula suffered a very severe heart attack on November 30, was confined to the hospital until December 23, and then released only with a full-time nurse. Beer-Hofmann noted in *Daten* that the doctors had offered virtually no hope of her survival; he added, "The young physician, Dr. Aristid Kiss (from the heart ward) saved her." In the meantime, the other, uglier threat to their survival led Beer-Hofmann to change their place of residence again. He took rooms at the Pension Atlanta in the Währingerstrasse, and there he and Paula remained until arrangements were completed for their flight from Vienna the following year.

This period had to be one of terrible anxiety for Beer-Hofmann and Paula, plunged abruptly from a pleasant, well-ordered life into one of imminent flight. The following, very moving passage from *Paula, ein Fragment* suggests the extent to which their love sustained them:

> *Frühjahr 1939*—Wir fahren am späten Vormittag zurück. . . . Sie blickt zum St. Michael hinauf: "Die hebräischen Buchstaben haben sie vom Schild doch nicht heruntergenommen," und wie sie hinaufblickt, leuchtet die Sonne durch den silberweissen Strähnen an ihren Schläfen. Ich blicke auf die Uhr, und es ist Mittag, und mit einem Mal läuft es durch mich: wie wir zuerst hier um Mittag uns trafen, und St. Michael in Salzburg, und in Eppan, und bei dem Graveur in der Rotenturmstrasse, und das gestickte Bild von St. Michael, das sie mir an einem Geburtstag schenkte, und erschüttert denke ich, wie rasch unser Leben verfloss und ich sage—denn ich weiss, auch sie denkt daran—"zwölf Uhr schlug es, wie du kamst—weisst du noch?" und ich sehe zur Seite und sie nickt, streift den Handschuh von ihrer Rechten, und fasst nach meiner Hand, und dann hält sie meine Hand . . . und ich fühle, was für uns auch kommen mag, wenn wir auch in die Fremde müssen—solange meine Hand in ihrer ruhen darf, bin ich geborgen—nichts kann mir geschehen. Ich neige mich über ihre Hand, meine Lippen gleiten leise über ihre Finger und verschieben den honigfarben leuchtenden Bischofsring, der ihr ein wenig zu gross geworden ist. Sie fühlt es, und ihr Blick weist auf den Ring: "Damals als du ihn auf dem Markusplatz in Venedig kauftest, war er auch ein wenig zu gross . . . und du hast mich gefragt, ob ich den Ring auch manchmal tragen werde—und ich hab gesagt: Immer! Und du hast gesagt: 'versprich's nicht, sag nicht Immer—was weisst du denn, was nicht alles kommen kann—du bist ja noch so jung!' Jetzt bin ich nicht mehr jung—und immer hab ich ihn getragen, und dass alles, was gekommen ist, schön gewesen ist—das weisst du doch—mein Richard—nicht wahr?"—"Ja." (*GW*, 854–55)

[Spring 1939—We're returning in the late morning. . . . She glances up at St. Michael's: "They haven't removed the Hebrew letters from the sign after all," and as she looks up the sun gleams through the silver white strands at her temples. I glance at my watch, it's noon, and suddenly it courses through me: how we first met here at midday, and St. Michael's in Salzburg and in Eppan, and at the engraver's in the Rotenturmstrasse, and the embroidered picture of St. Michael she once gave me for my birthday, and deeply moved I think, how quickly our life has passed, and I say—for I know she is thinking of it, too—"it was striking twelve when you came—do you still remember?" and I look to the side and she nods, peels the glove from her right hand and reaches for mine, and then she holds my hand . . . and I sense that whatever may come for us, even if we must go into exile—as long as my hand may rest in hers I am safe—nothing can happen to me. I bend over her hand, my lips glide gently across her fingers, displacing the shining, honey-colored bishop's ring that has become a bit too large for her. She senses it, and her glance points to the ring: "When you bought it on St. Mark's Square in Venice it was also a bit too large . . . and you asked me whether I would sometimes wear the ring—and I said: always! And you said: 'don't promise, don't say always—how do you know what might yet come—you're still so young!' Now I'm no longer young—and I did wear it always, and everything that came was beautiful—you do know that—my Richard—don't you?"—"Yes."]

On the evening of August 19, 1939, thirteen days before the Nazi invasion of Poland and the outbreak of World War II, Beer-Hofmann and Paula left Vienna for the last time, en route to the United States via Switzerland. He was seventy-three years old; Paula, sixty. She was still convalescing from the heart attack she had suffered the preceding winter, and Dr. Aristid Kiss travelled with them. They were met at Buchs on the Swiss border by Sam Wachtell and Herbert Steiner, and by Bernhard Altman at the railway station in Zurich.

Paula's condition compelled them to proceed in slow stages; they were still in Zurich on September 7 when she suffered a complete collapse. After weeks in the hospital she seemed to rally; then her condition grew suddenly worse. She died on October 30 and was buried in the Friesenberg cemetery at Zurich on November 2. Unable to obtain permission to remain in Switzerland, Beer-Hofmann continued the journey alone, sailing from Genoa aboard the *Conte di Savoia* on November 14. His arrival in New York on the 23rd was followed by Mirjam's (from England) on the 24th. The two lived for the next year and a half in a flat on Waverly Place.

At the invitation of friends, Beer-Hofmann and Mirjam spent the summer of 1940 at Woodstock in the Adirondacks. In April of that year Beer-Hofmann had recorded two dreams about Paula; he continued to record such dreams at Woodstock, although he had not yet decided to compose a book about her. By the winter of 1940, however, Beer-Hofmann had finished "Herbstmorgen in Österreich" ["Autumn Morning in Austria"] and now resolved to form this and other fragments into a book of memoirs whose central theme would be Paula.

The lyric poetry Beer-Hofmann had written over the years was published in book form for the first time in 1941 by Bermann-Fischer (New York and Stockholm) under the title, *Verse*. In the spring of that year, Beer-Hofmann, Mirjam and her husband, Ernst Lens, and Naemah had moved into an apartment on Cathedral Parkway, overlooking Morningside Park and the Cathedral of St. John the Divine. This was to be Beer-Hofmann's home until he died. As in 1940, the summer of 1941 was spent at Antoinette Kahler's summer home in Woodstock.

The next years were devoted to the *Paula* volume. In 1944 the now seventy-eight-year-old writer gave a series of lectures—on March 22 at Harvard, on April 25 at Yale, in May at Columbia, and in October at Smith College. "Herbstmorgen in Österreich," one of the longest of the *Paula* fragments, was published that year as a separate piece by the Johannespresse (New York).

In February, 1945—not knowing how much time remained for him, but assuming that *Paula* in its entirety would be published only posthumously—Beer-Hofmann wrote detailed instructions for the compilation and ordering of the *Paula* fragments. Edited by Otto Kallir, the book was published in New York in 1949.

Beer-Hofmann was granted United States citizenship on March 14, 1945. Two months later, on May 18, the National Institute of the American Academy of Arts and Letters presented to him the "Institute Award for Distinguished Achievements," given annually to an eminent foreign artist living in America. The presentation was made by William Rose Benét in the auditorium of the American Academy of Arts and Letters in New York, and Beer-Hofmann accepted the award with the following speech, the only one he ever gave in English:

> Mr. President, Members of the Academy and the Institute, Ladies and Gentlemen: I am deeply touched by your generous words of appreciation—as I have been by the great honor bestowed upon me since I first received the good news. It so happened that the letter of your secretary . . . arrived almost the same day on which this country accepted me as a citizen. More than seventy years of my life I spent in the country of my birth—surrounded by what seemed as self-evident as my existence itself. When I came to these shores, I could by no stretch of my imagination foresee that I was to receive again what had been taken from me by tyranny: a home, a working place, a country that was to be mine by choice and by right, and now—this proof of human sympathy, of under-

standing and recognition. To me—this has come as a lesson in democracy. For: respect for the dignity of man, the basis of democracy, is at the same time the very foundation of any sincere artistic endeavor. A writer's work can never hope to be complete. Yet it was worth trying—if only to learn this lesson. I thank you.[95]

Four months later, on September 26, 1945, Richard Beer-Hofmann died of pneumonia in New York.[96]

2

The Prose Works

The five works to be examined here are *Camelias (1891), Das Kind* (1893), *Der Tod Georgs* (1900), *Gedenkrede auf Wolfgang Amadé Mozart* (1906), and *Paula, ein Fragment* (posthumously published in its entirety for the first time in 1949). Attention will focus upon the themes that recur in these works, and upon the language, artistic techniques, and literary conventions that Beer-Hofmann employs. Treatment of *Camelias* and *Das Kind* will also include brief plot summaries, since these early stories are not contained in the 1963 edition of the collected works.

Of the titles listed above, *Paula* is the only one that is not fiction in the strictest sense of the word. Beer-Hofmann himself called it a biographical "book of reminiscences." It is included here on the grounds that, although the story he tells has its basis in historical biography, the work as a whole is as much fiction as fact. Beer-Hofmann may honestly have believed what he told Werner Vordtriede about the writing of *Paula*: "What I am writing does not stem from me at all. I am merely describing how things actually were."[1] Still, the work has little in common with the standard factual biography; in its language and style and in its author's very conscious artistic ordering of his material, *Paula* is more closely akin to the highly subjective modern work of prose fiction.

Beer-Hofmann's aphorisms and other short prose fragments will not be treated individually. They will, however, be used where appropriate to enhance the discussion of the major prose works.

Camelias

Arthur Schnitzler, one recalls, spoke of *Camelias* as "a sketch"; that designation seems more appropriate than "novella," the title under which the story was published. It contains no external action, and certainly no "unheard-of event"; indeed, the "action" consists almost exclusively of the ruminations of the protagonist and his resulting decision. The plot, briefly, is this:

Freddy, a Viennese dandy on the verge of middle age, is infatuated with Thea, a seventeen-year-old girl whose family he has known since before she was born. On a sudden impulse he determines to sever relations with his mistress of many years and marry Thea, but as he weighs the pros and cons of the matter while preparing for bed, he is overcome by misgivings—provoked by fear of approaching old age, the recollection of friends whose young wives had eventually deceived them, and not least of all, by the sight of his middle-aged face (smeared with cold cream) and figure (corseted) in the mirror. His fear of disrupting the familiar, comfortable pattern of his carefully ordered life finally leads him to give up the idea of marriage, and he goes to bed, having left instructions for his valet to send camellias to his mistress on Sunday as usual.

It scarcely needs to be said that there is nothing new or original about the plot of this story or the figure of Freddy. Both are familiar to the reader as typical subject matter of the so-called decadent works written around the turn of the century; Schnitzler's *Anatol* is probably the best known among them.

The structure of *Camelias* and the author's techniques are not original either, but they are indicative of certain changes that prose fiction began to undergo about this time: first of all, the story is constructed in a manner that conveys everything to the reader from the perspective of one person only, Freddy. Limited perspective is not a new development in prose fiction, of course—one need only think of the fairly long history of the epistolary novel. The only such novels that achieve a similar effect, however, are those in which all the letters have been written by one person.[2] The degree of subjectivity in *Camelias* is further heightened and a certain dramatic quality introduced by the fact that the author dispenses with artificial means (such as the letter) and simply opens the protagonist's mind, allowing the reader to eavesdrop on and learn directly of his mental associations and reflections.

Another aspect of *Camelias* which points to subsequent trends in prose fiction is the marked decrease in the amount of exposition. An absolutely minimal number of narrative passages introduce the characters, render their past history, set the scene, and otherwise orient the reader. The story begins with the brief sentence, "Das Haustor schloss sich, und Freddy stand auf der Strasse" ["The house door closed, and Freddy stood on the street"]. The reader has no idea who Freddy is, what house he has just left, or what street he is standing on. Wolfdietrich Rasch named this abrupt beginning as a typical feature of the narrative style of the period (1890–1914): ". . . with calculated artistry . . . the opening sentence is formed in such a way that it denies its epic character . . . and creates the impression of being in a context. The narrator gives the impression of taking up the thread at an arbitrarily selected point."[3]

Beer-Hofmann does conform to the traditional technique of telling his story in the third person, but the reader is scarcely aware of this since the narrator never intrudes as such, never attempts to explain his hero or provide a commentary of his thoughts and feelings. Despite the use of the third person, the prevailing impression is one of immediacy and direct contact with the protagonist.

It is clear that Thea (although the reader never actually meets her) is meant to bring Freddy's decadent qualities into sharper relief by being his opposite in almost every detail: she is fresh, vigorous, and full of youthful zest for life. These are precisely the qualities that attract Freddy to her. Significantly, however, his misgivings and fear of change prevail over his desire to marry Thea. In sketching Freddy with all of his decadent characteristics (acutely sensitive nerves, ennui, extreme preoccupation with self, and a kind of pervasive tiredness that paralyzes his will to act), Beer-Hofmann succeeds best in portraying his protagonist's fear of change as a decadent quality. One is reminded of Hofmannsthal's observation about Beer-Hofmann himself: "You are too fearful of the idea of decisive changes." To say that this or that aspect of the story is more successful than another, however, is small praise. *Camelias* scarcely qualifies as literature, and it is understandable that Beer-Hofmann later dismissed the sketch as a youthful endeavor not worthy of much attention.

Das Kind

Only two years lie between *Camelias* and the completion of *Das Kind,* but an examination of the second story shows that the twenty-seven-year-old Beer-Hofmann had undergone considerable maturation, both as a writer and as a young man in the process of coming to terms with himself and the world. *Das Kind* is still a youthful work that reflects its young author's groping and searching, but it is much superior to *Camelias* in depth of content and artistic skill. It also contains some indications of the direction the mature Beer-Hofmann was later to take.

The plot is not complicated, the subject matter still quite typical of "Viennese decadence." Paul—a young man whose occupation the author never troubles to tell us, but who is obviously refined and well-educated—has had a protracted affair with Juli, a Viennese servant girl. For some time he has wanted to break off with her, but feels he cannot because she is pregnant with his child. Neither willing nor able to keep the child after its birth, Juli arranges for it to be given to a peasant family in the country near Vienna. Shortly thereafter she receives word that the child has died. Paul's first reaction to the news of the child's death is one of well-concealed but enormous relief: the sole obstacle to his freedom from Juli is gone. Soon, however, he is overcome by pity for the helpless infant, whom he imagines as unwanted and neglected by the peasant family, and then by remorse and guilt, which drive him finally to the village to talk to the peasant couple and visit the child's grave. Upon his arrival he learns that their financial straits had forced them to leave the village to search for a better life elsewhere. At the cemetery he is unable to single out his child's grave, which is unmarked. On the return trip to Vienna, Paul's reflections about the entire experience lead him, for the first time in his life, to an awareness of his own past selfishness and indifference to others, and to some tentative conclusions about the nature of life.

Upon analyzing *Das Kind,* one is first struck by the fact that it reflects a degree of artistic independence largely lacking in *Camelias.* Beer-Hofmann is now clearly more inclined to look inward, to rely on his own judgment and instincts as a writer, than he had been two years before. His choice of language is the first indication of this. Most of the expository passages are impressionistic: "Nur langsam verschwamm das kalte, matte Blau des Frühlingshimmels in ein wässeriges Lichtgrün . . . ["Slowly the cold, faint blue of the spring sky melted into a watery light green . . ."].[4] Beer-Hofmann, however, now does not hesitate to use the realistic, indeed naturalistic, device of dialect when it will heighten the effectiveness of a passage or enhance his characterization of one of the figures in the story:

> Er fuhr heftig auf: "Gieb jetzt Antwort, was ich Dich frag'. Wie hat das Kind ausgesehn,—was für Farb' haben die Haare gehabt, was für"—Juli schüttelte erstaunt den Kopf: "Na, was Dich das jetzt noch interessirt? So mehr dunkles Haar hat's g'habt, und ausg'schaut—no wie sie halt alle

in dem Alter ausschaun, a sehr a hübsches Kind war's—die Hebamm hat's auch g'sagt, no jetzt ist ihm ohnehin besser oben im Himmel als Engerl, was hatt's auch gut's g'habt hier unten auf dera Welt?" (*Novellen,* pp. 36–37)

[He started up vehemently: "Answer what I'm asking you. What did the child look like—what color was its hair, what"—Juli shook her head, astonished: "Well, why does that interest you now? It had sort of dark hair, and it looked—well, the way they all look at that age, a pretty child it was—the midwife said so, too. Well, it's better off now as a little angel in heaven, what good would it have had in the world here below?" Note: in the original Juli speaks in Viennese dialect.]

Like its forerunner, *Das Kind* is told in the third person, but again without any intrusion into the story by the narrator, about whom the reader learns nothing. The repeated effect is one of direct exposure to the protagonist's reflections and impressions.

One difference between the two stories is that *Camelias* contains virtually no dialogue, while *Das Kind* has much more. *Camelias* consists almost exclusively of the reflections of Freddy, and most of them relate to the immediate past (i.e., the earlier events of the evening), the present, and the future. The levels of time have been expanded in *Das Kind,* and the author deals with them in a somewhat different way: as the story opens, Paul is about to keep a rendezvous with Juli, at which she will tell him that the child is dead. Only after this scene does the reader learn of all that preceded their meeting, becoming acquainted with the history of their relationship through Paul's recollections, interspersed with his reflections, as his mind moves back and forth between the remembered past and the present. Past conversations are not recalled in indirect discourse, but are given as direct dialogue.

Despite the increased use of dialogue in *Das Kind,* the preponderant note is still one of reflection, even in the second half of the story, after Paul's sense of guilt has driven him to act. He thinks primarily about death and its relation to life (a problem which more than any other preoccupied the young Beer-Hofmann and his contemporaries), about man's fate and the transitoriness of his existence:

Die Natur! Wusste er es denn jetzt erst, dass sie immer von Neuem brünstig und zeugend und trächtig und gebärend war, und vernichtend, was sie geboren—und stumm blieb auf alle unsere Fragen? Und die "Stimme" liehen wir ihr nur, weil uns vor ihrem Schweigen graute! . . . Und dann folgten wir ihrer Stimme, und lehnten uns gegen sie auf, und wir sündigten gegen sie, und schlossen mit ihr Frieden, als wäre sie

unseres Gleichen, und wir mehr, als Keime, von einer Welle an den
Strand des Daseins geschleudert—und hinweggespült von der Nächsten.
(*Novellen,* pp. 79–80)

[Nature! Did he realize only now that she was fertile and lustfully
productive, that she gave birth and destroyed what she bore—and
remained mute to all of our questions? And we gave her a "voice" only
because we were horrified by her silence! . . . And then we followed her
voice, and rebelled against her, sinned against her, and made peace with
her, as if she were one of us, and we more than grains of sand, hurled
upon the shore of existence by a wave—and swept away by the next one.]

Although he refers to nature rather than to God, Beer-Hofmann also
has Paul wrestle with the ancient problem of the existence of suffering
and evil in the world:

Gesündigt, gegen sie [die Natur], gegen göttliches Gebot hatte er, zuerst
als er ein Kind in die Welt gesetzt, und dann, als er es hilflos, elend
umkommen liess? Und Strafe war es gewesen, dass er darum litt? W e n n
es Sünde war, um die man leiden musste, was litt dann sie, die Natur,
die grosse Sünderin, die A l l e in die Welt setzte, und A l l e n elend,
hilflos umkommen liess, die uns zuerst schuldlos zum Leben verdammte,
und dann zum Tode begnadigte? (*Novellen,* p. 79)

[He had sinned against nature, against divine law, first when he had
sired the child and then when he had allowed it to die, helpless and in
misery? And it had been punishment that he was suffering for it? *If* it
was sin for which one had to suffer, then what did nature suffer, the
great sinner, she who put *all* of us into the world and allowed *all* of us to
die, helpless and in misery, she who first condemned us, innocent, to life
and then pardoned us with death?]

Despite his tormenting doubts and his knowledge that nature "remains
mute to all of our questions," Paul believes that "nicht bloss Form und
Farbe hatten die Dinge—hinter ihnen war ein geheimer Sinn, der sie
durchleuchtete, sie standen nicht fremd nebeneinander—e i n Gedanke
schlang ein Band um sie!" (*Novellen,* pp. 78–79). ["things had not only
form and color—behind them was a secret purpose that suffused them;
they did not stand beside each other like strangers—*one* thought wound
a unifying band about them!"] This reference to a mysterious and
unifying sense or purpose in life is made only in passing in *Das Kind*;
in later years Beer-Hofmann was to return to this theme again and
again, developing it most fully in the Biblical dramas. The willingness
to believe in such a purpose—despite profound, tormenting doubt—is

touched upon only briefly in this early story, but toward the end of his life Beer-Hofmann told Werner Vordtriede that "again and again the poet must become the exculpator of God. The role of *advocatus Dei* is a much more difficult office than that of *advocatus diaboli*. Nothing is more difficult than to excuse and justify the course of events in the world."[5]

Paul's doubt emerges in another passage of *Das Kind* as a very positive and constructive force. He has been thinking about his sense of guilt; now, as he regards the peacefully sleeping Juli, his thoughts turn to her possible sense of guilt and to how she has coped with it:

> Wenn in ihr etwas aufgedämmert war, wie Schuldbewusstsein, wenn sie sich sündig fühlte—war sie in die Kirche getreten und ihr kindisch-verworrenes Empfinden hatte sie ausgeschüttet vor dem Heiland am Kreuze; dem Mittler zwischen ihr und ihrem Gotte hatte sie im Beicht-stuhle ihre reuige Selbstanklage anvertraut. Und wenn dann durch weih-rauchduftende Gitterstäbe feierlich geflüsterte Worte zu ihr drangen, die sie lossprachen von ihren Sünden—war sie aufgestanden . . . in froher Zuversicht, dass . . . "das Lamm Gottes, welches hinwegnimmt die Sünden der Welt," auch ihre Schuld von ihr genommen habe. (*Novellen,* pp. 56–57)

> [If something like a sense of guilt had dawned in her, if she felt sinful—she had entered the church and poured out her childishly confused feelings before the saviour on the cross; in the confessional she had confided her remorseful self-accusation to the intermediary between her and her God. And then, when the solemnly whispered words which absolved her of her sins penetrated to her through the incense-scented bars, she had arisen . . . happily confident that "the Lamb of God, which taketh away the sins of the world," had also removed her guilt from her.]

At first Paul envies her, but his reflections eventually lead him to another realization: "Er hatte ja nie geleugnet, nur gezweifelt, und war nicht Zweifeln auch ein Glauben, zumindest ein Glaubenwollen an Ihn, ein Suchen nach Ihm, ein Drang, Ihn zu finden, der tieferem Fühlen entsprang, als der ruhig-naive Kinderglauben?" (*Novellen,* p. 57). ["He had never denied, only doubted, and was doubt not also a form of belief, or at least a desire to believe in Him, a searching for Him, an urge to find Him, that arose from a deeper feeling than did untroubled, naive, childlike faith?"] Doubt as a means to faith is presented here in the form of a question, a tentative possibility of which the young Beer-Hofmann was conscious. In his later works it appears as an answer.

In the passage quoted on page 36, Paul speaks unequivocally of life as a state of damnation and death as a state of grace. By the end of the story, however, a change has clearly taken place. Life, not death, is now the object of his yearning: "Und Sehnsucht kam über ihn, heisse Sehnsucht, zu leben, sich am Leben zu freuen, ehe die Nacht von den dunklen Bergen her, in missfarbene Schleier gehüllt, lauernd heran- kroch" (*Novellen,* p. 83). ["And longing overcame him, an intense longing to live, to rejoice in life before the night, wrapped in discolored veils, crept down from the dark mountains."] Paul has not lost his awareness of death, but his longing for life is at the same time an affirmation of it, and unlike Hofmannsthal's Claudio, he has acquired his insight before it is too late.

Der Tod Georgs

On August 9, 1893, only a few days after Beer-Hofmann had begun work on *Der Tod Georgs,* the *Frankfurter Zeitung* published an essay on Gabriele d'Annunzio by the young Hugo von Hofmannsthal. "Two things seem to be in vogue today," he wrote, "analysis of life and flight from life. People take little pleasure in plot, in the interplay of the external and internal forces of life, in learning to know life in the manner of Wilhelm Meister, or in the course of world events as repre- sented by Shakespeare. One undertakes the dissection of the life of one's own soul, or one dreams. . . . In vogue is a psychological listen- ing-to-the-grass-grow, and a splashing about in the magical world of pure phantasy . . . in vogue is the dissection of a mood, a sigh, a scruple; and in vogue is the instinctive, almost somnambulent surren- der to every manifestation of beauty."[6] Hofmannsthal then applies these observations to d'Annunzio's *L'Innocente* and *Elegie Romane.* The extent to which his remarks also apply to *Der Tod Georgs* is striking, though not surprising: it was Hofmannsthal's and Beer-Hofmann's practice to discuss their works in progress, and though the actual writing of *Der Tod Georgs* had barely begun when the d'Annunzio essay appeared, we may certainly assume that Beer-Hofmann had discussed his conception of the novel with Hofmannsthal.

A letter which Hofmannsthal wrote to Beer-Hofmann from Göding on June 16, 1895 confirms that he did see some marked similarities between d'Annunzio and Beer-Hofmann: "D'Annunzio, too, is affect- ing me unbelievably on second reading. Like you, he seeks the slice of life that runs through neither pure appearance nor the *ultimae rationes,* but rather through the richly varied fabric in the middle. And really, he sometimes evokes in one the monstrous feeling of sensing a soul in its entirety (which one usually experiences only with one's own self), not through a sudden, very characteristic gesture, but rather through a wonderful accumulation of little facts, insignificant characteristics, recollections, associations, and the thousandfold effects of the environment" (*Hofmannsthal/Beer-Hofmann Briefwechsel,* p. 54). Beer-Hofmann knew d'Annunzio's works and read them with enthusiasm; he once recommended a German translation of *Il Piacere* to Georg Brandes and gave him a copy of the novel.[7]

In the letter just quoted, Hofmannsthal summarizes the literary techniques d'Annunzio and the young Beer-Hofmann had in common; the two writers were also drawn to the same motifs: death, the relation of the dream to life, and the problem of decadence, particularly its lack of will.[8] These major themes of *Der Tod Georgs* are joined by a fourth, which may simply be labeled "Woman." There is no representation of great events on the Shakespearean scale in Beer-Hofmann's treatment of these themes, and no long process of learning to know life, as found in Goethe's *Wilhelm Meister.* It is indeed difficult to understand why Alfred Werner placed *Der Tod Georgs* in the tradition of the German *Bildungsroman.*[9] The only external action is Georg's death, and even that is vital to the subsequent development of the story only because it provides the impetus for the hero's wide-ranging thoughts and ultimate transformation. Virtually everything else transpires within the mind and fantasy of the hero, Paul.[10]

Structurally, the novel is divided into four parts. The first presents Paul's conversation with an acquaintance about Georg's arrival for a visit, Paul's reflections on this conversation, his walk along the river, his encounter there with a young woman he "recognizes," his reverie about "the woman in the clouds," and his confusion of the two female figures. Part II consists of Paul's dream (which ranges from the dying "wife"—whose name is never mentioned—to his life before he met her, to the love-death rites in the Syrian temple, and finally, to the death of the "wife") and his reflections on the dream upon waking. Part III, during which Paul is taking Georg's body to Vienna for burial, is devoted to his reflections on Georg's sudden death (which lead to thoughts of death in general and to reflections on the sadness and hopelessness of old age) and to his recollection of the story of the youths of Argos, to whom the gods showed special favor by allowing them to die young. The fourth and final part traces Paul's walk through a Viennese park, highlighted by his encounter with the two women at the fountain, which leads to his transformation and ensuing affirmation of life.

The woman motif dominates Part I. Before its two representatives are introduced, however, the reader is given an early clue to the character of Paul, the decadent protagonist—not in the traditional form of a descriptive passage, but rather through his own mental comparison of himself and his friend, Georg. Paul had told an acquaintance about Georg's call to a professorship at Heidelberg, and the acquaintance had replied, " 'Der hat's gut!' . . . seine Stimme klang neidisch traurig. . . . 'Ja—Glück muss der Mensch haben!' " [" 'How lucky he is!' . . . his voice sounded enviously sad. . . . 'Yes—one has to be lucky!' "]. Having said goodnight to the acquaintance, Paul is left alone with his thoughts:

> "Glück muss der Mensch haben!" Der traurig neidvolle Ton klang in ihm nach. "Glück!" Freilich nicht so, wie der Doktor es meinte. Er horchte auf die ruhigen kräftigen Atemzüge des Schlafenden [Georg] im Nebenzimmer. So hätte er sein mögen, wie der! So stark und gesund im Empfinden, wie der da drinnen; und den Willen, den starken Willen, und den Glauben an das, was er wollte, hätte er haben mögen! (*GW*, 523–24)

> ["One has to be lucky!" The sadly envious tone echoed in his mind. "Luck!" To be sure, not the kind the doctor meant. He listened to the strong and peaceful breathing of the sleeper [Georg] in the adjoining room. How he wished to be like him! As strong and healthy as he was in his perceptions; and how he would have liked to have Georg's will, that strong will, and that belief in what he wanted!]

The decadent Paul sees his friend as everything he himself is not and would like to be: strong of will and sound in mind and body—in short, entirely fit for life.

The two female figures who dominate Part I are actually variations of the same image in Paul's fantasy. The first of these representatives of the woman motif is the girl Paul encounters on his walk beside the river:

> Schön war sie ja eigentlich nicht, aber etwas in ihr erinnerte an vieles Schöne. . . . Wenn ihre schlanke knabenhafte Gestalt, von einem eng-anliegenden Kleid umschlossen, ruhig dastand, den Kopf leicht zur Seite gewandt, die Hand vor sich hingestreckt auf dem zu hohen Griff des Schirmes ruhend, musste er an Bilder denken, auf denen Erzengel in stählernem goldtauschiertem Panzer ihr Schwert vor sich hin in den Boden stemmten. (*GW*, 525)

[She was not actually beautiful, but something in her reminded him of many beautiful things. . . . When her slender boyish body stood there quietly, enveloped by a close-fitting dress, her head bent lightly to one side and her outstretched hand resting on the high handle of her umbrella, he was reminded of pictures in which archangels in golden armor planted their swords in the ground before them.]

Beer-Hofmann's model for this figure was almost certainly the young Paula. He had not even met her when he began *Der Tod Georgs,* but he had known her for five years when the novel was published and he had worked on it during all of that period. There is a striking similarity between the passage just quoted and Beer-Hofmann's description of his wife in *Paula, ein Fragment* (see especially *GW,* 787). Nevertheless, the biographical elements should not be overemphasized; the women of the novel are fictitious figures, and Beer-Hofmann did not hesitate to add or omit whatever he deemed necessary for their characterization.

The reader has learned on the second page of the novel that Paul lacks "strong and healthy perceptions" and the strong will necessary for life. The women of Part I are, in a sense, extensions of Paul—or at least are very much like him: in the world but not of it, they stand on the periphery of life.[11] This is conveyed about the girl by the river in terms of her latent, as yet unawakened sexuality: "Hart und ungefügig bewegten sich ihre hagern Kinderarme, als hätten sie noch nicht gelernt, umarmend sich um den Hals des Geliebten zu schlingen, und ihre verschlossenen knospenden Formen schienen den Tag zu erwarten, an dem die Liebe schwellen und öffnen würde, was jetzt noch verschüchtert schlief" (*GW,* 526). ["Her lean arms, like those of a child, moved stiffly and awkwardly, as though they had not yet learned to encircle the neck of a lover in an embrace, and her concealed but budding form seemed to await the day when love would swell and open what now still shyly slept."] As Paul studies the face and form of the "woman in the clouds," he muses: ". . . über allem, was er sonst sah, so blass es schien, lagen doch noch die warmen dunkelnden Schatten des Lebens; aber was sich um den dürftigen Leib dort weich und taudurchfeuchtet legte, war ein Sterbekleid. . . . Nichts von dem, was um sie war, konnte sie sehen; über alles Nahe hinweg ging unter halbgesunkenen Lidern der Blick ihrer Augen . . . zu ihm" (*GW,* 528). [". . . above everything else that he saw, however pale it seemed, there still lay the warm darkening shadows of life; but what wrapped itself softly and moist with dew about this slight body was a shroud. . . . She could see nothing that surrounded her; disregarding everything near her, the glance from her half-closed eyes travelled . . . to him."]

Throughout Part 1, Paul returns repeatedly to the doctor's remark about luck. In thinking about what constitutes happiness or good fortune, Paul first ponders the kinds of happiness he does *not* mean:

—Nicht das des helldampfenden Frühlingsmorgens, wo man auf weissem Pferd über braunen lockern Acker reitet, und feuchtduftende Erdkrume zu einem aufsprüht, und alles noch vor einem liegt: der Tag und das weite Land und das Leben. ... Und nicht das träge liebesmatte Glück windstiller Sommernachmittage, wo man in schwülen Lauben verlassener Gärten mit der Geliebten ruht, das Gesicht an ihre Brust geschmiegt ... und die satten Sinne träumen und alle Sehnsucht ist eingeschlafen. (*GW*, 527)

[—Not the happiness of a brightly steaming spring morning, when one rides on a white horse over yielding brown acres, and moistly fragrant crumbs of earth spray up, and everything is still before one: the day and the expansive countryside and life. ... And not the languid lovespent happiness of windstill summer afternoons, when one rests in the sultry arbors of deserted gardens with one's beloved, face pressed to her breast ... and the sated senses dream and all yearning has been stilled.]

Since it is neither the happiness of anticipation nor that of actual experience which Paul longs for, one is tempted to conclude that for him happiness lies in death. That is not what he yearns for, however: "Und auch nicht das letzte grosse todesmütige Glück des Untergangs, wenn eine Sonne in goldene Wolken verblutet und man ein freies prunkendes Sterben ersehnt" (*GW*, 527). ["And not the last great happiness of brave resolution in the face of downfall, when the sun bleeds to death in golden clouds and one yearns for a free and splendid death of one's own."] Although in this passage Paul refers to death as "the last great happiness," he does not want to die:

Wovon er träumte, war ein Glück so still und voll Frieden, dass es sich nur wenig von Wehmut und Entsagen schied. Manchmal hatte er es geahnt, wenn er am frühen dämmernden Morgen am Waldrand stand. ... Von den gelben Lilien im Wasser hatte der Morgenwind noch nicht den Tau geweht, und in den unbewegten Teichen fingen sich blass errötende Wolken wie in matten silbernen Spiegeln. Da hatte er die kühle ruhevolle Schönheit der Dinge gefühlt, über die das Leben noch nicht gekommen war, und sein heisser Atem. (*GW*, 528)

[What he dreamed of was a happiness so quiet and full of peace that it differed only a little from sadness and renunciation. Sometimes he had sensed it, standing at daybreak on the edge of the forest. ... The morning breeze had not yet wafted the dew from the yellow lilies in the water, and in the motionless ponds faintly blushing clouds were reflected as in delicate silver mirrors. Then he had felt the cool, restful beauty of things over which life and its hot breath had not yet passed.]

Paul wants to live, but aloof from life and all its turmoil, strife, and ugliness, in a spiritual limbo where he can enjoy aesthetic pleasures undisturbed.

It would be a mistake, however, to assume that he is simply another Epicurean or hedonist. Proof that he is not lies in his longing for the very qualities that make Georg so strong and fit for life. By the end of Part I, Paul has emerged as a young man with basically conflicting desires—for aloofness from life and for involvement in it—although at this early point in the novel, his "decadent" desires and impulses clearly dominate.

The shock effect of Part II is considerable, largely because the dream of which it consists begins without any introduction whatever. The unsuspecting reader realizes, of course, that the love-death rites in the Syrian temple are products of fantasy, but he naturally assumes that all of the other developments (the dying wife, Paul's recollections of his life with her, etc.) are "real." Only at the end of Part II does the reader learn—to his surprise and consternation—that everything was a dream. At least one early reviewer of *Der Tod Georgs* could not suppress a note of indignation at this literary trick: "He [Beer-Hofmann] causes the dream to pass before us as life and the characters as shadow pictures, and he links dream and reality in a strange and fascinating way. To be sure, this is not accomplished without . . . a trick. Probably every reader will at first feel repelled when he realizes that Paul's entire marriage, the tragic death of his wife, and a number of other things are only dream fantasies. No one likes to be duped, least of all where his feelings are concerned."[12]

The dream as reality becomes a major motif in Part II. Like Hofmannsthal, Beer-Hofmann here carries on a tradition that dates back to the Baroque, a tradition represented by Calderon, Shakespeare, and later by Grillparzer. Looking first at the nature of the dream, one finds that for Paul the impressions of the waking state cannot begin to compare with those of the dream in vividness and intensity; moments after waking, he realizes that the dream's images are already beginning to fade. Everything in the dream, moreover, had an importance to him for its own sake, and a connection with him: "Es schien ihm, als wäre der kurze Schlaf mit unendlich vielem erfüllt gewesen; nichts Gleichgiltiges hatte es da in seinem Leben gegeben. Keine leeren Stunden,

die nur die Brücken zu erhofften reicheren waren; und nichts, das
wertlos am Wege stand und an dem man fremd vorüberging" (*GW*,
568). ["It seemed to him that his brief sleep had been filled with an
infinite number of things; and there had been nothing in it of indifference to him. No empty hours that were merely bridges to hoped for,
richer ones; and nothing worthless along the way that one passed by
like a stranger."] Paul recalls that in the dream he experienced a very
keen sense of relationship with all things: "Ihm hatten alle Dinge ihr
Antlitz zugewandt—er konnte nicht an ihnen vorüber; um seinetwillen
waren sie da, und ihr Schicksal vermochte er nicht von dem seinen zu
lösen" (*GW*, 568). ["Toward him all things had turned their faces—he
could not pass them by; they were there for his sake, and he could not
separate their fate from his own."]

Paul differs from the heroes of earlier dream literature (such as
Rustan in Grillparzer's *Traum ein Leben*) in several important respects:
he is infinitely more sophisticated and—a true child of his time and
milieu—further characterized by inordinately delicate sensibilities,
high-strung nerves, and a kind of paralysis of the will. He is also
different (and this likewise marks him as a child of his time) in that he
tries to fathom the psychological implications of the dream and its
relation to life. Upon waking, he analyzes his dream, attempts to
interpret it and draw some conclusions from it:

> Aber wenn er nur geträumt hatte, warum war dann noch jetzt, da
> er wach war, dieser Schmerz in ihm? Als wäre ihm wirklich die ge-
> storben, von der er geträumt. Die gab es ja doch gar nicht! . . . Wie
> sonderbar doch der Traum dichtete! Er kannte ja gar kein Haus, das
> dem glich, von dem er geträumt hatte . . . und er selbst war auch ein
> anderer gewesen; oder kannte er sich im Traum besser als im Wachen?
> (*GW*, 568)

> [But if he had only dreamed, then why was there still, now that he was
> awake, this pain in him? As if the woman in his dream had actually died.
> But she didn't really exist at all! . . . What strange fictions dreams
> created! He knew no house that resembled the one in his dream . . . and
> he himself had been a different person; or did he know himself better in
> dreams than in the waking state?]

This last question appears to be a casual one, appended as an after-
thought, but it has far-reaching implications. With it, as with Paul's
earlier admission that his dreams were "mehr sein wahres Leben als
das, das er lebte" ["more his real life than the one he lived"] (*GW*,
538), Beer-Hofmann raises the question of what actually constitutes

reality. His answer is not a denial of the reality of the waking state, but rather an assertion that the dream is equally valid and, as far as vividness and intensity are concerned, even more "real" than the waking state. Paul himself does not realize this fully or understand why it is so until Part IV:

> Und über dem Leben seiner Tage war ein zweites—das seiner Nächte—gewölbt. Aus allen Früchten des wachen Lebens war der Saft in Träume so gepresst und gedichtet, wie die Taten vieler Jahre in ein Lied, das man zu singen anhebt, wenn es dämmert, und das zu Ende ist, ehe es Nacht geworden. Träume lösten alle Schwere des Lebens von den Sohlen; keine leeren Stunden gab es, die nur Brücken zu erhofften reicheren waren, und Jahre wogen nur das, was sie werteten. *Der träumte, schuf eine Welt und setzte in sie, nur was für ihn bedeutete: von ihm gesteckt, waren die Grenzen ihrer Himmel und ihrer Erden, allwissend war er in ihr, und alles wusste von ihm.* Nicht unterjocht von Zeit und Raum, freier als das Leben der Tage, lebten Träume . . . (*GW*, 619; italics added)

> [And arched above the life of his days was a second one—that of his nights. The juice from all the fruits of waking life was compressed into dreams like the deeds of many years into a song that one begins to sing at twilight and that is finished before night falls. Dreams removed all the heaviness of life from one's soles; they contained no empty hours that were only bridges to hoped for, richer ones, and years weighed only as much as they were worth. *The person who dreamed created a world and placed in it only what had meaning for him; he set the boundaries of its heavens and its earth, in it he was omniscient, and all things knew of him.* Not subject to time and space, the life of one's dreams was freer than the life of one's days . . .]

The italicized lines of this passage point to Beer-Hofmann's conviction that the dream is not only a valid complement of the waking state, but also a necessary one. In an era already profoundly influenced by psychological theory and experimentation, particularly Freud's, a deterministic view of human behavior was becoming increasingly prevalent—a view that Beer-Hofmann shared, not unequivocally, but to a considerable degree. This view, of course, applies to human behavior in the waking state; in the dream, by contrast, man satisfies the need to exercise the creative power, omniscience and control that he does not have over the events of "real life."[13] Beer-Hofmann has Paul realize in Part IV that this is precisely why he had always feared life and sought to remain detached from it: "Fremd und sie nie erfassend, war er in die Welt geworfen, in der er im Wachen lebte; wovon er nicht wusste, rührte an ihn, und was er tat, wirkte ins Unbekannte. Aber aus ihm geboren war die Welt, in der er träumte; von ihm gesteckt waren die Grenzen ihrer Himmel und ihrer Erden. Allwissend war er in ihr, und alles wusste von ihm" (*GW*, 607). ["Like a stranger he had been tossed into the world in which he lived in the waking state, never understanding it; things of which he knew nothing touched him and what he did had an effect unknown to him. But the world in which he dreamed was born of him; he set the boundaries of its heavens and its earth. In it he was omniscient, and all things knew of him."]

Not only the predetermined nature of human behavior makes the dream a necessary complement of the waking state; it is also necessary because the ever-advancing science and technology of the modern world have brought about the "de-secretizing" of virtually everything that was once a mystery. Beer-Hofmann expresses this idea in one of his (undated) prose fragments:

> The "de-secretizing" of all events of life continues unchecked. A waste of time to deplore this or hail it. Certainly through this casting of light into many dark corners, through . . . this opening of windows, a great deal of stale air has been removed. But ties that were also present . . . have [likewise] fallen away. Man has more freedom of movement, but he is lonelier. . . . This supra-sharp, often painful light (one should never forget that it is not sunlight, but the light of the laboratory) that now falls equally on much that previously remained in twilight, leaves many innate instincts unsatisfied. Just as we could not endure a perpetually even distribution of light, we are not content when everything appears clear—"de-secretized." The soul will seek a substitute. And in addition to the growth of occult movements (especially among those too dull to be amazed by the daily miracle of life), the need for occasional twilight will find refuge in dreams—in the second, better half of life. The people of the future will dream more, will *have* to dream more, in order to achieve balance. ("Entgeheimnissung," *GW*, 635)

Beer-Hofmann's view and artistic treatment of the dream as a state infinitely richer and more vivid than life itself make this aspect of the novel an expression of the "flight from life" that Hofmannsthal mentions in the d'Annunzio essay—but not in the negative sense usually associated with escapism; the flight has become a constructive, indeed therapeutic activity. Paul's ultimate realization is that the world of dreams should not dominate, but neither should the world of the waking state; both are valid and necessary realms of life.

One aspect of Paul's dream—namely, his sense of oneness with all things in it—requires separate consideration because it relates to a different problem: that of the poet and his efforts to communicate his experience of life. Within the dream itself, Paul's sense of oneness applies to things past as well as present:

> In anderer Menschen Gedächtnis lag das Wissen von diesen Dingen wie das Korn in trockenen Speichern. . . . Nicht wie ein Wissen von Geschehenem empfand er es; es war sein Eigen. . . . Er fasste es nicht, dass es gewesen, und er hasste alle, die in selbstverständlichem Begreifen, unerschauernd, an dem Wunder vorüberschritten, das sie Zeit nannten. . . . Was Macht besass, an seine Seele zu rühren, das lebte. . . . Er sprach nicht davon wie von gewesener Herrlichkeit, und wie man von Toten spricht, die man geliebt: Mit Sehnsucht und Mitleid und vielem Erinnern. . . . Ihm lebte es . . . (*GW*, 538)

> [In other people's memories the knowledge of these things lay like corn in dry storage bins. . . . He did not experience it as a knowledge of past events; it belonged to him. . . . He couldn't grasp that it was past, and he hated all those who, unmoved and with matter-of-fact understanding, passed by the miracle they called time. . . . Whatever possessed the power to touch his soul, lived. . . . He did not speak of it as past splendor, or as one speaks of loved ones who have died: with yearning and pity and much remembrance. . . . For him it lived . . .][14]

Despite Paul's sensitivity to all things in the dream and his feeling of oneness with them, he cannot communicate what he feels, and here Beer-Hofmann—a year before the publication of Hofmannsthal's *Brief* (*des Lord Chandos*)—transforms into a literary work of art the Lord Chandos phase of his own life:

> So flocht sich wundervoll und beängstigend ein Netz um ihn, engmaschig und alle Freiheit ihm nehmend. Alles war mit allem unlösbar verknotet, Gewesenes stand neben ihm aufrecht wie Lebendiges. . . . Wäre er ein Dichter gewesen, er hätte, was schwer und verworren auf seinem Nacken lastete, mit leichten Fingern formend über sein Haupt gehoben; und was zahllos und ohne Ende um ihn wallte, hätte er in Lieder gepresst und gedichtet. . . . Aber er vermochte es nicht . . . (*GW*, 551; see also note 43, chapter 1)

> [A tight net wove itself strangely about him, creating anxiety and robbing him of all freedom. Everything was indissolubly bound to everything else, past things stood upright beside him like living things. . . . Had he been a poet, he would have raised above his head what lay heavy and jumbled upon him, forming it with deft fingers; and the countless things that swirled endlessly about him he would have compressed into songs. . . . But he could not . . .]

Death is by far the most important motif of Part II, represented primarily by the dying "wife" to whom Paul has been married for seven years. She is the woman in the clouds who appeared to be wearing a shroud and the young woman whom Paul encountered on his nocturnal walk along the river in Part I.

In Part II several more details are added to the earlier characterization of the young woman as a person on the periphery of life. Now she is not merely unawakened to life, but is unfit for it: she has never been able to bear children; she is dying in her early adulthood of an incurable disease. Part I provides the first suggestion that she is Paul's female counterpart; in Part II he has very consciously molded her into an extension of himself. When thinking about their life together, he recalls that

> es quälte ihn, dass er sie so anders wusste, als er selbst war. Schlicht und festgebettet lag ihre Seele in dem, was man sie gelehrt und was sie von Jugend auf um sich gesehen. Oft nur mit einem Lächeln und dann wieder mit scheinbar spielenden klugen Worten rührte er an dem, was ihr unantastbar geschienen. Er nahm ihr den Glauben an einen gütigen Gott, der ihr Schicksal lenkte, und liess ihr nichts als verzehrende Sehnsucht nach Glauben; wo sie frei und ahnungslos auf sicherem Boden geschritten war, liess er sie auf die dunkeln gurgelnden Wasser des Abgrunds unter ihr horchen und lehrte sie, in ihr eigenes Leben mit Zweifel und fragenden Augen zu sehen. (*GW*, 535)

> [he was tormented by the knowledge that she was so different than he himself was. Simply and firmly anchored, her soul rested in what one had taught her, what she had seen about her, from childhood on. Often with only a smile and at other times with seemingly playful, clever words he questioned what to her had seemed sacred. He robbed her of the faith in a benign God who directed her fate, and left her nothing but the gnawing hunger for faith; where she had walked, free and unafraid, on sure ground, he caused her to hear the dark gurgling waters of the abyss beneath her, and taught her to look into her own life with doubt and questioning eyes.]

But Paul also enriches her life. He teaches her to be receptive to beauty in all of its manifestations and to cultivate her senses: "Er zeigte ihr die Schönheit alltäglicher Dinge, an der sie achtlos vorübergegangen ... und sie begriff, dass es nicht nur Schönheit gab, die auf ererbten Thronen prunkend sass und der alles opferte, sondern dass um uns, so weit wir sahen, Throne leer standen, harrend der Schönheit, die jeder Augenblick neu gebar" (*GW*, 535). ["He showed her the

beauty of everyday things, which she had passed by without noticing
. . . and she grasped that there was not only beauty which sat resplen-
dent on inherited thrones and to which all things were sacrificed, but
that round about us, as far as we could see, thrones stood empty,
awaiting the beauty that every moment brought forth anew."] These
passages also provide further evidence that Paula Beer-Hofmann was
the model for this figure; one is reminded of Erich Kahler's observation
that Beer-Hofmann "shaped her into a perfect companion . . . one is
hard put to distinguish which qualities destined the one for the other
and which were attributable to his own shaping."[15]

The long, slow death of the wife evokes a variety of emotions in
Paul. He feels sadness and the pain of loss, but in a very self-centered
way. He also feels guilt. This is already evident on the first page of
Part II, but there it is simply the vague, inexplicable guilt of a man
who is alive and in good health while his wife is dying: "Scheu und
verstohlen aß er . . . und dass er essen konnte, empfand er wie schamloses Unrecht an ihr, die unten seit Wochen sterbend lag" *(GW, 530)*.
["Shyly and furtively he ate . . . and that he was able to eat struck him
as a shameless injustice against her, who for weeks lay dying downstairs."] Later he feels a more specific sense of guilt when he realizes
that he has divested this woman of her identity and given her his own,
placing on her a burden she is ill-equipped to carry:

> Geschlechtslos schien sie ihm; nur mehr etwas, was litt und starb, und
> vorher lange neben ihm geschritten war, mit hungernden Augen von
> ihm den Inhalt des Lebens sich erbettelnd. Denn an ihn hatte sie ge-
> glaubt, als wäre ihm die Kraft und Tugend aller Dinge zugewachsen, die
> er ihr zerstört und die schwächer gewesen als sein Wort. Und nun starb
> sie; voll von schweren unruhigen Gedanken, die er in sie geworfen.
> Hilflos . . . verfangen in die prunkende Vielfalt seiner Seele, in die er sie
> gehüllt. Er hatte geglaubt, sie trüge, frei von aller Schwere . . . das
> Wissen, das lange verworren auf ihm gelastet war; und er fühlte jetzt:
> Mit der ganzen Last der Sehnsucht hatte er sie beladen, und sie trug
> kaum ihre Gewande. (*GW,* 561)

> [She seemed sexless to him; something that was suffering and dying,
> that previously had walked beside him for a long time, begging from him
> the content of life with hungry eyes. For she had believed in him, as
> though in him resided the strength and virtue of all the things he had
> destroyed for her, that were weaker than his word. And now she was
> dying, full of heavy, restless thoughts with which he had burdened her,
> helplessly trapped in the resplendent diversity of his soul, in which he
> had enveloped her. He had believed that she bore, weightlessly, the

knowledge that had long weighed confusedly upon him, and now he felt: he had encumbered her with the full burden of longing, and she was scarcely able to carry the weight of her garments.]

Paul's life with this woman, as it emerges in his recollections, had been one of serenity, beauty, and self-imposed detachment from all ugliness and pain. Confronted now by the reality of her suffering and death, he simply cannot grasp it: "Wie er wusste, dass er auf einer Erde stand, die wirbelnd im weiten Weltenraum rollte, und es dennoch nicht fasste, er hätte sonst schwindelnd taumeln müssen—so wusste er, dass sie sterben müsse, und fasste es nicht" (*GW*, 531). ["Just as he knew that he stood on an earth that rolled about in the vast universe and yet did not understand that—otherwise he would have staggered dizzily—so he knew that she must die, and could not grasp it."] The attitude of the dying wife is clearly meant to show that life, despite the suffering it entails, is infinitely precious:

> Neidisch tastete ihr Blick über die Ringe an ihren Fingern und den lichten geschnitzten Ahornschrank an der Wand; das alles lebte ja nicht, aber es durfte noch dauern. Ein unerhörtes Unrecht geschah ihr; höhnend lebte eine Welt weiter, und sie allein musste sterben. Keines half ihr zum Leben, niemand starb mit ihr—und in ihren Augen war der hilflose Hass der Sterbenden gegen alles, was lebte. (*GW*, 565)

> [Enviously her glance moved across the rings on her fingers and the carved oak cupboard against the wall; these things were not alive, to be sure, but they could continue to last. An incredible injustice was happening to her; mockingly a world went on, and she alone had to die. Nothing helped her to live, no one died with her—and in her eyes was the helpless hatred of the dying toward all that lived.]

This passage also illustrates two other themes which were to recur frequently in Beer-Hofmann's work: the indifference and apparent cruelty of nature and the loneliness and isolation of the individual, particularly in death. The second theme found its most succinct expression in the famous line from the "Schlaflied für Mirjam": "Keiner kann Keinem Gefährte hier sein" ["No one can be a companion to anyone here"].

The preciousness of life is also the major motif of Paul's lurid fantasy of the orgiastic love-death rites in the Syrian temple.[16] This dream within a dream, fraught with eroticism,[17] ends with the question,

Was trieb sie denn barfuss durch den Staub der Strassen und die stein-
starrenden Wege der Gebirge zum Tempel hin, was drängte sie gebietend weg von der Gewohnheit ihres Lebens? . . . Fühlen wollten sie—
endlich ihr Leben fühlen; den Kreis gleichverrinnender Tage, in den es
gebannt, sprengen, und—wie sie die eingeborenen tiefen Schauer vor
dem Tode kannten—die schlummernde Lust des Lebendigseins jubelnd
aufwecken. (*GW,* 547–48)

[What drove them barefoot through the dust of the streets and the stony
paths of the mountains to this temple, what drew them imperiously away
from the routine of their lives? . . . They wanted to feel—at last to feel
their lives; to break the circle of monotonous days to which their lives
were condemned, and—knowing the innate, deep horror of death—to
awaken, jubilantly, the slumbering lust for life.]

Like the attitude of the dying wife, the motives of the ritualists reflect
both a horror of death and an awareness of the preciousness of life.

The Syrian temple of this episode has been interpreted as "the work
of a community," i.e., the thousands of people who helped to build it,
". . . pushing aside their personal life, served only the common task."[18]
This is true as far as it goes, but there are indications that in a higher
sense the temple symbolizes the work of the artist, his joy and pain in
creating, and his motivation to create: "Über ihr eigenes Leben hinaus
ihre Macht zu weiten, schaffend den Marmor zum Verweser ihrer
Herrschaft zu bestellen, dass er noch in kommenden Tagen an Seelen
zu rühren vermochte, wenn die ihre längst entflattert, gab so viel
Glück—dass es schien, als wäre dem Leiden aller Stachel gestumpft
und selbst der Tod um seinen Sieg betrogen" (*GW,* 540). ["Extending
their power beyond their own lives, making the marble the agent of
their dominion, so that in days to come it might move souls when their
own were long departed—this provided so much happiness that it
seemed as though suffering had lost its sting and even death had been
cheated of its victory."][19] Further evidence that the temple represents
the work of the artist is found in Beer-Hofmann's reference to the
temple-builders as "unruhig irrende Seelen, deren Schaffen vielleicht
Gebet war und vielleicht ein Freveln" (*GW,* 540) ["restlessly erring
souls, whose creation was perhaps a prayer and perhaps an outrage"]—
a reference reminiscent of Beer-Hofmann's statement that the poet
barely escapes committing an outrage (see note 44, chapter 1).

Paul's character develops considerably in Part II: he wrestles with
the problem of death, not as an abstraction but in concrete form; he
experiences a growing sense of oneness with all creation, past and
present; and his tentative feeling that life has meaning and purpose,

however obscure they may seem, strengthens into conviction. This becomes clear from Paul's reflections on *A Thousand and One Nights*— the only book he has been able to read in the months that his wife has lay dying:

> Mit klaren ungequälten Augen sahen die Menschen dieses Buches. . . . In gewundenen labyrinthischen Wegen lief ihr Leben, mit dem anderer seltsam verkettet. Was einem Irrweg glich, führte ans Ziel. . . . Kein blindes Geschick schlich hinter ihnen und schlug sie tückisch von rückwärts zu Boden; in weiter Ferne, regungslos, mit unerbittlich offenen Augen, harrte ihr Schicksal ihrer; sie wandelten den Weg zu ihm, wenn sie vor ihm flohen. (*GW, 532*)

> [The people in this book saw with clear, untroubled eyes. . . . Their lives moved along labyrinthine paths, strangely linked to the lives of others. What resembled a false path led to the goal. . . . No blind fate crept up insidiously and felled them from behind; at a distance, motionless, with inexorably open eyes, their fate awaited them; they travelled toward it even when they fled it.][20]

The dream of Part II is presented, finally, as the prophetic shaper of life: in it Paul experiences virtually everything that will happen to him in the waking state in Parts III and IV, and the development of his character in these last two parts corresponds to that in the dream of Part II. In this sense Part II is a prophecy, and Parts III and IV are the representation of its fulfillment.

The death motif is represented in Part II by the dying wife, in Part III, by Georg's death. There is no account of his actual dying; the reader learns of his unexpected death through Paul's thoughts, as he accompanies Georg's body to Vienna the next day. At the beginning of this reverie Paul's thoughts dwell less on Georg himself than on the reactions of others who learned of his death. Their behavior had clearly appalled him:

> Zuerst das Staunen darüber, dass ein so junger gesunder Mensch über Nacht gestorben sei; die Rührung über die Schicksalstragik, die sie darin fanden, dass Georg kurz vorher eine Professur erhalten hatte . . . und wenn sie hörten, dass seine Eltern tot seien und dass er keine Geschwister habe, trösteten sie sich . . . und erklärten, dass schliesslich ein Tod durch Herzschlag, ohne Schmerzen und Krankheit, jedenfalls der schönste Tod sei. Gereizt und erstaunt starrte Paul auf ihre Lippen, die so unfehlbar sicher, geschäftig dieselben Worte formten. . . . alle glichen unheimlich verzerrt einander, wenn, wie fertige rasch gewechselte

Masken, erst Staunen, dann Trauer, und Trost, und sichere Lebens-
weisheit, über ihr Antlitz sich legte. (*GW,* 570)

[At first astonishment that so young and healthy a person had died
overnight; then emotion at the fateful tragedy they saw in the fact that
Georg had received a professorship only shortly before . . . and when
they heard that his parents were dead and that he had no brothers and
sisters, they comforted themselves . . . and declared that death by heart
attack, without pain and illness, was at any rate the best kind of death.
Irritated and amazed Paul stared at their lips, which busily formed the
same words with such infallible certainty. . . . in an eerily distorted way
they all resembled each other when first astonishment, then sadness,
comfort, and sure wisdom descended upon their faces like ready-made,
quickly changed masks.]

Paul soon recognizes, however, that for all his revulsion he is not much
different than they. First comes the realization that "was ihn jetzt
erschütterte, war nur der Tod, nicht G e o r g s Tod" (*GW,* 572). ["what
now moved him was merely death, not *Georg's* death."] He is shocked
to realize that even if the day ever comes when he mourns Georg,
"auch das würde nur der Schmerz sein, dass Georg i h m gestorben
war, nicht dass Georg nicht mehr leben durfte" (*GW,* 572–73). ["that
too would only be the pain of knowing that Georg had left *him*, not
that Georg had been denied a longer life."] Paul consciously acknowledges here the same self-centered grief that he experienced more or
less unconsciously in his dream of the dying wife.

Paul's vivid, imaginary picture of what Georg's life might have been,
had he lived to old age, represents the young Beer-Hofmann's gradually emerging conception of the true poet's life: Georg, a physician,
would not have lived a life of detachment, insensitive to the world's
suffering, nor would he have been one of those "die bloss mit gehäuf-
tem Wissen und Händen, geschickt wie gute Werkzeuge, ihr Handwerk übten. Wie die Augen der Künstler an allen Dingen tasten und
die Form um ihr Schicksal fragen . . . so hätten seine Augen voll Frage
auf leidenden Menschen geruht" (*GW,* 575). ["who practice their craft
merely with accumulated knowledge and hands like good tools. As the
eyes of artists touch all things and seek their fate in form . . . so would
Georg's eyes have rested questioningly upon those who suffer."][21] Paul
imagines how Georg would have turned his patients' beds toward the
window, with its view of the sun and the clouds, "nur damit die
Sehnsucht nach dem Leben draussen und die Hoffnung in ihnen nicht
stürbe" ["so that hope and the yearning for life outside would not die
in them"].

Paul extends his mental picture to include the thoughts, feelings, and recollections of Georg's patients; through one of them, Beer-Hofmann reintroduces the motif of human isolation and loneliness. The patient recalls an experience from his young manhood: standing alone on the desolate shore of a deserted lake, he had been overwhelmed by the feeling that he was alone:

> Keine Brücken führten von ihm zum Duft der Pflanzen, zum stummen Blick der Tiere, und zur Flamme, die nach oben lechzte, und zum Wasser, das zur Tiefe wollte, und zur Erde, immer bereit alles zu verschlingen und alles wieder von sich zu speien. Und Blicke und Worte und erratene Gedanken der Menschen waren lügnerische Brücken, die nicht trugen. Hilflos und niemandem helfend, einsam nebeneinander, lebte sich ein jedes, unverstanden, stumm, zu Tode. (*GW*, 580)

> [No bridges led from him to the fragrance of plants, to the mute glance of animals, to the flame that licked upward and the water that sought the depths, and to the earth, ever ready to devour all things and spew them forth again. And people's glances and words and divined thoughts were deceptive bridges, not strong enough to carry them. Helpless and helping no one, side by side in loneliness, each one lived himself to death, mute and not understood.]

Now, as the patient lies dying, he feels that this, and indeed all his life's experience had meant little to him because

> der graue Schutt gleich verrinnender Tage hatte es bedeckt und verborgen. Wie Kostbarkeiten in verschütteten Schatzhäusern geflohener Könige, hatte es lange geruht, *bis Georgs Wort es gehoben*. Vorher hatte es wenig bedeutet: ein Duft in der Nacht, das Verhallen einer Stimme, Wasser, das verrann, und ein Schatten um Mittag. Mutter – Jugend – Liebe – Erkenntnis – hiess es jetzt, und war genug, ein ganzes Leben reich zu erfüllen. (*GW*, 580; italics added)

> [the grey ash of monotonously elapsing days had covered and concealed it. Like costly objects in the ruined treasuries of fleeing kings, it had rested long, *until raised by Georg's words*. Earlier it had meant little: a fragrance in the night, the echo of a voice, water that trickled away, a shadow at midday. Now it meant mother – youth – love – understanding – and it was enough to fill a whole life richly.]

The earlier comparison of Georg to the artist and the phrase "Georg's words" in the passage just quoted are scarcely accidental. Like the temple-builders of Part II, Georg symbolizes the artist, and particularly the writer. Different from other human beings, yet one of them; sensitive to all things; full of compassion and understanding; at once an observer of life and a man deeply engaged in it—Georg has the power to ease men's suffering, satisfy their longing, and open their eyes to things which "the grey ash of monotonously elapsing days" had previously obscured.[22]

It is noteworthy that Paul imagines Georg's days as happy: "So waren seine Tage glücklich sich wiegend einhergezogen, trunken vom Gefühl der grossen Macht, die Georg übte. Denn nur um seinetwillen, damit er helfen könne, schien alles da zu sein" (GW, 580). ["Thus his days passed, happily cradled, intoxicated by a sense of the great power Georg exercised. For everything appeared to exist only for his sake, so that he could help."] This shows a significant change from Part I, where Paul's conception of happiness was a state of detachment in which all things were untouched by life "and its searing breath." It also reflects the same sense of oneness he had felt with everything in the dream of Part II.

Paul makes a determined effort to turn his thoughts away from Georg entirely, for "etwas in ihm, das er gern verleugnet hätte . . . redete leise, hartnäckig, im Tone von aller Welt, hässliche Allerweltsworte: dass Georg nun einmal tot sei und dass alle sterben müssten . . . und dass es dumm sei, sich damit zu quälen, wie Georgs Leben und Sterben vielleicht geworden wäre" (GW, 584–85). ["something in him that he would have liked to deny . . . spoke the ugly words of the world, softly, stubbornly, and in the common tone of the world: that Georg, after all, was dead and that we all had to die . . . and that it was stupid to torment himself with how Georg's life and death might have been."] Paul is deeply dismayed, but he cannot help himself; he senses that "tief in ihm, geweckt durch Georgs Tod, die Freude am eigenen Lebendigsein schamlos aufjubelte" (GW, 585). ["deep within him, awakened by Georg's death, the joy at being alive welled up in shameless jubilation."] The ruthlessness of life and nature was conveyed in Part II primarily from the perspective of the dying wife; here it is experienced—with an accompanying sense of shame—by the living.

Paul's "joy at being alive" is revealed by his impressions and feelings as he watches the passing scenery from the window of the train: "Eine neue, junge Schönheit, die er noch nicht gekannt, schien den Dingen geschenkt, die er sonst kaum sah" (GW, 585). ["A new and youthful beauty, previously unknown to him, seemed given to things which otherwise he scarcely noticed."] The passage is replete with symbols of life: a swarm of bees in a field of clover, a peasant boy in the grass with a girl, and a profusion of blossoming flowers are just a few. As he sees these things with new eyes, Paul realizes "dass er nur sich selbst belog, wenn er an diesen frühen Tod wie an etwas dachte, was Georg vor vieler Qual behütet hätte" (*GW,* 587–88). ["that he was only deceiving himself when he thought of this early death as something that had protected Georg from much agony."]

In the ensuing pages, however, Paul seems to change his mind, for in wishing that Georg had lived to enjoy fame, power, and a happy old age, Paul is struck by the realization that he has never seen old age and happiness together in a human face. He recalls a winter morning when he had stood before the display window of a toy shop. Gazing at the toy theatre in the foreground with its puppet figures of warriors, a king, an old man, an executioner, and a princess, Paul had realized that in children's play, no matter where their vivid imaginations carried them, "kein Verirrtsein gab es, wie in den Strassen begrenzter Städte; in Grenzenloses, in Zeit und Raum schien man zu sinken und—sich darin verlierend—fühlte man sich ein Teil von dem, darin man sich verlor" (*GW,* 590). ["there was no going astray, as in the streets of narrow cities; children seemed to sink into limitless time and space and—losing themselves therein—felt part of that in which they lost themselves."] Their play, a preparation for life, somehow went beyond mere imitative motions: "Am Faden des Lebens selbst schienen sie zu spinnen, der unzerreissbar—von andern kommend zu anderen—durch ihre schweren Hände glitt; Spinner und—wie sich ihr Leben mit hinein-verflocht—Gespinst zugleich für die nach ihnen" (*GW,* 591). ["They seemed to spin the thread of life itself, which—coming from and passed on to others—glided, unbreakable, through their heavy hands; spinners and—as their own lives were woven in—also the spun thread for those who came after them."][23] Unconsciously, children seemed to sense "dass in der Erde alle Schicksale sich vorbereiteten. . . . Ihr entstammt alles, was in ein Leben sich lenkend verflocht. Nicht tot und ohne eigenes Schicksal waren die Dinge. . . . Aus der Tiefe stiegen sie nach oben und wanderten—von einander nicht wissend—auf vielverschlung-enen, unerkannten Strassen uns zu. Zur vorbestimmten Zeit waren sie an unserem Weg . . ." (*GW,* 591–92). ["that all fates readied them-selves in the earth. . . . From it stemmed everything that wove the fabric of a life. Things were not dead and without a fate of their own. . . . They rose up from the depths—unaware of each other—and trav-elled toward us over unrecognized, intricately entwined paths. At a pre-determined time they stood before us. . . ."]

All of this only seems to confirm the sense of a mysterious purpose in life and to continue Paul's development toward an affirmation of it, but as he glances upward his eye is caught by the sign above the entrance to the toy shop. It consists of several luridly painted masks: "Grauenhaft verzerrt waren hier die Hässlichkeiten des Alters gehäuft" ["Accumulated here in horrible distortion was all the ugliness of old age"]. In his mind's eye, Paul sees the faces of all the old people he has ever encountered: a ghastly, endless procession of feebleness, infirmity, and physical deterioration in every repulsive detail, old people in whom "der Tod gegen die abgenützte Haut sein Antlitz drängte, ungeduldig wartend, begierig zu erscheinen" ["death's countenance pressed against the worn-out skin, waiting impatiently, greedy to appear"]. Comparing these hideous images to Georg's vitality and youthful handsomeness at the time of his death, Paul concludes at the end of Part III that Georg had been spared after all: "Glücklich durfte man Georg nennen, wie man die beiden Jünglinge glücklich und Lieblinge der Götter nannte, von denen Paul als Knabe gelesen" (*GW*, 598). ["Georg could be called fortunate, like the two youths Paul had read about as a boy, who were called the favorites of the gods."] Paul has not thought of the story of the youths of Argos in many years, but now he effortlessly recalls its concluding lines: "Da erlangten sie das beste Lebensende, und es zeigten die Götter dadurch an, dass dem Menschen besser sei zu sterben als zu leben" (*GW*, 598). ["Thus they attained the best end of life, and thereby the gods made known that it was better for man to die than to live."] According to *Daten*, the title Beer-Hofmann originally intended to give the novel was *Götterliebling* [*The Favorite of the Gods*], an obvious reference to the story of the youths of Argos. Beer-Hofmann's view of early death as fortunate clearly changed in the years he worked on the novel, which ends with Paul's affirmation of life. This necessitated a change in the original title, which was no longer compatible with the novel's conclusion.

Several months have elapsed between Parts III and IV, though the reader has no immediate indication of this. In past years Paul's autumn walks had brought him a sense of peace: "Klar schien sich alles um ihn zu gliedern. Wie es sich sonderte und stufte, erkannte er die Zusammenhänge. . . . Gerechter als vorher, vermochte er im stillen klärenden Licht des Herbstes den stummen Willen der Landschaft zu erfassen, durch die er schritt, und ihr Gesetz" (*GW*, 600). ["Everything around him seemed clearly arranged. As things took distinguishable form he recognized their connections. . . . In the still, clarifying light of autumn he was able to grasp, more justly than before, the silent will of the landscape through which he walked, and its law."] These are not at all his impressions now: "Er fand überall dasselbe: eine Landschaft, die hässlich geschrumpft schien, oder öde sich dehnte; die keinen Zwecken mehr diente und nichts mehr erhoffte; nur mehr wartend lag" (*GW*,

603). ["Everywhere he found the same thing: a landscape that seemed ugly and shriveled or that stretched away like a wasteland; a landscape that served no further purposes and hoped for nothing more, but only lay there waiting."] Unlike the countryside teeming with life which Paul had observed from the window of the train, this is a dying landscape.

Paul is also vexed by the disturbing sensation of having forgotten something that he feels is important for him to remember: "Und er begriff es nicht: Wie konnte etwas, das einmal sein gewesen, ihm so verloren gehen, dass er auch nicht mehr wusste, was er verloren? Was ihn einmal so erschüttert hatte, musste es nicht von jeher und für immer, unverlierbar in ihm ruhen? Was war noch sicher, wenn sein eigenes tiefes Empfinden ihn so verriet?" (*GW*, 602). ["And he could not understand it: how could something that had once been his become so lost that he no longer even knew what it was? What had once moved him so deeply, did it not have to remain in him from then on and forever, impossible to lose? What was still safe or certain, if his own innermost feelings betrayed him in such a way?"] A series of associated questions follows, the last of which is the major question Beer-Hofmann attempts to answer in this concluding section of the novel: "Und gab es nichts, das unvergänglich in ihm war, das ihn nicht verlassen konnte, dessen er sich sicher fühlen durfte, und das immer ihm, und n u r ihm, so gehörte, wie das Blut in seinen Adern?" (*GW*, 602). ["And was there nothing in him that was not transitory, that could not leave him, of which he could feel certain and that would always belong to him and *only* him, like the blood in his veins?"] This seemingly casual reference to his blood will unexpectedly assume crucial significance as the novel reaches its conclusion.

What Paul is vainly attempting to remember is the dream of Part II and the insight it had given him. His encounter in the park with the mother and her daughter sets in motion the process of recall; the daughter bears a striking resemblance to the girl by the river (Part I) and the dying wife (Part II). Now Paul remembers in sharp detail the dream and his impressions of its richness and fullness, his feeling of oneness with everything in it. He now understands why he has found the world of dreams so much more satisfying than life itself: it is the uncertainty of life, the lack of control over its events, that have made Paul try to remain aloof from it.

As in earlier parts of the novel, his reflections lead him to the intuition of an all-encompassing purpose in life. Now, however, this purpose is not merely unifying; despite the inability of finite human beings to comprehend this, the guiding purpose behind all life is also just:

> Unbegangene dunkle Strassen gab es, auf denen, ehe man starb, alles noch den Weg zu einem finden konnte. . . . Denn ehe noch der letzte Atem über klaffende Lippen wehte . . . konnten unerkannt vielleicht Vollstrecker nahen, die h i e r Verworrenes h i e r noch lösten, die an noch Lebenden Urteilssprüche vollzogen, irdisches Unrecht zu irdischem Recht richteten, und die . . . qualvolle Tode verhängten, und Verlassene wieder einführten in die Heimat, und Gefesselte hinaus, in Seligkeiten.
>
> Ziemte es sich nicht, auch vor der verhüllten Möglichkeit gerechter Lose, ehrfürchtig seine Augen zu beschatten? (*GW*, 609–10)

> [There were dark untravelled streets on which, before one died, everything could find its way to one. . . . For even before the last breath wafted through parted lips . . . executors, perhaps unrecognized as such, might yet approach who would resolve chaos not in the beyond but *here,* who would execute sentences upon those still living, set earthly injustice right . . . ordain agonizing deaths, lead the abandoned to their homes and the enslaved to blissful freedom.
>
> Was it not proper to shield his eyes reverently before the hidden possibility of just fates?]

Here Beer-Hofmann still presents his conviction in the form of a question, but it is clearly a rhetorical one. More than in any of the earlier passages of the novel, he emerges here as the *exculpator dei.* In the ensuing pages he dispenses with rhetorical questions and has Paul conclude: "Gerechte Wege ging alles; ein jedes das Gesetz erfüllend, das ihm vorgeschrieben. . . . Und Unrecht k o n n t e nicht geschehen; denn Irdischem war nicht die Macht gegeben, G e s e t z e zu beugen, die in der buntverworrenen Vielfalt des Geschehens, herrlich, klar, einfältig, geboten" (*GW*, 616). ["All things travelled a just path, each fulfilling the law prescribed for it. . . . And injustice *could* not occur, for the earthly was not empowered to bend *laws* that prevailed, splendid, clear, and simple, in the colorfully tangled diversity of events."]

In the final pages of the novel, the theme of a just and purposeful universal order is given a new and unexpected dimension: Paul's experience of it is linked to the Jewish tradition. The reader learns for the first time that Paul is a Jew, and he is convinced that his Jewish blood and heritage are what have led him to his new insight: "Denn über dem Leben derer, deren Blut in ihm floss, war Gerechtigkeit wie eine Sonne gestanden, deren Strahlen sie nicht wärmten, deren Licht ihnen nie geleuchtet, und vor deren blendendem Glanz sie dennoch mit zitternden Händen, ehrfürchtig ihre leidenerfüllte Stirne beschatteten" (*GW*, 621). ["For above the life of those whose blood flowed in him, justice had stood like a sun whose rays did not warm them, whose light had never shone for them, yet before whose blinding radiance they nevertheless reverently shielded their suffering brows with trembling hands."]

The Israelites' conception of a just God stands at the center of Paul's vivid mental picture of his ancestors:

> Vorfahren, die irrend . . . wanderten . . . von den Niedrigsten noch verworfen—aber nie sich selbst verwerfend; . . . in Leiden nicht zum barmherzigen Gott—zu Gott dem Gerechten rufend. Und vor ihnen viele, deren Sterben ein grosses Fest . . . war . . . sie selbst an Pfähle ge-schnürt, das Feuer erwartend, schuldlos Sünden sich erdichtend und ihre Qualen "Strafe" nennend, nur dass ihr Gott ein Unbezweifelter, Gerechter, bleibe. Und hinter ihnen allen ein Volk, um Gnaden nicht bettelnd, im Kampf den Segen seines Gottes sich erringend. . . . Und langsam ihren Gott von Opfern und Räucherungen lösend, hoben sie ihn hoch über ihre Häupter, bis er, kein Kampfesgott von Hirten mehr—ein Wahrer allen Rechtes—über vergänglichen Sonnen und Welten, unsicht-bar, allem leuchtend, stand. (*GW*, 621–22)

> [Forebears who wandered the earth . . . rejected even by the lowliest—but never rejecting themselves; . . . crying out in their suffering not to a merciful God but to God the just. And before them many, whose dying had been . . . a great festival . . . they themselves bound to stakes, awaiting the fire, in innocence inventing sins and calling their torment "punishment," so that their God might remain undoubted, just. And behind them all, a people not begging for grace, but wresting for them-selves through struggle the blessing of their God. . . . And gradually removing their God from sacrifices and incense-burning, they raised Him high above their heads until He stood—no longer the battle god of shepherds but the preserver of all justice—above transitory suns and worlds, invisible, shining for all.]

This passage is also like a first sketch of the vast panorama of Jewish character, history, and religious tradition that Beer-Hofmann was later to create in the *David* cycle; the reference to a people who struggle for the blessing of their God certainly suggests that Beer-Hofmann was already considering a work about Jacob and his experience at Peniel.

Arthur Goldschmidt, in his early review of *Der Tod Georgs*, regretted this unexpected turn the novel takes, saying, ". . . it is a great pity that the story ends thus."[24] Unfortunately, he does not elaborate. If he meant that there is insufficient preparation for this association of Paul's affirmation of the world order with his Jewishness, and that its sudden introduction in the very last pages weakens the novel's unity, his contention would have some justification. The passage just quoted, with its exalted language, expresses far more than ethnic pride, but there has been no previous indication that Paul, though concerned throughout the novel with philosophical questions, feels any interest in an established religion. Of course, Beer-Hofmann may have deliberately introduced this motif so belatedly and unexpectedly in order to surprise his readers. Conscious craftsman that he was, this is entirely possible and it certainly would not be the only such literary "trick" in the novel. Although probably not part of Beer-Hofmann's original conception of the work, it was in all likelihood both a literary device and the expression of his growing sense of pride in and identification with his Jewish heritage. In any case, it is a theme which in time was to engross him more and more.

It has been said that the decadent heroes portrayed by young Austrian writers of the turn of the century "inevitably . . . reach the same conclusion—namely, that they have no free will and are mastered by their nerves or life or fate. They have reached the last stage of civilization, and there is no tomorrow."[25] Beer-Hofmann's young hero definitely does not conform to this type by the end of the novel, where the problem of detachment from versus involvement in life is resolved in favor of involvement. This resolution is not presented in vague generalities, but in specific relation to Paul and his future life. For him there is a tomorrow, and it will be very different from his past.

There is, to be sure, a strong note of determinism in Paul's affirmation of life. He realizes that life itself—"a powerful master"—can compel him to involvement; his new awareness that no one may live for himself alone is followed by a passage which clearly demonstrates Beer-Hofmann's conviction that the mysterious world order makes involved human beings of us all, whether we will it or seek to avoid it (GW, 617). Nonetheless, Paul's affirmation of life is an act of will, for he goes far beyond a resigned acceptance of what he cannot change. He recalls his past life with contempt, and envisions a new one in which he will be no passive tool of fate, but an active participant who, by virtue of voluntary involvement, will achieve the sensitivity to and the sense of oneness with all creation that he previously had experienced only in his dreams:

Verschlungen in ein grosses von Urbeginn gemessenes, feierliches Kreisen, trieb sein Leben, mitdurchtönt von ewigen Gesetzen, die durch alles klangen. Kein Unrecht konnte ihm geschehen, Leiden waren kein Verstossensein, und der Tod schied ihn nicht von allem. Denn, vermählt mit allem, allem notwendig und allem unentbehrlich, war jede Tat vielleicht ein Amt, Leiden vielleicht Würden, und der Tod eine Sendung vielleicht. (*GW,* 619)

[Entwined in a great and solemn circle measured from the beginning of time, his life pulsed, resounding with eternal laws that rang through all things. No injustice could happen to him, suffering was not a matter of being cast out, and death did not separate him from all things. For wedded to all, necessary and indispensable to all, every deed was perhaps an office, suffering perhaps honor, and death a mission perhaps.]

With this passage the last vestiges of decadence disappear: death is neither "the ultimate happiness" (as it was in Part I) nor a longed-for escape—the earlier the better—from the suffering and ugliness of life (Part III). It has become the culmination of a pilgrimage.

Life and the human community are symbolized at the close of the novel by the excavating street workers in front of the park entrance—they stand hip-deep in the ground. Paul follows a group of them whose work shift has just ended. It has been suggested that Beer-Hofmann strives here to establish a link between his hero and the human community, but fails to do so: "Paul is a youthful representative of the Jewish *bourgeoisie* in Austria with its inherited culture. He does not work . . . he is alone."[26] That Paul does not overtake or join the workers seems to support this interpretation, as does the sentence, "Sie sprachen miteinander in einer fremden Sprache, die Paul nicht verstand" ["They spoke to each other in a strange language that Paul did not understand"]. The next sentence, however, strongly suggests that this whole passage is meant to show Paul's *newness* to life, not his failure to enter it: "Langsam ging er hinter ihnen, unbewusst in den schweren Takt ihrer Schritte verfallend" (*GW,* 624). ["Slowly he followed them, unconsciously falling into step with the heavy beat of their footsteps."] The heavy rhythm of their footsteps also suggests Beer-Hofmann's realization that the affirmation of life and a just universal order is extremely difficult; the *advocatus Dei,* as he was later to observe, has a much more demanding task than the *advocatus diaboli,* for nothing is harder than to justify the course of events in the world.

Having examined the content of *Der Tod Georgs,* we can turn to a discussion of it as a representative novel of that turn-of-the-century movement known as *Jugendstil,* or *art nouveau.* Early critical essays on *Jugendstil,* which attempt to define the essence of the movement, scarcely mention Beer-Hofmann, and even later studies of literary

Jugendstil do not discuss *Der Tod Georgs* as being exemplary of that style.[27] Perhaps the reason for this surprising omission lies in the very pluralism, not to say profusion, of styles that flourished at the turn of the century. Many were similar to each other, yet different enough to merit separate names: in addition to familiar terms like Impressionism, Symbolism, Neo-Romanticism, and *Jugendstil* (*art nouveau*), one also encounters such designations as "biologische Romantik," "Manierismus," "Dekorativismus," and (particularly in connection with Viennese trends) "Sezessionismus." Walter Lennig recognized the problem this pluralism poses when he noted that "one of the difficulties of identifying literary *Jugendstil* is that it did not develop a binding linguistic style, as the plastic arts developed a style of form."[28]

More recently *Der Tod Georgs* has received critical attention in connection with *Jugendstil*.[29] Fischer associates the novel with the movement, but recognizes the difficulty of placing it squarely in that stream and nowhere else. He attributes this difficulty to the novel's stylistic pluralism: "All of these observations certainly do not suffice to justify the label '*Jugendstil*-story.' The work is indeed a strikingly rich repository of motifs and images that may legitimately be ascribed to *Jugendstil*, but it surely would not be difficult also to find evidence in it of Impressionism, Neo-Impressionism, Symbolism, etc."[30] In terms of its motifs, language, and imagery, *Der Tod Georgs* is indeed a *Jugendstil* novel, but its ending represents a renunciation of the decadent attitudes and impulses commonly associated with that movement. Far more than the novel's stylistic pluralism, that ending—which reflects a decided shift in Beer-Hofmann's philosophical base—prevents *Der Tod Georgs* from being classified unequivocally and exclusively as a work of *art nouveau*. As noted in chapter 1, Beer-Hofmann's early decadence was not an end, but a beginning, first marked by his affirmation of life and the universal order in the closing pages of *Der Tod Georgs,* and then culminating in the *Historie von König David* and *Paula*.

The word *Jugendstil* itself provides a useful point of departure for a discussion of the nature of the movement, for one of its most striking characteristics is its preoccupation with youth. This sometimes (as in *Der Tod Georgs*) finds expression as a pronounced fear and horror of old age and death. The emphasis upon youth also influenced the movement's concept and image of woman, one of the dominant motifs of *Jugendstil* art and literature (and already discussed as one of the major motifs of *Der Tod Georgs*).[31] Sternberger has noted the period's "erotic attitude toward the childlike," and described the resulting view of woman as ". . . an ideal of delicate slenderness, the suggestively touching qualities of angular elbows and shoulders, of thin, pale, still undeveloped girls' bodies."[32] Jost has drawn attention to still another aspect of this image of woman: "Female figures, engrossed in solipsistic reveries, are the exclusive creatures of a sustained cult of beauty that has a secret affinity to the sick, the declining, the decaying, to exhaustion, paralysis, and dull passivity."[33] Many passages already quoted from *Der Tod Georgs* readily identify the girl by the river, the woman in the clouds, and Paul's "wife" as belonging to this type.

The male counterpart of this *Jugendstil* woman is the aesthete, or in more extreme form, the dandy.[34] One need only think of Paul's aesthetic sensibilities, his fastidiousness, his (to use Hofmannsthal's phrase) "almost somnambulent surrender to every manifestation of beauty," to recognize in him a representative of this type.

In sharp contrast to Naturalism, the literature of *Jugendstil* seldom deals with social and political problems, and if at all, only marginally. Its subject matter instead reflects a decided preoccupation with the exotic (often taking the form of the Oriental or Middle Eastern), the fantastic, the opulent, the sensual. Again one recognizes that the dream which comprises the largest part of *Der Tod Georgs* reflects these same preoccupations. Jost has pointed out that *Jugendstil* also shows "a marked inclination to the nocturnal side of nature . . . to the macabre and lustful, to the monstrous and the satanic. . . ." He also refers to the "linking of ecstatic religiosity with an eroticism that inclines toward hysteria."[35] Regrettably, he cites no examples; none would have served better than the Syrian temple episode of *Der Tod Georgs.*

Another characteristic of *Jugendstil* literature is its pronounced symbolism and imagery. As Schmutzler notes, floral and avian images prevail.[36] Favored birds are the swan and the peacock, universally associated with grace and exotic beauty. The preferred flowers are the lily and the lotus blossom. These are usually associated with water, another popular image and symbol of *Jugendstil* literature. An example from *Der Tod Georgs* is Paul's recollection of the forest pond at daybreak, adorned with yellow lilies and still untouched by "life and its searing breath." This, of course, is not the only point in the novel where the water image is used; it figures symbolically in every part of the book: the river of Part I, the artificial lake in the Syrian temple of Part II, the deserted lake in Part III (recalled by one of Georg's patients), and the fountain of Part IV.

The language of *Der Tod Georgs* likewise marks it as a *Jugendstil* work. The antithesis of tight, terse prose, the novel's language is fraught with symbolism (at times a bit too insistent, as, for example, the phallic symbolism of the temple episode), richly detailed and reflecting an intense awareness of colors, shapes, and sounds. Particularly illustrative are the passages describing Paul's sensitivity to the phenomena of nature, beautiful artifacts, etc. (*GW*, 524, 525, 528, 542ff., 562, 586–87, 604, to cite only a few.)

The language of the novel also reflects Beer-Hofmann's intense and abiding concern for the renewal of the word. One indication of this is the passage in which Paul recalls the language of heroic tales he had read as a boy: "Wenn er sprach, meinte er das Antlitz seiner Worte zu sehen, die der mühevolle Dienst des Alltags verzerrt und kraftlos und niedrig gemacht. Aber tot und verklärt und entrückt allem unedlen Dienen war die Sprache, in der von jenen Helden geschrieben stand; sie redete nicht von Geschehenem, sie war Magie, die es heraufbeschwor" (*GW*, 538). ["When he spoke, it was as though he could see the countenance of his words, whose laborious service in everyday life had distorted them and made them common and powerless. But dead and transfigured and removed from all mean or common service was the language that told of those heroes; it did not merely tell of past events, it was magic that conjured them up."] One could also point to the passage (*GW*, 584–85) in which the phrase *hässliche Allerweltsworte* ["the ugly words of the everyday world"] occurs, and to the one in which Paul recalls the meaningless platitudes of his acquaintances when they learned of Georg's death (*GW*, 570).

Beer-Hofmann strives very consciously to avoid "Allerweltsworte," the worn-out language of the everyday world. This, of course, is true of all creative writers, who seek to renew the word by using it in fresh, imaginative ways, on multiple levels of meaning. For the *Jugendstil* writer, however, it is often also an expression of the "instinctual, almost somnambulent surrender to every manifestation of beauty." *Der Tod Georgs* contains many passages in which its author seems utterly intoxicated by the word *per se* as he describes various manifestations of beauty: a landscape, an art object, precious stones, a beautifully woven piece of cloth. Perhaps the most notable example is the long introductory passage to the Syrian temple rites: Beer-Hofmann sets the scene in elaborate detail, conjuring up brilliant images of the building of the temple, its structural beauties, and the wealth of treasure it contains. With this in mind, it is easier to understand one reviewer's assertion that " 'Der Tod Georgs' only appears to be a story; it is really a connected series of linguistic jewels, of sparkling sentences and splendor-laden images."[37] The word itself becomes an ornament, a decoration existing for its own sake.

At the same time, the language of *Jugendstil* represents a desperate effort to revitalize both language and life: "Literary language had again become almost as sterile as in the seventeenth century, when it was in its beginnings. Thus one either had to break with that language or examine it with utmost exactness in search of charms that were hidden or previously overlooked. This is precisely what the *Jugendstil* masters did, and in the process they became great craftsmen, probably more from necessity than intentionally. Their so-called aestheticism consisted merely of a strict distinction between worn-out effects and those that had not been exhausted."[38] As Lennig notes, however, this intense effort often led to "artificiality, however much that was in contradiction to the renewal of life which they had set themselves."[39]

A number of critics have recognized that with *Der Tod Georgs,* Beer-Hofmann emerged as an innovator, anticipating the techniques of Proust, Joyce, Virginia Woolf, and Hermann Broch years before their works appeared. Indeed, some seem to regard him as the inventor of stream-of-consciousness writing in German literature.[40] There is some justification for that view: except for the very brief conversation with which *Der Tod Georgs* begins, the entire story unfolds in Paul's mind.

Since there is an unfortunate tendency to use the terms "stream of consciousness," "interior monologue," and "erlebte Rede" ["indirect interior monologue"] as though they were completely synonymous, it seems necessary to begin the discussion of Beer-Hofmann's techniques with some definitions. The difference between interior monologue and "erlebte Rede" has been formulated very concisely by Rasch: " 'Erlebte Rede' is a narrated, not a quoted, interior monologue."[41] Interior monologue (as in Schnitzler's *Leutnant Gustl*) transmits the character's thoughts and sensations without benefit of any intermediary, while "erlebte Rede" (as in *Der Tod Georgs* and the earlier stories, *Camelias* and *Das Kind*) maintains the convention of a narrator. As will be shown, however, the line of demarcation can be erased almost completely, if—as is the case in Beer-Hofmann's prose fiction—the narrator as such is not permitted to intrude or interrupt in the slightest.

Both "erlebte Rede" and interior monologue fall within, but constitute only one level of, the very broad category known as "stream of consciousness"—namely, the language level on which thoughts are actively formulated into words.[42] The stream-of-consciousness technique, however, can also include the rendering of a vast range of consciousness lying below the language level; the attempt to express the sub-lingual level is often called the technique of "sensory impression," distinguished from interior monologue and "erlebte Rede," but, like them, a sub-category of the stream-of-consciousness technique.[43] (Probably one of the most skillful representations of sub-lingual consciousness is the latter part of Molly Bloom's reverie in *Ulysses,* where

Joyce succeeds in conveying the increasingly nebulous and inchoate thoughts, sensations, and images that immediately precede sleep.)

Such categories and definitions are valuable as working tools; one of the pitfalls of their use is that they can easily become ends in themselves, molds into which literary works are sometimes forcibly poured. What the following discussion will attempt to show is that Beer-Hofmann's technique, while corresponding most closely to "erlebte Rede," does not fit perfectly or completely into any one of these categories, but contains elements characteristic of several of them, and that in addition to these, he uses a number of much older and more conventional literary devices.

There is no question that *Der Tod Georgs* is a stream-of-consciousness novel. Its content alone provides ample evidence of that. As noted earlier, *Der Tod Georgs* contains amazingly little external action, and what little is there has importance only as a supporting phenomenon, i.e., as a means of setting the scene or of establishing a certain framework. The novel's internal action is clearly of far greater interest and importance to the author. Robert Humphrey's conclusion about stream-of-consciousness writing in general can readily be applied to Beer-Hofmann's novel: ". . . the realm of life with which stream-of-consciousness literature is concerned is mental and spiritual existence—both the whatness and the howness of it. The whatness includes the categories of mental experiences: sensations, memories, imaginations, conceptions, and intuitions. The howness includes the symbolizations, the feelings, and the processes of association. It is often impossible to separate the what from the how."[44] This does not mean that stream-of-consciousness writers are any more concerned than earlier novelists were about rendering character and human experience as faithfully as possible; it simply means that they concern themselves with different areas of human existence—the earlier novelist with "motive and action," the stream-of-consciousness novelist with "psychic existence and functioning." It is the difference, Humphrey remarks, "between being concerned about what one does and being concerned about what one is."[45]

In Beer-Hofmann's novel, as in many other modern works of prose fiction, the problem of technique centers about two much-disputed conventions: the narrator and his role, and the treatment of time, including use of tense.[46] Beer-Hofmann's technique is not interior monologue in the strict sense, since thoughts and utterances are related, rather than quoted; his technique conforms to that of "erlebte Rede" in its use of a narrator, but the narrator of *Der Tod Georgs* functions solely as storyteller, and interrupts his narration neither to tell us anything about himself nor to analyze or interpret the protagonist's thoughts, sensations, and impressions. Thus, what is strictly speaking an objective technique is used to present the most highly subjective material. The "objectivity" gained by the use of a narrator is more than offset, however, by his lack of intrusion, often carried to such an extent that long passages of reflection or reverie are developed without any introductory phrase at all (such as "Paul thought," or "Paul wondered"):

> Und wenn man n i c h t mehr erwachte? Wenn in die Mitte buntverkleideter hastiger Träume ... der Tod, der wirkliche Tod trat, und alle Türen zum Leben hinter ihm zuschlugen? . . . Träume waren es, solange man noch aus ihnen erwachen konnte. . . . Aber, wenn aus dunklen Klüften hervorgebrochene, flüchtig rauschende Träume nicht mehr ins wache Leben mündend sich ergossen, wenn sie am Tod, der sperrend in die Mündung trat, sich stauten—erstarrten sie nicht? Wurden sie nicht hart, schwerlastend, unwiderruflich wie das Leben, das einzige Leben für den, der vor dem Tod von keinem anderen mehr erfuhr? (*GW*, 608; for other examples see pp. 538, 575, 595–96, 609)

> [And if one did *not* awake? If in the middle of rapidly moving, colorfully garbed dreams . . . death, real death entered and all doors to life slammed shut behind it? . . . They were dreams, as long as one could awake from them. . . . But if swiftly thundering dreams, broken forth from dark chasms, no longer emptied into waking life, if they were obstructed by death, which blocked the estuary—would they not be paralyzed? Would they not solidify, weighing heavily, irrevocable as life, the only life for him who learned of no other before death overtook him?]

The questions which constitute this passage are not set off by quotation marks; the reader is obviously meant to regard them as directly transmitted thoughts that are crossing the protagonist's mind at that moment.

While the narrator's lack of intrusion gives the work virtually the same sense of intimacy and immediacy that interior monologue conveys, it also creates a problem of credibility. The reader's willingness to accept the literary convention of the omniscient author is strained considerably when an obviously existent but completely anonymous narrator tells him things about the protagonist and the workings of his mind that no outsider could possibly know. Since the narrator never does tell us that Paul has confided his story to him and he in turn is telling it to us, we assume that the narrator is telling the story on the basis of his own recollections and observations. The "observations" he makes about the setting and the external action (e.g., Paul's walk along the river, his train trip to Vienna) are entirely plausible. These sections, however, constitute only a small part of the narrative and are important largely as a means of establishing the mood and setting the scene. Much more significant are those passages of the novel that deal with what is transpiring in Paul's mind, and these are the ones that create a problem of credibility. How, for example, could an observer-narrator possibly know what Paul is thinking when he wakes from his dream?

> Er neigte sich der Wand zu und presste seine Stirne an die kalte Mauer. Wie gut das tat; nun konnte er wieder denken. Was war *denn* geschehen? *Also:* Er war am Abend den Fluss entlang gegangen—*ja* . . . Und dann?— Dann hatte er sich schlafen gelegt und hatte lebhaft geträumt—und jetzt war er wach—das war alles. Aber wenn er nur geträumt hatte, warum war dann noch jetzt . . . dieser Schmerz in ihm? Als wäre ihm wirklich die gestorben, von der er geträumt. Die gab es *ja doch* gar nicht! . . . Jetzt schon schien alles zu verblassen, und er musste ein wenig nachdenken, wenn er sich an das Zimmer erinnern wollte, in dem er im Traum gewesen. . . . Er kannte *ja* gar kein Haus, das dem glich, von dem er geträumt hatte; und was war das *doch* für ein Landgut gewesen, auf dem er bei seinen Grosseltern das Frühjahr verbrachte? Er hatte *doch* seine Grosseltern gar nicht gekannt! (*GW*, 567–68; italics added)

[He leaned toward the wall and pressed his forehead against its coldness. How soothing that was; now he could think again. What, *then,* had happened? *All right:* in the evening he had walked along the river—*yes* . . . And then?—Then he had gone to bed and had a vivid dream—and now he was awake—that was all. But if he had only dreamed, then why was there still this pain in him? As if the woman in his dream had really died. But she didn't *even* exist, *after all!* . . . Already everything seemed to fade, and he had to think a bit, if he wanted to remember the room in which he had been in the dream. . . . He didn't *even* know a house that resembled the one he had dreamed of; and what sort of country estate was that, *anyway,* where he had spent the spring with his grandparents? *Why,* he had never *even* known his grandparents!]

This passage provides an excellent example of Beer-Hofmann's technique of alternating description and "erlebte Rede" within the same paragraph, and without the use of quotation marks to signal the transition. The first sentence is conventional description by the narrator (as is the sentence that begins, "Jetzt schon schien alles zu verblassen . . ."); the rest of the passage is "erlebte Rede," imbedded in the paragraph and not set off by quotation marks. In making the transition, Beer-Hofmann instead relies on the use of adverbs and particles (italicized above), dashes (which suggest the associative pattern of Paul's thoughts), and questions designed to create the illusion that Paul, at this precise moment, is mentally reconstructing his dream and the events that led to it.

The problem of credibility also stems from Beer-Hofmann's language and style. Despite the use of a narrator, the reader's prevailing impression is one of direct exposure to the protagonist's immediate and most intimate thoughts and feelings—virtually the same impression that interior monologue evokes. Again, however, the reader's good will is put to a hard test: it is difficult to believe that anyone couches his immediate thoughts (to say nothing of fleeting impressions and sensations) in such formal, lofty language and flawless grammar. An example of this is found in Part IV:

> Aber wusste er denn, ob nicht auch dies aus vielem, das ihn fremd umgab, nur herangeweht an ihn war? Aus dem Erinnern an einen Traum, aus dem Schatten fremder Frauen, der über ein dunkles totes Wasser fiel, aus Wolken und dem Abend und dem Wind? Welches Zeichen war ihm denn gegeben, dass dies nicht vergänglich in ihm war, dass es ihn nicht verlassen konnte, dass er sich dessen sicher fühlen durfte? (*GW*, 621)

> [But did he know whether this, too, had not merely been wafted to him from among the many strange things that surrounded him? From the memory of a dream, from the shadow of unknown women which fell upon dark, dead water, from clouds and the evening and the wind? What sign had been given him that this was not transitory in him, that it could not leave him, that he could feel certain of it?]

As Bowling observed, "To be convincing, interior monologue must be no more logical and formal than ordinary speech."[47] In *Der Tod Georgs*, however, the language in which the hero's immediate thoughts are transmitted is often decidedly flowery, and the rules of conventional syntax are almost always observed.

The attempt to apply objective narrative technique to highly subjective material is indicative of Beer-Hofmann's ties to both the literary past and the future: like many later writers, he is far more interested in what his characters think and feel than in what they do, but he is not yet prepared to go as far as his successors in experimenting with or relinquishing conventional techniques. In this sense, his consistent use of the third person and the narrative preterite is a concession to the past. Except for the novel's opening conversation, the third person is used throughout; the narrative preterite is seldom abandoned, and then usually to express (in the past perfect tense, albeit with fairly consistent omission of the auxiliary verb) recollections of events lying farther back in time. This is true not only of the novel's "real" situations and events, but of its imaginary ones as well. Less conventional, by contrast, is the grammatical usage in Paul's hypothetical musings about the course of Georg's life, had he lived to old age. After a few conventionally constructed sentences in the subjunctive, there is an almost imperceptible shift to the indicative, narrative past:

> Zwischen Leiden und Genesung und Tod hätte Georgs Weg geführt. Jede bunte und überschätzte Tracht, die Menschenschicksale untereinander schied, war wie versengter wertloser Lappen von ihnen gefallen; nackt und allen gemein, ging aller Handel der Menschen um Leben und Tod. Von dort, wo Georg stand, waren alle Eitelkeiten weggegangen. . . . Und wenn sein Wissen schwieg, war sein Tun noch nicht zu Ende. . . . Wenn er sich über Kranke neigte, fühlten sie, dass sie in den Schutz dieser Augen sich schmiegen durften, und seine Worte stiegen langsam, wie aus tiefen Brunnen, zu ihnen, schwer, vollgeschöpft voll Weisheit und Güte. . . . (*GW,* 576)

> [Georg's path would have led him between suffering and convalescence and death. Every colorful and over-valued costume that distinguishes one human fate from another had fallen from them like scorched and worthless rags; naked and common to all, the whole traffic of men was a question of life and death. From the place where Georg stood all vanities had departed. . . . And when his knowledge failed, his activity was still not finished. . . . When he bent over the sick they felt that they could cling to the protection in his eyes, and his words rose slowly to them, as if from a deep well, heavy and brimming with wisdom and goodness. . . .]

This shift from the subjunctive to the indicative heightens the realism of the passage, and causes the reader to forget, at least momentarily, that Georg is in fact dead, and never actually had these experiences.

One of the important new trends in prose fiction that *Der Tod Georgs* heralds is a subtle but fundamental change of attitude toward the reader. It no longer startles us today, but it was still new when Beer-Hofmann's novel appeared. The change can best be seen in the absence, or at least in the drastic reduction in the amount, of exposition, i.e., passages which provide explanations, background information, or otherwise orient the reader. Either the author presupposes a more sophisticated reading public than his predecessors were wont to do or he does not feel so obliged to explain to the reader. If we are baffled about the context of a given situation or train of thought, no matter; the author may orient us later—and then again he may not. Beer-Hofmann usually does, but only after the fact; thus, we do eventually learn that Part II of the novel is a dream.

Another aspect of this change in attitude toward the reader has already been mentioned in connection with Beer-Hofmann's early novellas: Rasch, it will be recalled, names the abrupt beginning as a typical feature of turn-of-the-century narrative style. *Der Tod Georgs* conforms to this pattern. After a relatively brief description of the physical setting, for example, Part II continues with the lines: "Scheu und verstohlen aß er dann; und dass er essen konnte, empfand er wie schamloses Unrecht an ihr, die unten seit Wochen sterbend lag" (*GW*, 530). ["Shyly and furtively he ate; and that he was able to eat struck him as a shameless injustice against her, who for weeks lay dying downstairs."] It is apparent that someone is dying, but who is she? We do not know, and it will be some time before we find out. This, of course, is an effective means of maintaining the reader's interest; one is not likely to put the book down before discovering what it's all about.

The change in attitude can also be seen in the passages which present the protagonist's recollections, reveries, and mental associations. Every writer (no matter how dedicated he may be to the concept of art for its own sake) attempts to communicate something to somebody; Beer-Hofmann spoke in his later years of the beauty and pleasure art brings to the lives of others as one of the primary justifications of its creation. Still, the reflections and reveries of *Der Tod Georgs* are written, in a sense, for no reader at all. They are akin to the soliloquy in that they are couched in very smooth, correct, indeed elegant prose (in contrast to the freely associative and sometimes ungrammatical ramblings of convincing interior monologue), but they differ from the conventional soliloquy in this important respect: soliloquy assumes, at least tacitly, a direct and immediate audience, whereas the reflective passages of *Der Tod Georgs* do not. Paul is not conveying his thoughts to another character within the novel, and one does not have the impression that he (or his creator) is particularly bent on conveying them to the reader either; his reflections are as uninhibited as though he really were alone. This does not signify actual indifference to the reader, of course; the author creates this illusion in order to heighten the realism of these passages, to make them more like the thought processes of real life. As noted earlier, however, the formality and grammatical flawlessness of the language sometimes detract from the illusion the author is attempting to create.

Still another new trend to be found in *Der Tod Georgs* is the author's treatment of time, which often involves a device that Ford Madox Ford called "eccentric chronology." "It became very early evident," Ford said, ". . . that what was the matter with the novel . . . was that it went straight forward, whereas in your gradual making acquaintanceship with your fellows you never do go straight forward. . . . You could not begin at a man's beginning and work his life chronologically to the end. You must first get him in with a strong impression, and then work backwards and forwards over his past. . . ."[48] This last statement describes precisely Beer-Hofmann's approach to the treatment of time in *Der Tod Georgs*: the external events of the novel—Georg's arrival for a visit, his death, Paul's train trip to Vienna, etc.—occur in chronological sequence, but the crucial internal action does not conform to this time scheme at all. The author "first gets his hero in with a strong impression" in Part I, and then proceeds to "work backwards and forwards over his past." The external, chronological events are interrupted repeatedly and at length (the longest interruption being the dream of Part II) by reflections, sensations, and recollections which relate to other points in time, ranging from antiquity to the immediate past to the future. Paul's dream, by the time it is ended, has ranged over a gigantic span of time, and not in chronological order. It begins with "the present," in which Paul's wife is dying; moves next to the immediate past, with memories of his courtship of the girl by the river; approaches the present again when he reflects on their seven years of married life; next moves still farther back in time to his childhood; and then takes an enormous leap backward to antiquity and the Syrian temple episode, returning finally to "the present" and the death of the wife (*GW*, 530–69). At this point, moreover, still another level of time is introduced: as Paul wakes and it becomes apparent that he had dreamed everything in the preceding pages, we find ourselves in the novel's "real present," as opposed to "the present" of the dream.

Occasionally, the transition from the novel's present to earlier points in time resembles the technique of the flashback in motion pictures.[49] An example of this is the smoothly achieved shift (in Paul's dream) from the present to the time of his childhood: "Er fühlte es, dass er weniger litt, seitdem sie neben ihm lebte, und er begriff es, wenn er an seine eigene Jugend dachte. Abseits von andern Kindern war er aufgewachsen . . ." (*GW*, 536). ["He sensed that he had suffered less since she lived beside him, and he understood that, when he thought of his own youth. He had grown up apart from other children. . . ."] Another example is the transition (in Part III) from the present, in which Paul is travelling to Vienna with Georg's body, to his earlier experience in front of the toy shop: "Paul schloss das Fenster, dann trat er zurück ins Coupé. Er lehnte sich müde in die Ecke . . . 'Ein glückliches Alter!' Wusste er von einem? Oder hatten seine Augen jemals in der Menge fremder Menschen, auf einem Antlitz Alter und Glück beieinander gesehen? Er erinnerte sich an einen Wintermorgen; die Strassen waren noch leer, and die Kaufleute öffneten erst ihre Läden . . ." (*GW*, 588). ["Paul closed the window and stepped back into the compartment. He leaned wearily in the corner . . . 'A happy old age!' Did he know of one? Or had his eyes ever seen, in a crowd of strangers, old age and happiness together in one human face? He recalled a winter morning; the streets were still empty and the shopkeepers were just opening their stores. . . ."] At other times, when the author concentrates with great intensity and infinite detail upon a given image, the effect is that of the close-up in a film—for instance, the masks above the toy shop entrance (*GW*, 592–93). In such close-ups, the reader feels that time has been suspended altogether.

The use of dream and fantasy is one innovation that may be regarded as a fundamental characteristic of stream-of-consciousness fiction. Dating back to the Baroque, the use itself is not new, nor is the fact that the dream is as vivid as "real life," if not more so. "The peculiarity of the new method," as Joseph Warren Beach said, "lies in the author's neglect to indicate where the actual leaves off and the imaginary begins."[50] In this Beer-Hofmann is a forerunner of such writers as Joyce, Dorothy Richardson, Kafka, and Broch. He does orient the reader, letting him know that all but the last few pages of Part II was a dream—but only afterward.

The similarity between Beer-Hofmann's technique and Joyce's, however, lies less in the employment of such devices than in the use of recurring motifs as a formal means of organizing and unifying their material.[51] A first reading of *Der Tod Georgs* leaves one with the impression of chaos, of a bewildering mass of thoughts, impressions, sensations, and images all jumbled together. A closer examination reveals that this is a very deceptive first impression; beneath the seeming chaos of the surface, one becomes aware of very strict and rigorous attention to form, reflected above all in Beer-Hofmann's use of recurring motifs.[52] This is the unifying principle that gives the novel form and brings order to its chaos. In a discussion of the novel in general, Alfred Döblin spoke of "a dynamic net, which gradually extends itself over the entire work, fastened to certain conceptions, and actions and persons are imbedded in this net. . . . If one asks, what do works with these laws of form resemble . . . [the answer is]: symphonies."[53] The development of themes in a symphony is indeed the best analogy with which to describe Beer-Hofmann's organization of his motifs, which, to recapitulate, are death, woman, the dream and its relation to life, the problem of decadence, aloofness from life versus involvement in it, and the question of a just and purposeful universal order. After its original introduction, each of these motifs is reintroduced at various points throughout the novel and either examined each time from a different perspective or developed further. Thus, the representative of the woman motif is characterized in Part I as unawakened to life and in Part II as unfit for it; she ultimately realizes its preciousness, but only when she is dying. The young woman in Part IV is so much like her that her appearance causes Paul to recall the dream he had been struggling vainly to remember. These representatives of the woman motif are brought into even sharper relief by the contrasting image of woman Paul has in the moment of insight that leads to his affirmation of life: "Und ihre ganze Seele trugen Frauen in demütigen Händen dem entgegen, den sie liebten; in allem was sie taten, wollten sie sich an ihn verschenken" (*GW,* 613). ["And women carried their whole soul in humble hands to him whom they loved; in everything they did, they wanted to give themselves to him."] Belatedly, Paul recognizes that the "wife" of his dream had been like that, too, but in his self-centeredness he had not realized it and, in fact, had stripped her of her identity and imposed on her his own.

The death motif undergoes similar development and variation. It is treated from the perspective of the dying (Part II) and of many diverse representatives of the living: the sensitive, high-strung protagonist, the temple-builders and the Astarte-worshippers of Part II, the sick and infirm in Paul's reverie of what Georg's life might have been like, the aged (evoked by Paul's memory of the toy shop in Part III), and even the acquaintances in Part III who reacted to Georg's death with such irritating platitudes.

The question of a mysterious but purposeful world order and the unity of all life within it is likewise taken up repeatedly after its original introduction. Beginning early in Part II with Paul's reflections on *A Thousand and One Nights* (*GW,* 531–32), and followed by many, increasingly insistent re-introductions (*GW,* 537, 552, 560, 568, 573–74, 580–82, 589–92, 600, 609–10, 614, 616–18, 621–22), the development of this theme indeed resembles a musical crescendo—moving from the "pianissimo" of Paul's tentative, groping questions to the "fortissimo" of his affirmation of the universal order in Part IV.

The language in which a motif is reintroduced sometimes undergoes slight variation, but frequently the reintroduction is more obtrusive, taken verbatim from an earlier passage. The author, moreover, does not limit himself to brief phrases (e.g., "inexorable fate," which almost invariably approaches along "labyrinthine paths"), designed, as they recur, to set in motion in the reader's mind the process of association; complete sentences and even whole paragraphs recur, almost or totally unchanged. The sentence, for example, with which the flashback to Paul's childhood begins, reappears after the Syrian temple episode in almost the same form: ". . . und er fühlte, dass er weniger litt, erst seitdem die neben ihm lebte, die jetzt da unten starb" (*GW*, 551). [". . . and he sensed that he suffered less, only since she, who now lay dying downstairs, had lived beside him."] The nature of the love-death rites is such that the reader has completely forgotten the dying wife; the repeated sentence refocuses attention on her and at the same time— through the addition of the word *jetzt*, ["now"]—returns us to the time level of the dream's present.

The recurrence of whole paragraphs is particularly striking in the treatment of the dream and its relation to life (Parts II and IV). Paul's reflections on the nature of his dream are repeated several times in Part IV (*GW*, 607, 612, 619). Such pronounced use of the leitmotif in the treatment of this particular theme serves several purposes: it is in Part IV that Paul finally recalls his dream, and the fact that the language of his recollection corresponds almost exactly to his original reflections underscores the profound impression the dream made on him. In addition, the author hereby reinforces his representation of the dream and the waking state as closely related, complementary realms of life. The dream, it will be recalled, is prophetic in nature: almost everything that happens to Paul in it he re-experiences in the waking state in Parts III and IV. In Part IV, the recollected observations and reflections on the dream become the basis of Paul's transformation, as he uses them to examine himself and his past life, and to plot the course of his future life. Finally, the pronounced use of the leitmotif in connection with this theme underscores Paul's ultimate affirmation of life. The word *gleichgültig* ["indifferent"] or a variant of it, serves as a key. The dream contained "nichts Gleichgiltiges"; after Georg's death, by contrast, Paul's thoughts return repeatedly to Georg's visit and to the fact that they had spoken of "fast gleichgiltigen Dingen" (*GW*, 571, 585, 597–98). In each instance the entire paragraph is repeated; the final recurrence of this passage is found on pages 622 and 623, but now several lines have been added that reflect Paul's newly acquired insight: "Sie sprachen von fast gleichgiltigen Dingen; aber wenn Georg den Kopf leicht zur Seite wandte, fiel Licht auf seine Lippen. Dann sah Paul die ruhigen gütigen Linien seines Mundes, die er lange kannte. Und gleichgiltige Worte, die Georgs Lippen formten, lösten sich von ihnen und sanken schwer, vollgesogen von Weisheit und Güte" (*GW*, 623). ["They spoke of almost indifferent things; but when Georg lightly inclined his head, light fell upon his lips. Then Paul saw the good and quiet lines of his mouth, which he had known for a long time. And the indifferent words that Georg's lips formed detached themselves and sank heavily, weighted by wisdom and goodness."] Paul now realizes that the "real" world also contains "nothing of indifference"; for the person who is voluntarily and unreservedly involved, it is as full, as rich and satisfying, as the world of dreams.

Written at the close of one age and on the threshold of another, *Der Tod Georgs* reflects much of the old but even more of the new. Later writers refined the techniques, were more subtle in their symbolism and imagery, less obvious in their use of the leitmotif, and more daring in their willingness to experiment, but Beer-Hofmann's novel remains a significant prelude to many subsequent trends in modern prose fiction.

Gedenkrede auf Wolfgang Amadé Mozart

This brief commemorative piece was first published in the *Frankfurter Zeitung* in 1906. The great difficulties Beer-Hofmann encountered in writing it were discussed in chapter 1; in later life he told Werner Vordtriede that he had resolved them by relating Mozart's life as a fairy tale.[54] In some respects that designation is appropriate; in others, to be discussed later in this section, it is questionable.

The opening paragraphs of the *Gedenkrede,* which provide a rich and colorful description of the geography and history of the Salzburg region, are clearly intended to create at the outset a fairy tale atmosphere, an impression of Mozart's birthplace as a fabled city. Should this have escaped the reader, the point is soon made more explicitly with the observation, "Andere Kinder mögen auf Märchen hören . . . aber dieses Kindes wunderbaren Fingern ist früh Kraft gegeben, die Welt sich aufzublättern wie ein Märchenbuch" (*GW*, 649) ["Other children might listen to fairy tales, . . . but this child's marvelous fingers are early endowed with the power to open the world like a book of fairy tales"], and with the repeated rhetorical question, "Ist dies ein Märchen?" (*GW*, 650). ["Is this a fairy tale?"]

In vivid language which evokes the glittering splendor of eighteenth-century court life, Beer-Hofmann recalls episodes in the life of the child, Mozart, which were indeed like the events of a fairy tale: his reception by the King and Queen of England and the court of the Holy

Roman Emperor, and the Pope's bestowal of the Order of the Golden Spur.

In a passage that skillfully links the famous landmarks of Salzburg with many of Mozart's musical themes, Beer-Hofmann touches upon the now familiar motif of the artist and his task—this time in language which emphasizes not the artist's suffering, but his *Auserwähltsein*:

> An einem Sinnbild mag dann der Knabe hier zuerst erkennen, was ihm— wie allen, die Gott zu Schöpfern aufgerufen—verliehen ist: Auf kleiner Menschen tägliche Hast und geschäftiges Mühen, vergängliche Lust und endliches Leid, mildlächelnd, ihrer Buntheit sich freuend, zu horchen—und zugleich dem Lobgesang zu lauschen, der aus der lärmenden Unruhe ihres Treibens feierlich sich hebt; und zu wissen, dass e i n Quell beides bewegt. (*GW*, 649)

> [Here in an image the boy perhaps recognizes for the first time what is granted to him—as to all those God calls to be creators: to listen to the daily hustle and bustle of common men, their transitory pleasure and ultimate suffering, smiling gently, rejoicing in the rich variety of it all— and at the same time to hear the song of praise that rises solemnly from the noisy restlessness of their activity; and to know that *one* source gives rise to both.]

The last line also expresses the familiar theme of the unity of all life in the universal order.

Although the general impression of the *Gedenkrede* is one of lightness and charm, the tone becomes darker when Beer-Hofmann traces the human passions, the joys and sorrows of men, expressed in Mozart's music. The author leads a long procession of Mozart's operatic characters before the reader, from Idomeneo to Don Juan and Donna Anna. His awareness of the death motif in Mozart's music is expressed by the questions, "Nimmt der Zug kein Ende? . . . Ist niemand mehr hinter euch?"—to which he replies: "Schweigt, ich brauche nicht Antwort! Denn die Augen dessen, der jetzt hinter euch tritt, kennt auch der, der ihn noch nie gesehen. Auch dir, du Ernster, der du jeden Reigen schliessest, hat der Meister Stimme gegeben . . ." (*GW*, 651–52). ["Is the procession not yet over? . . . Is there no one else behind you? . . . Be silent, I need no answer! For the eyes of him who hoves in sight behind you are known even to those who have never seen him. To you, too, earnest one, who closes every circle, the master has given voice. . . ."] This is reminiscent of the somber note which Eduard Mörike injected into *Mozart auf der Reise nach Prag* [*Mozart on the Journey to*

Prague], reflected in the *memento mori* theme of the poem that brings the novella to a close.

According to an acquaintance, the two artists Beer-Hofmann most loved and admired were Shakespeare and Mozart.[55] The *Gedenkrede* contains at least one passage which suggests that he saw certain similarities between himself and the composer: "So steht der Meister— vom Schicksal gestellt—an der Grenze zweier Zeiten. Ihm . . . ist es geschenkt, das Antlitz seiner Welt, ehe es sich wandelt, allen Kommen- den zu künden, und zugleich ein seliger Bote dessen zu sein, was, hinter aller Zeiten wechselndem Antlitz, ewig sich birgt" (*GW*, 652). ["Thus the master stands—placed by fate—on the boundary of two eras. It is given to him to proclaim to those of the future the counte- nance of his world before it is changed, and at the same time to be a blissful messenger of that which is eternally hidden behind the chang- ing countenance of all ages."] The radical changes which the new age will bring are expressed in musical terms, through a comparison of Mozart and Beethoven:

> Noch dürfen seine [Mozart's] Gefangenen hinter goldenen Gartengittern die freie Luft des Meeres schlürfen, und ihr Wächter heisst "Osmin"; es kommt die Zeit, wo ihr Leib, zwischen feuchtem Gestein, im Finstern fault, und ihr Herr wird "Pizarro" heissen. Noch jauchzt auf Don Juans Festen ein Maskenchor ein "Lebehoch" der Freiheit; es kommt die Zeit, wo Chöre von Gefangenen in düsteren Kerkerhöfen um Freiheit auf zum Himmel stöhnen. (*GW*, 652)

> [From behind the golden latticework of a garden Mozart's prisoners may still breathe the free air of the sea and their guard is called "Osmin"; the time is coming when their bodies will decay in the darkness of damp stone, and their master will be called "Pizarro." At Don Juan's revelries a masked chorus still shouts a jubilant "Long live freedom!"; the time is coming when choruses of prisoners in dark dungeons will moan to heaven for freedom.][56]

Continuing the comparison of Mozart and Beethoven as representa- tives of a waning and an ascending age, Beer-Hofmann, for all his love of Mozart's music, confesses: "Nicht immer will unsere Seele bei dir weilen. . . . Zu sehr hat man uns gelehrt, in unseres Wesens geheim- sten Schächten zu schürfen, und wir wissen von vielzuviel Leid. Von Jupiters weisser leidloser Stirn wenden wir unsere Augen, und suchen den tiefen mitleidsvollen Blick, der unter des Prometheus wehevoll geballten Brauen wohnt" (*GW*, 652). ["Our soul does not always want to remain with you. . . . We have been too thoroughly taught to dig in the most secret levels of our being, and we know of far too much suffering. We turn our eyes from Jupiter's white, untroubled brow and seek the deep and sympathetic gaze that dwells beneath Prometheus's painfully concentrated brows."][57] We admire Mozart as one reveres a god; we understand Beethoven and the Promethean drives which much of his music expresses.

Mozart's music, the author concludes, is for times of joy. Thus, in the closing passage Beer-Hofmann reintroduces the charming, fairy tale quality which characterizes the beginning of the *Gedenkrede,* and ends the piece with the same sentence with which it began.

The extent to which the *Gedenkrede* can be considered a fairy tale now needs to be examined more closely. Certain parallels do exist; the physical setting of the piece as described in the opening paragraphs certainly has a fairy tale atmosphere. Description, however, is not really characteristic of the fairy tale at all; as Max Lüthî observed: "The very fact that the fairy tale seldom describes its characters and physical settings, but only tersely names them, gives them a certain exactness. The fairy tale seldom grants a substantive more than one adjective: as if it feared to give us confusing variety instead of a clear picture, to entice us into the depths and therewith into formlessness."[58]

There is also a degree of similarity between the extraordinary fame and honor bestowed upon Mozart as a child of relatively humble origins and the fabulous adventures of his humble counterpart in the fairy tale. Again, however, the form and style of the *Gedenkrede* are not characteristic of the fairy tale: Mozart's adventures are *described*; those of the fairy tale hero are *shown*, with great singleness of purpose, in terms of action.[59]

The most compelling reason for questioning the designation of the *Gedenkrede* as a fairy tale, then, is the style and form in which it is written. In terms of its origins, at least, the fairy tale is folk literature (or *Naturpoesie,* as the Brothers Grimm said), and its style and language are correspondingly simple and uncontrived. This clearly cannot be said of the *Gedenkrede,* which also lacks the pronounced juxtaposition of "cruel punishments and glittering rewards, the sharp conditions and prohibitions and the black/white depiction of morality" that are such characteristic features of the fairy tale.[60] In other words, the *Gedenkrede* reflects too much of *fin-de-siècle* Vienna to be a fairy tale in the traditional sense. It is a work of description and reflection, not action; this is especially true, of course, of the brooding, melancholy passages which introduce Mozart's operatic characters and compare his music to Beethoven's.

It is almost certain that when Beer-Hofmann spoke of the *Gedenkrede* as a fairy tale, he was thinking of the Oriental genre, or even more specifically, his beloved *Thousand and One Nights*. In this light, the designation seems more appropriate; one of the major differences Lüthi notes between the European and the Oriental fairy tale is the latter's "love of description."[61] In any case, the fact that Beer-Hofmann attempted to resolve his difficulties with the Mozart piece by making it a fairy tale provides some insight into the temperament and aesthetic sensibilities of the man; like *Der Tod Georgs,* the *Gedenkrede* shows his predilection for the realm of fantasy. This does not mean that he was indifferent to the real world and what was happening in it; on the contrary, Beer-Hofmann and contemporaries like Hofmannsthal recognized the signs of decline and decay in their era and its culture far better than most people did. The signs were grim for those who had eyes to see, and it must have been tempting indeed to turn from them to fantasy. For the writer, however, this involved more than mere daydreaming; creating in this realm a much more beautiful world than the real one brought a measure of relief. Hofmannsthal, one recalls, warned Beer-Hofmann of the dangers that lay "in the disintegration of unrealized fantasies." The realm of fantasy, as a setting, also lent itself well to the representation of the moods, impressions, and sensations that Beer-Hofmann so often strove to convey.

Paula, ein Fragment[62]

That Beer-Hofmann's last work is not a biography in the conventional sense has already been noted, though his phrase "biographical book of reminiscences" does describe the work as far as content is concerned. The fragments are preceded by a foreword Beer-Hofmann wrote on January 19, 1944. It begins with a quotation (from Dante's *Vita Nuova*) that clearly states his purpose in writing *Paula*: "Und so darf ich denn—wenn es Ihm, in welchem alle Dinge leben, gefällt, dass mein Leben noch einige Jahre dauere—hoffen, von ihr zu sagen, was von Keiner jemals noch gesagt worden . . ."(*GW,* 677). ["And so I may hope—if it pleases Him in whom all things live, that my life last for a few years more—to tell of her what has never been told of any woman. . . ."] The foreword closes with a second quotation, also from *La Vita Nuova,* which could be regarded as the underlying theme not only of *Paula,* but of Beer-Hofmann's entire oeuvre: "Siehe ein Gott, stärker

denn ich; er kommt und wird über mich herrschen!" (*GW,* 679).
["Behold a God, stronger than I; He comes and will rule over me!"]
With this Beer-Hofmann not only expresses his profound conviction of
a guiding purpose in people's lives, but affirms his faith in a God whose
ways are wise and just—despite all the questions "to which nature
remains mute" and despite the fact that "we know of far too much
suffering." It needs to be emphasized that Beer-Hofmann made this
affirmation not only in his early adulthood, in the final passages of *Der
Tod Georgs,* and in all the dramas of the *David* cycle, but again at the
close of his life, after the indignities, injustices, and anguish he had
suffered at the hands of the National Socialists.

The writer of fiction, Beer-Hofmann says in the foreword, "mag,
was erwachte Phantasie ihm zuträgt, in sein Werk aufnehmen, es—mit
dem Schein eines Anfangs und eines Endes—zum Gleichnis eines Gan-
zen formen, Licht, Rhythmus, Farbe, schicksalhafte Verflochtenheit
des Geschehens frei wählen" (*GW,* 677). ["may include in his work
whatever his awakened fantasy brings him, form it—with the appearance of a beginning and an end—into an image of the whole, freely
choose light, rhythm, color, the fateful interweaving of events."] *Paula,*
he continues emphatically, has nothing whatever to do with fiction:
". . . in n i c h t s ist ihm [meinem Unterfangen] freie Wahl gelassen,
und ruhigen Herzens unbefangen zu bestehen, ist ihm nur gestattet,
wenn es Kraft hat, seine Reinheit zu hüten, nichts anderes sein zu
w o l l e n, als ein wahres, frommes, beglückendes Erinnern" (*GW,*
677). ["In *nothing* did this undertaking have free choice, and it will be
permitted to last with a peaceful heart only if it has the strength to
protect its purity, to *want* to be nothing other than a faithful, devout
remembering that inspires happiness."]

Despite this assertion, Beer-Hofmann did indeed form *Paula* "into
an image of the whole," even one "with the appearance of a beginning
and an end," the fragmentary nature of the work notwithstanding.
Beer-Hofmann acknowledges the book's fragmentary character in his
foreword: "So mag vieles unausgewogen erscheinen, vieles überstark
betont, vieles zu flüchtig gestreift, vieles verschwommen ins Dunkel
tauchend, anderes, überscharf umrissen, in zu grellem Licht . . . ver-
wirrend wird vieles bleiben . . ." (*GW,* 678). ["Thus many things may
appear insufficiently weighed, others unduly emphasized, some touched
upon too fleetingly, many things blurred and submerged in darkness,
others too sharply outlined, in too bright a light . . . much will remain
confusing. . . ."] He himself defends this with the observation that
Paula "wird nicht launenhafter, nicht ruheloser, nicht verwirrender,
nicht dunkler, nicht m e h r Stückwerk sein, als das Leben" (*GW,* 678).

["will not be more capricious, more restless, more confusing, darker, more of a fragment than life itself."] This is precisely the kind of selectivity and variation in emphasis that the writer of fiction exercises, and Beer-Hofmann, perhaps without being conscious of it himself, exercises it in *Paula,* too.[63] In this respect, as in others, his "biographical book of reminiscences" shows some similarities to his early works of prose fiction.

Paula is divided into five main parts of greatly varying length. Some of the fragments within each part bear sub-titles, others do not. The fragments derive their external unity from the fact that Beer-Hofmann and Paula are the central figures throughout—each fragment relates an episode or describes an experience from the life of one or the other, or both. As a literary work, the fragments have an internal unity, too, which stems from Beer-Hofmann's use of recurring motifs as an organizing principle and his application of techniques employed many years earlier in his prose fiction.

The first fragment, "Donnerstag, der fünfte Dezember, 1895" ["Thursday, 5 December 1895"], provides an account of Beer-Hofmann's family history, his own childhood, school and university years, and finally, the events of December 5, 1895: Beer-Hofmann's decision to give up writing until after he had travelled extensively; his encounter with Paula; and his thoughts, impressions, and emotions during and immediately after the encounter.

Entitled "Winter-und Frühjahrswochen 1896" ["Winter and Spring Weeks, 1896"], the second fragment relates the author's first acquaintance with Paula and the early weeks of courtship. This is followed by "Herbstmorgen in Österreich" ["Autumn Morning in Austria"], which begins with Beer-Hofmann's discovery—some months after his arrival in New York—of a seven-page manuscript written in Alt-Aussee in September, 1935. His re-reading of the manuscript leads to recollections of summer life in Aussee, a trip to Italy with Paula and the children, and further recollections of his courtship of Paula, including their trips to the Lake of St. Wolfgang and to Scandinavia.

The fourth fragment, "Alcidor," is Paula's story of her grandparents' poodle, with many details of her family history woven into the account. This section also includes "Der grosse Fürst Michael" ["The Great Prince Michael"], which tells of Beer-Hofmann's St. Michael's medal and his encounter with the Jewish engraver; "Frühjahr 1939" ["Spring 1939"], quoted in chapter 1; and "Aus vielen Jahren" ["From Many Years"], which provides brief but poetic recollections of Paula, Beer-Hofmann's relationship with her, and his pain and sense of loss at her death. The fifth part of *Paula,* "Träume," recounts six dreams Beer-Hofmann had of his wife after her death.

Although the first edition of *Paula* (edited by Otto Kallir) was not published until four years after Beer-Hofmann's death, the organization of the fragments stemmed from the author himself. In February, 1945, he wrote very detailed instructions for ordering the material, based on "dispositions" he had written earlier: "Beer-Hofmann wrote out no fewer than thirteen such 'dispositions,' the first on November 12, 1941, the last dated 'November – December, 1944.' Tormenting anxiety, deriving from the uncertainty about how much more time would be granted him, and the determination to transmit the book to the world exactly as he envisaged it, caused the poet to decide the place of each completed part within the entire work. Since the individual parts of the book did not originate in chronological order, the necessity of new 'dispositions' arose again and again, in order to provide guidance to the future editor."[64] Mention of this is not meant to minimize the editor's task, but simply to show that *Paula* is not a loose, haphazard collection of anecdotes, held together only by a common set of characters. Like the fictional works, it reflects Beer-Hofmann's very deliberate and purposeful ordering of his material.

Two themes dominate the work: love and destiny. In a sense Beer-Hofmann fuses them into one motif: the reader has an overwhelming sense of destiny at work in the lives of these two people (as indeed the author intends him to)—in their meeting each other at all, in their love for each other and their marriage despite great obstacles, in their life together. This is already evident from the fact that Part I, although dealing primarily with Beer-Hofmann's life before he met Paula, is entitled "Donnerstag, der fünfte Dezember 1895"—the date of their first encounter. The author is not content with this; with the insistence that also characterizes his development of themes in the fictional works, he interrupts his narration to say:

> Seite um Seite füllt sich, und noch ist Paulas Name nicht genannt worden. Von meinen Vätern und Ahnen ist die Rede, von Menschen, Zeiten, Orten, ihr fremd, scheinbar durch nichts mit ihr verbunden.— Und doch: da Paula und ich zum erstenmal uns sehen, ist sie sechzehn, ich neunundzwanzig—und zartes Erinnern frühester Kindheit, heitere Knabenjahre, Ungestüm und sorglos Frohes meiner ganzen Jugend . . . all das muss ja mit mir den Weg langer Jahre zu ihr hin finden. (*GW,* 695)

> [Page after page is filled and still Paula's name has not been mentioned. My forebears and ancestors have been the subject, persons, times,

places foreign to her, seemingly in no way connected with her.—And yet: when Paula and I see each other for the first time she is sixteen, I twenty-nine—and the tender memories of earliest childhood, the bright boyhood years, the turbulence and carefree happiness of my whole youth . . . along with me, all these things must find the way to her over the path of many long years.]

The author's conviction that he and Paula were destined to meet and to love each other is expressed again, more explicitly, in the closing pages of Part I: "Vorher war alles ein wirr verschlungener Knäuel, den ich nicht verstand—wo war der Sinn? Von Tag zu Tag hatte ich gelebt—nun war alles sinnvoll der Weg gewesen zu diesem Augenblick . . ." (GW, 767). ["Everything before was a chaotically tangled skein that I did not understand—where was its meaning? I had lived from day to day—now everything made sense as the path to this moment. . . ."]

This "chronicling of fate" reminds one of the brief, undated prose fragment, "Chronist des Fatums," in which Beer-Hofmann says: "Of everything created with words, the narrative tale is spiritually the purest form, or at least can be, if it reports the author's own experience. . . . Only he who takes it upon himself to relate his own experience, who—speaking of himself—nevertheless . . . only reports the will of fate . . . can, with a pure heart, be a reverent chronicler of fate while appearing to speak of himself" (GW, 637).[65]

The fragments which comprise *Paula* are designed not only to give the reader a vivid picture of this woman's appearance, personality, and character, but also to shed light on the many facets of Beer-Hofmann's love for her and hers for him. How completely this love dominated his life as a man is suggested by this passage:

Manchmal, wenn ich den Kindern beim Spielen zusehe, und Zärtlichkeit in mir aufquillt, erschrecke ich plötzlich, denn wie ein Blitzen leuchtet es in mir auf, dass ich die Kinder nicht anders denken kann, als "ihre Kinder" . . . und wie ich ihre Wangen liebe, und i h r e Hand—so liebe ich die Kinder, die ein Teil von ihr sind . . . und vielleicht haben die Kinder das—nicht g e w u s s t aber doch, ohne es zu wissen, gefühlt. (GW, 857)

[Sometimes, when I watch the children at play and tenderness surges up in me, I am suddenly alarmed, for it flashes through me that I cannot think of them except as "*her* children" . . . and just as I love her cheeks and *her* hand—so do I love the children, who are a part of her . . . and perhaps the children have—not *known* that, but somehow sensed it.]

His love for Paula dominated his life as a writer to an equal extent. *Der junge David* bears the dedication, "Für Paula, als ärmlichen Dank für unermessliches Schenken" ["For Paula, as poor thanks for immeasurable gifts"], and the volume of Beer-Hofmann's lyric poetry (*Verse*) published in 1941 is likewise dedicated to her. While such tributes may not have displeased Paula, she was deeply offended by Beer-Hofmann's inclusion of her, not in disguise but as the playwright's wife, in the "Vorspiel auf dem Theater zu *König David.*" Despite her displeasure, she eventually said, ". . . jetzt lass schon alles so, wie dus gemacht hast—es wird schon das Richtige sein" (*GW,* 820), [". . . just leave everything as you wrote it—it will probably be the right thing"], a remark which suggests that she shared Beer-Hofmann's conviction that things happen as they are meant to.

Beer-Hofmann's narrative technique in *Paula* differs in some respects from that of the earlier works, as dictated by the biographical and historical nature of the material. He not only relates his and Paula's story in the first person, but occupies a distinct place in the work as narrator—not in the sense of the author who is nowhere and everywhere present in his work, but as a person who tells a story and interrupts it occasionally to inject his own observations, to comment, and to explain. This is the case in the already-quoted passage (*GW,* 695) in which Beer-Hofmann explains why he is describing his own childhood in great detail. He concludes this interruption of the narration: "So mag mir auch noch weiterhin gewährt sein, von den Jahren meiner Jugend auszusagen, und von den Menschen, zwischen denen ich aufwuchs. Nur leicht umrissen soll all dies werden—gerade soviel, dass, was Paula und mich später umgibt, schon Vertrautes ist—nicht Fremdes, das Erklärung verlangt" (*GW,* 696). ["Thus I hope I may be further permitted to tell of the years of my youth, and of the persons among whom I grew up. All of this shall only be outlined—just enough so that what later surrounds Paula and me will be familiar to the reader, and not something strange that requires explanation."] Despite the matter-of-factness, this interruption is a literary device that takes us from the level of narrated time to "the time of the telling." In addition, the author-narrator creates the impression of taking us into his confidence: by explaining the reason for developing his story as he does, he offers a glimpse of the creative process itself.

Occasionally, the shift in time is effectively used to introduce or set the scene for recollections of earlier events; here it has the quality of a film flashback. At the beginning of "Herbstmorgen in Österreich," Beer-Hofmann describes the belated receipt of a suitcase (whose contents he no longer remembered) after his arrival in the United States.

The manuscript in the suitcase evokes a mental image of the place and time he had written these lines, and the shift in time is smoothly achieved: "Nicht anders als an jenem Herbstmorgen steht ja wohl noch das kleine Bauernhaus, in dem ich jene Seiten schrieb . . ." (*GW,* 777). ["The little farmhouse in which I wrote those pages probably still stands, no different than on that autumn morning. . . ."]

The shift to narrative time in the epilogue to "Alcidor" has the quality of editorial comment. Having related the story of "Alcidor" as Paula had told it to him (in language and style which the reader is to regard as hers), Beer-Hofmann appends an excerpt from a letter by Adalbert Stifter, and then comments: "In diesem Brief Adalbert Stifters ist die Situation äusserlich und seelisch dieselbe, wie in einer Stelle der kleinen Erzählung 'Alcidor' " (*GW,* 851). ["In this letter of Adalbert Stifter's the situation is outwardly and inwardly the same as in one passage of the little story, 'Alcidor.' "] The editorial tone is strengthened by Beer-Hofmann's observation that the wife of Dr. Otto Kallir had only that day called this similarity to his attention. At the close of the epilogue, the association of "Alcidor" with Stifter's experience reemphasizes the motif of the unity of all life, past and present: "Hier habe ich diesen wundervollen Brief angefügt, weil es mir ist, als würden durch ihn Adalbert Stifter, und Paula, und die zarten vornehmen Menschen, die ihre Mutter und ihre Grosseltern waren, und ich—der Herrschaft alles Zeitlichen entgleitend—von einem gemeinsamen, freundlichen, vertrauten Band sanft umschmiegt" (*GW,* 852). ["I have appended this wonderful letter here because it seems to me as if through it Adalbert Stifter, and Paula, and the gentle, refined people who were her mother and grandparents, and I—escaping the dominion of time—were gently encircled by a friendly, unifying, familiar bond."]

In some passages of *Paula,* Beer-Hofmann employs a technique that is more closely akin to later stream-of-consciousness writing than is the "erlebte Rede" of *Der Tod Georgs.* These passages seem more convincing, not only because they are written in the first person, but also because their language and syntax make them more realistic representations of the processes of thought. The episode in which Beer-Hofmann conveys what he felt during the first encounter with Paula provides a good example:

Auf dieser Flut treibt alles Erinnern hinab—meine Jugend, meine Kindheit, ich fühle Bangen—aber was ist Jugend, was Kindheit—Neues hat begonnen—was vorher war, war ein Eingepupptsein—dies hier ist meine wahre Geburt . . . um mich herum nicht die Welt, die Dinge—um mich der Weltenraum. Ich—nicht mehr einem Ziel zustrebend, nicht mehr auf

einem Weg, der endet—einbezogen—aufgenommen—kreisend in einer
Bahn—anfang- und endlos—Stern unter Gestirnen . . . (*GW*, 766)

[Borne by this tide, all memory courses down—my youth, my childhood,
I feel fear—but what is youth, what is childhood—something new has
begun—what was before, was a chrysalis—this is my true birth . . . not
the world, things, surrounding me—around me the universe. I—no longer
pursuing a goal, no longer on a path that ends—included—accepted—
circling in a path—a star among constellations, without beginning or
end . . .]

With the highly charged language of this passage, couched not in
complete sentences but consisting mostly of a welter of phrases linked
together by dashes, Beer-Hofmann comes close to expressing "was
sich nicht ausdrücken lässt" ["what cannot be expressed"].[66]

Beer-Hofmann's poetic license with his biographical material lies
partly in the very lyrical language in which much of *Paula* is written.
It also becomes clear at times that he exercised a certain amount of
license with historical fact for the reader's benefit. An example of such
exposition in disguise is the fragment sub-titled "Vor dem Laden" ["In
Front of the Shop"], in which Beer-Hofmann tells of eavesdropping on
the conversation of Paula's brother and Fräulein Karolin. The conversation seems rather contrived: it strikes one as unlikely that so many
details of the Lissy family's history and present circumstances would
have been discussed in a casual chat between Paula's brother and a
girl with whom she worked. The fact that Beer-Hofmann allowed
himself certain liberties is not really the important point—poetic license,
after all, is not something for which a writer needs to apologize. More
important is the fact that in private conversations and in the work
itself, Beer-Hofmann was extremely anxious to persuade the public
that *Paula* was not fiction in any sense of the word (in addition to his
emphatic assertion in the foreword, he interrupts the narration repeatedly to assure the reader that his representation of past events is
"accurate"). These protestations can only be understood in the context
of Beer-Hofmann's intense desire to be believed and his fear that he
would not be. The Western world had undergone devastating changes
that had erased virtually every trace of the life and times about which
he was writing. Quite aside from that, the conversations with Vordtriede (which took place during the writing of *Paula*) reveal that Beer-
Hofmann the writer had always been tormented by the question, "Who
will ever again believe anything I say, if I excite myself in words with
imaginary situations?" He may indeed have felt that his love of fantasy

had now come back to haunt him. One gains that impression from his description of the struggle to keep *Paula* free of fictitious elements: "I am doing nothing else than to defend myself with all my strength against flashes of fantasy. In times past I only needed to close my eyes and immediately the most diverse fancies presented themselves. Now I have all I can do just to ward them off."[67] There is no reason to doubt these words, but one is reminded of Thomas Mann's perceptive observation that literary works have a will of their own. Beer-Hofmann did not succeed in his efforts to write a strictly factual biography—and *Paula, ein Fragment* is the better for his failure.

3

The Dramatic Works

The dramatic oeuvre of Richard Beer-Hofmann consists of the five-act play, *Der Graf von Charolais,* which had its premiere in 1904 and first appeared in print in 1905; the pantomime, *Das goldene Pferd,* completed in 1922, but first published in its entirety in 1955; and the Biblical cycle, *Die Historie von König David,* to which the playwright devoted himself more and more exclusively after 1905, but which he did not complete. This chapter will explore the dramas' development of themes that were first introduced in the early prose fiction and will examine the language, style, and techniques that characterize Beer-Hofmann's theatrical works.

First, however, some general observations may be made which apply to all of Beer-Hofmann's dramas and to his life-long love of the theatre. He was intensely interested in everything theatrical and certainly regarded the drama as his principal genre; indeed, virtually everything he did after 1900 was connected with the theatre in some way. His almost unerring theatrical sense and great technical skill in staging and production were admired and respected by Max Reinhardt and many other contemporaries in the theatre. In 1918, when Leopold von Andrian was being considered for the directorship of the Burgtheater, Hofmannsthal wrote to Hermann Bahr: "I wrote to Poldy . . . that in the event of his appointment he would be in the happy position of finding in close proximity all the persons with whom it would be of inestimable value to talk, before his actual assumption of his duties: among these I meant first of all you, then Reinhardt . . . also Richard

B.H. and Strauss. . . . B.H. is . . . full of imagination and competence as an advisor in this sphere, however impossible he would be as director."[1] Although Hofmannsthal considered Beer-Hofmann unsuitable for the position, it clearly was not because he thought him incompetent; he was probably thinking of Beer-Hofmann's stubbornness and his imperious tendencies, especially in matters of art—traits which undoubtedly would have made it difficult for him to work with others as director-general of Austria's most important theatre.

Perhaps the word "stubbornness" does Beer-Hofmann an injustice— one might do better to use Schnitzler's apt term, "perfectomania." Many people, including some who knew Beer-Hofmann well, did not fully understand this "perfectomania," especially in theatrical matters. A letter Beer-Hofmann wrote to Erich Kahler in 1933 explains his reasons for the use of certain dramatic techniques and sheds considerable light on his artistic convictions in general:

> The breadth of comment that attempts to lay hold of landscape, lighting, costuming, position, tempo, dynamics, the shading of a word, mimic detail—this breadth does not stem from the unspent instincts of a director, or from lost chances, or a lost sense of artistic balance that places too much value on the *unimportant.* This breadth attempts to restore to the drama only important things that in the epic and lyric genres were always recognized as decisive and that have been lost to the drama . . . to far too great an extent. . . . I am trying to rescue for the drama, which today—as never before—is writhing in the throes of death and birth, a little of the marvelous, mystical union in which all things of the soul live. For: readied by the primacy of technology over our external lives, our sense of time and space is engaged in a still painful process of change. . . . And so I am trying to establish a healthier, more life-like, more organic, divinely intended relationship between everything that is seen, breathed, smelled, tasted, passed over in silence and done, and that which is spoken. . . . I realize that the reader is sometimes taken aback by this, and that he becomes impatient, but I *will* not, above all I *cannot* do otherwise without blaspheming what I call *art.* This strange soup that (presumably under some sort of mandate) I *must* brew, the reader will either have to eat or leave on the table. (*GW,* 877–78)

These remained Beer-Hofmann's principles and purposes for the drama throughout his life; his revision (as late as 1940–41) of the scenario of *Der Graf von Charolais* is evidence of that.[2] How he attempted to fulfill his purposes will be seen in the following examination of the dramas themselves.

Der Graf von Charolais

The text of the play is preceded by Beer-Hofmann's acknowledgment that the names of the main characters and several preconditions of the story are taken from the seventeenth-century English play, "The Fatal Dowry," by Philip Massinger and Nathaniel Field (*GW*, 323).[3] Except for the names and the historical setting, however, *Der Graf von Charolais* bears little resemblance to the earlier English play, and it is misleading to refer to Beer-Hofmann's drama as an adaptation of it, as several critics have done.[4]

In some respects *Der Graf von Charolais* seems to be a renunciation of earlier themes, rather than a restatement of them.[5] The world order presented in *Charolais* is mysterious but certainly does not appear to be just. This bitterly pessimistic drama, which has been called "a complete surrender of free will to blind 'chance,' "[6] and whose characters are presented as helpless puppets of fate, seems to negate the affirmation of life made earlier in the final pages of *Der Tod Georgs*. It will be seen, however, that the motifs are essentially the same; in *Charolais* Beer-Hofmann simply focuses our attention on their dark and fearsome side. The young hero of *Der Tod Georgs* came to realize that he had feared life and sought to remain detached from it because of its uncertainty and his lack of control over its events. Beer-Hofmann now carries this realization to its ultimate conclusion, showing in *Charolais* the catastrophic effects this lack of control can have. "So wirf mir nicht noch Zweifel auf den Weg, / Das Eine lass mir doch: den sichern Schritt!" ["So cast not doubt upon my path, / Leave me at least this: the certain step!"], Charolais says at the close of act I, later to be forced to the bitter insight that in life there is no certain step.

One of the most frequent criticisms of *Charolais,* especially among its early reviewers, was that the play lacked unity, that Beer-Hofmann had attempted—unsuccessfully—to fuse what were actually two dramas, one about filial love and loyalty (acts I–III), the other about marital infidelity (acts IV–V).[7] This criticism shows little understanding of the drama's dominant motif—namely, the mysterious and unpredictable workings of fate; it is precisely this that ties the two parts together and gives the drama unity. Through a series of apparent accidents and coincidences, Charolais, by the end of act III, has not only achieved the release of his father's body from debtor's prison, but he also faces the completely unexpected prospects of marriage to the judge's beautiful and virtuous daughter, and a life of happiness and ease he had never dreamed possible for himself. In the last two acts of the play, it is the same unpredictable fate that destroys him utterly, and with him, those he loves. In the play's final scene Charolais says, *"bitterly mocking"*:

> Ich trieb sie ja wohl in den Tod! Ich "trieb" sie!
> "Trieb" ist das Wort—nicht wahr?
> (*Kopfschüttelnd*) Ich trieb sie nicht!
> (*Ernst und stark*) "Es" trieb uns—treibt uns! "Es"—nicht ich, nicht du!

> [I drove her to her death! I "drove" her!
> "Drove" is the word—isn't it?
> (*shaking his head*) I did not drive her!
> (*earnestly, forcefully*) "It" drove us—drives us! "It"—not I, not you!]

And to the anguished reproach of Desirée's father he says: "Nichts tat ich! Mir / Ward's angetan—(*er fasst sich und zuckt die Achseln*)—auch das nicht—es geschah!" (*GW*, 464–65). ["I did nothing! It / Was done to me—(*controlling himself and shrugging his shoulders*)—Not even that—it happened!"]

The unity provided by the fate motif is further strengthened by the structure of the play, which begins and ends at the same place: the inn is the setting for act I; in the second, third, and fourth acts the scene shifts to the judge's home, the courtroom, and back to the judge's home, returning in act V to the inn. Moreover, Charolais's reaction to the drama's two most crucial developments is exactly the same. In a passage reminiscent of the opening and closing scenes of Kleist's *Prinz Friedrich von Homburg*, Charolais responds in dazed bewilderment to the incredibly good turn his fortunes have taken at the end of act III:

> Dies ist ein Traum! Romont! Nicht wahr, wir reiten
> Durch Felder in der Nacht zur Stadt, ich hab'
> Geträumt, im Sattel bin ich eingeschlafen.   (*GW*, 406)

> [This is a dream! Isn't it, Romont? We're riding
> By night through fields to town, I've
> Dreamed, fallen asleep in the saddle.]

His reaction is the same after the seduction scene in act IV, as the evidence of Desirée's infidelity becomes more and more conclusive. In fact, Charolais himself refers to the sameness of his reactions:

> Dies kann nicht sein! Dies ist
> Ein Traum nur, Romont! Sagt' ich das nicht schon
> Einmal—als ich zuerst sie sah?—Doch damals

War's Wirklichkeit! So muss dies j e t z t ein Traum sein,
Denn, die dort oben leuchtend stand, kann nicht
Dieselbe sein, die jetzt—von ihrem Kind weg—
Den Weg—mit ihm—den Weg hinab dort ging!
Ein Traum! . . .   (GW, 433–34)

               [This cannot be! This is
Only a dream, Romont! Did I not say that once
Before—when first I saw her?—but then
It was reality! So must *this* be a dream,
For she who, radiant, stood up there, cannot
Be the same who now—away from her child—
Went down that path—that path—with him!
A dream! . . .]

The only difference here is that the first "dream" was a happy one
with a fairy tale ending, the second, a nightmare—a difference which
only emphasizes the unfathomable and unpredictable nature of fate.

Death is another important motif in *Charolais*, as it was in the early
prose works. The fear of death is best seen in Beer-Hofmann's characterization of Philipp. To the judge's secretary, whose antipathy he
senses, Philipp says:

Wer lebt, der wirbt! Wer tot ist—d e r entsagt! . . .
Ihr seid so klug! Merkt Ihr denn nicht die Hast,
Mit der ich's treibe? Ruhlos, sinnlos! so hetzt
Uns Angst, nicht Eitelkeit! Ich will nicht sein
Von denen, die mit "dann" und "dann" ihr Leben
Sich wie ein Mahl in Gänge teilen, sparend
Beim ersten Gang den Hunger für den letzten.
Da folgen klug geordnet: Lust, Geniessen,
Erwerben, Freien, Kinder, Macht und Ruhm,
Ein sanftes Sterben, wenn man satt der Welt—
Des Lebens Gastmahl aber gibt der Tod;
Der hebt die Tafel auf, wann's i h m gefällt!
Das "Dann" ist sein, mein kaum das "Heut," das mir
Im Atmen, da ich "heute" sag, entrinnt.   (GW, 372–73)

[Who lives, woos! Only who is dead—renounces! . . .
You're so clever! Mark you not the haste
With which I do it? Restlessly, senselessly! What
Drives us is fear, not vanity! I do not want to be
Like those who divide their lives with
"Now" and "then," like courses of a meal, saving

At the first course their hunger for the last.
In that way follow, cleverly arranged: lust, pleasure,
Acquisition, courtship, children, power and fame,
A gentle death, when one is sated with the world—
But the feast of life is given by Death;
He ends the meal, when it pleases *him!*
The "then" is his, mine scarcely the "today" that
Escapes me in the breath I take to say it.]

Philipp is not merely a bon vivant or an exponent of *carpe diem*. The secretary says to him: "So werbt Ihr also—" and Philipp, interrupting, replies:

Um mein Leben! Weiss ich,
Wie bald es endet? Dies muss mir dann bleiben:
Dass viele an mich denken, viele, viele!
D e m war ich Freund, d e n mahnt an mich die Narbe
Auf seiner Wang'; der Bursch da, dem ich, prahlend
—Ich weiss—den Dolch gesandt, der Bettler, dem ich
Statt Geld ein labend Wort in seinen Hut warf,
Die Mädchen an den Fenstern, rasch gegrüsst,
Mit Blicken, die die Miederschnüre lösten—
Und Ihr, zu dem ich so gesprochen, wie ich
Zuvor es nie getan—und andre, viele,
Hab' ich für mich erworben als Provinzen,
Die dann noch blühen, wenn dies Reich zerfällt!   (*GW*, 373)

[I woo for my life! Do I know
How soon it ends? This much must remain:
That many think of me, many!
To *this* one I was a friend, *another* recalls me by the scar
Upon his cheek! The fellow there, to whom I, boasting
—I know—sent my sword, the beggar, in whose hat
I tossed a word of comfort instead of money,
The girls at windows, swiftly greeted,
With glances that untied their bodice strings—
And you, to whom I've spoken, as I
Never did before—and others, many,
I've acquired like provinces,
That still will flourish when I am gone!]

By living so that he will be remembered by others, Philipp is attempting to thwart death, or at least to offset its finality.

Another aspect of the fear of death emerges in Charolais's impassioned outburst in the courtroom in act III. In painfully graphic language (reminiscent of many Baroque poems), Charolais envisions the deterioration of his father's body:

Doch wenn die Sonne kommt, die Sonne, die
Uns wärmt, uns schmeichelt, die, die gut ist, die—
So weiss ich, was sie vorhat, kenn' ihr Handwerk:
Sie stiehlt sich durch das Holz des Sargs, ist drinnen,
Betastet sanft den Leib, bis er geschmeidig—
Nein—heiss und weich wird, und zuerst dann nimmt sie
Die Augen sich, dann erst den Rest! Es schwillt—
Gärt, spannt sich, birst, hebt auf den Deckel—und—
(*aus tiefster Qual aufschreiend*) Herr, ich ertrag's, ertrag' es nicht, dass er
Da oben fault!   (*GW*, 398)

[But when the sun comes, the sun that
Warms us, flatters us and does us good—
I know what it intends, know its handwork:
It steals through the coffin's wood, is within,
Softly touches the body, until it becomes pliant—
No—hot and soft, and first it takes
The eyes, and then the rest! It swells—
seethes, stretches, bursts, raises the lid—and—
(*crying out in deepest torment*) Sir, I cannot bear it, that he
Should rot in there!][8]

Related to the fear of death is the motif of shameless "joy at being alive," already familiar to the reader from *Der Tod Georgs*. Evident in many of Philipp's speeches—indeed, in Beer-Hofmann's entire characterization of him—it is also voiced by the innkeeper's father when he learns of the death of General Charolais:

Um zwanzig Jahre war er jünger
Als ich—und tot! Seht, Herr, wenn ich von einem,
Den ich gekannt—und wo ich weiss, dass er
Gesund und jünger war als ich—wenn ich
Von dem dann hör', dass er schon tot ist—ja,
Da gibt's mir einen Riss durch alle Glieder,
Da sag' ich mir: Siehst du, du bist viel älter
Und nicht gesund! Schon morgen kann es aus sein.
Am andern Tag dann freilich freut's mich wieder,
Dass so ein alter zäher Kerl wie ich
Die Jüngern überlebt!—So ist er tot!   (*GW*, 328)

[By twenty years was he younger
Than I—and dead! Sir, when I hear of one
I knew—and if I know that he
Was healthy and younger than I—when I
Then hear that he is dead—well,
It makes me shudder from stem to stern,
I say to myself: look, you're much older
And frail in health!
Tomorrow the end might come.
The next day, to be sure, I'm pleased to think
That such a tough old one as I
Outlives the younger men!—so he is dead!]

The beginning and the end of *Charolais* are marked by two cases of death which contrast sharply with each other. Charolais's father is already dead when the play begins, but we learn the details of his death through Romont's conversation with the innkeeper's father in act I (*GW,* 329). Like his life, the General's death had been noble and honorable, indeed heroic. Desirée, by contrast, is a woman condemned by her own father (albeit against his will); at least outwardly her death is one of shame and dishonor.

Both cases, however, demonstrate the unpredictability of fate and its apparent capriciousness. Man is an utterly helpless creature who does not act, but to whom things simply happen. Death, in this context, becomes the ultimate capriciousness of fate, against which human beings are powerless. At several points in the play, however, Beer-Hofmann appears to voice the faint possibility of an answer to death. In the final scene, the dying Desirée says to her father *"in a tone of deep contentment"*: "Ja—Vater—Kind! / Das bleibt doch!" (*GW,* 464). ["Yes—father—child! / That indeed remains!"] The last lines of the drama suddenly focus our attention upon the child, who played no significant part in any of the preceding action. As Charolais leaves his father-in-law, he says:

> Noch eins! Da drinnen schläft ein Kind! Wenn es
> Erwacht—so wird es nach der Mutter rufen,
> Nach seinem Vater auch vielleicht—und sie
> Und ich—wir beide—werden's nicht mehr hören.
> Die Tür lass ich dir offen, alter Mann!
> Bleib in der Näh, dass dich sein Ruf erreicht!   (*GW,* 466)

> [One thing more! Inside sleeps a child! When he
> Wakes—he will call for his mother,
> For his father, too, perhaps—and she

And I—we two—shall not hear him any more.
The door I leave open for you, old man!
Remain nearby, so that his call will reach you!]

The idea of posterity as an answer to death, suggested in *Der Tod Georgs*, re-emerges in the passage just quoted and is expressed in terms of sexual union in the final scene of the play, when Charolais says:

Bei i h r war Zuflucht, Sicherheit bei ihr!
Ihr Arm, gelegt um meinen Nacken, barg mich,
Ihr Atem—Friede! Ihre Lippen—Glück!
Ihr Leib—Verheissung! Eins mit ihr zu werden,
Aus mir in sie zu flüchten, fasst' ich sie,
Umschlang sie, liess mein Leben in sie strömen—
Und hielt sie—meine Antwort an den Tod!   (*GW*, 449)

[In *her* was refuge and security!
Her arm about my neck protected me,
Her breath—peace! Her lips—happiness!
Her body—promise! To become one with her,
To flee from myself into her, I embraced her,
Clung to her, let my life flow into her—
And held her—my answer to death!][9]

Moreover, the relationship of family members, and especially of one generation to another, forms an integral part of the drama. This is evident not only in Charolais's filial love and loyalty, and in the relationship between Desirée and the judge, but also in the family relationships of the play's minor characters. In his own way the innkeeper is a representative of this theme: though he lies to his father and conceals the actual circumstances of their life, he does so out of love and a desire to shield his father from painful truths. When the innkeeper admits to Romont that he lies to his father, his wife says, "Das ist ja doch nichts Schlechtes?" ["Surely that is nothing bad?"], and Romont replies,

                    Nein. Du ehrst
Den Vater ja auf deine Art, auf dass
Er glaube, dass dir's wohlergeht auf Erden.   (*GW*, 336–37)

                    [No. You honor
Your father in your way, that
He might believe life goes well for you on earth.]

The theme is given its most powerful treatment in the scene in which Red Ike describes the death of his father to Charolais (*GW*, 355ff).

As in the earlier works, this answer to death, almost totally overshadowed as it is by other motifs, emerges at best as a very faint hope. The tone of *Charolais* as a whole is one of overwhelmingly bitter pessimism, but the inclusion of this idea is nonetheless an indication that in his search for an answer to death, Beer-Hofmann saw posterity—the continuity of the seed—as a tentative possibility.[10] That this eventually strengthened into conviction is shown by *Die Historie von König David*, in which Beer-Hofmann gives the theme of posterity far more extensive treatment, expanding it beyond the single family to include an entire people.

Another of the drama's major motifs is love. Many kinds of love are treated in *Charolais*, with almost as many variations and nuances as there are characters: the love between parent and child (Charolais and his father, Charolais and the judge, Desirée and the judge, the innkeeper and his father, Red Ike and his father); conjugal love (Charolais and Desirée); erotic love (Philipp, and the people who use the inn as a trysting place); the love between friends (Charolais and Romont); and, in a sense, even the question of love of God.

Charolais's childhood clearly was not easy, or what one would think of as "normal":

> Sieh, ohne Mutter,
> Im Zelt, im Sattel bin ich aufgewachsen,
> Und "Heimat" sag' ich mit so fremder Zunge,
> Als wär's ein Name unbetretner Küsten,
> Den staunend ich erlauscht von Weitgereisten.
> Was doch der ärmste Bauer gibt den Kindern—
> Mein Vater hat es mir nicht geben können
> Und hat's gefühlt und hat darum gelitten.   (*GW*, 344)

> [You see, without a mother,
> In tent and saddle I grew up,
> And "home" is as strange a word to me
> As the name of untrod shores I overheard, amazed, from travellers.
> What the poorest peasant gives his young—
> My father could not give me
> And sensed it and suffered from it.]

Still, his love for his father is unmistakable, as is his conviction that the spiritual legacy his father left him is infinitely more valuable than any tangible inheritance:

Und siehst du—weil mein Vater dies gewusst:
Dass er mir nicht Besitz, nicht Heimat und nicht
Den leichten Sinn, der's leicht vermisst, gegeben—
Gab er ein Lebenlang sich selbst: sein Beispiel!
. . . Sieh!—Dies Gefühl gab er mir mit ins Leben:
Langsamen Siechtum, Armut, Sorge, Tod—
Kann Eintritt in mein Leben ich nicht wehren,
Ich weiss—Gebieter sind sie, und sie lenken!
Doch nie darf R e u e auf der Stirn mir steh'n,
Nie Ekel sich auf meine Lippen legen—
Ich mein', vor mir, vor meinem Tun und Denken.
Herr ist das Schicksal über allen Dingen—
—Doch hier bin ich's! D a z u kann's mich nicht zwingen.

$\hfill$ (*GW*, 344–45)

[And you see—because my father knew this:
That he gave me neither estate nor home nor
The frivolous sense that misses them—
He gave throughout his life himself: his example!
. . . Look—This feeling he gave me as a life's inheritance:
Long slow illness, poverty, sorrow, death—
I cannot prevent from entering my life,
I know—they are masters who control!
But never may *remorse* be etched upon my brow,
Never loathing upon my lips—
I mean for myself, for my own deeds and thoughts.
Fate is lord over all things—
But in this *I* am lord, and fate cannot compel me!]

The latter part of this passage also indicates that Beer-Hofmann was not an unequivocal determinist; the sovereignty of fate does not absolve people of the responsibility to live in such a way that they have no contempt for themselves.[11]

The judge does not replace Charolais's father in the son's affections, but he fills the void left by the general's death and becomes the second father-figure in Charolais's life. Their relationship is one of mutual love, respect, and trust, and for Charolais, one of profound gratitude.

Red Ike is a moving spokesman for the traditionally strong bond between Jewish parents and their children—his effectiveness is underscored by his use of Jewish-German dialect (which unfortunately cannot be duplicated in English translation). In a wider sense, however, he speaks for all of the drama's characters and their various parent-child relationships:

Was das bedeut': "E Vatter"! Was?—ich sag Euch,
Vorgestern war noch aner auf der Welt,
Der hat nix anderes gekennt als Euch!
Dem hätts Ihr antun können, was Ihr wollts!
Dieb, Räuber, Mörder hätts Ihr werden können,
Er hätt nix aufgehört, Euch lieb zu haben,
Und hätt' gebettelt gern, wenn's Euch nur gut geht!
A n' unbescheidnen Wunsch hat er gehabt:
Dass Ihr die Augen sollts zudrucken i h m,
Und nix er Euch. Und jeden Abend hat er
Gebetet: "Herrgott! ehnder dass mei Kind
Etwas geschehen soll, lass lieber m i c h
Zehntausend Tode sterben!" Sehts Ihr, so,
So reich warts Ihr vorgestern noch! Und heut'?
Und wenn Ihr alt werdts h u n d e r t Jahr'—so findts
Ihr d a s nicht wieder . . .
So senn bei uns die Väter und die Mütter—
Viel anders wern se bei Euch auch nix sein!   (GW, 357)

[What that means: "a father!" What? I tell you,
Day before yesterday there was still someone in the world
Who knew nothing else but you!
To him you could have done what you wished!
Become a thief, a robber, a murderer,
He would not have ceased to love you,
And gladly would have begged, if only all went well for you!
Only *one* immodest wish he had:
That you might close *his* eyes,
And not he yours. And every night he prayed:
"Lord God! rather than that harm
Befall my child, let *me* die
Ten thousand deaths!" You see, so
Rich were you two days ago! And now?
Well, if you circle the globe—
And if you live to be a *hundred*—
You'll not find *that* again . . .
That's how fathers and mothers are among us—
Among you they can't be much different!]

Essentially the same sentiments are expressed by the judge and
reflected in Beer-Hofmann's characterization of all the drama's parents, including Charolais himself, who says with reference to his son:
"Verwalter. Für ihn! So fühl ich mich!" ["An agent. For him. That's
how I feel!"]. Later in the same conversation, he remarks of himself
and his wife:

> Doch wir beide,
> Wir waren wichtig nur, bevor er ward.
> Nun da er ist,
> Braucht uns Natur nicht mehr!   (*GW,* 413, 415)

> [But the two of us
> Were important only before he came.
> Now that he is here
> Nature no longer needs us!]

This attitude is also seen in the innkeeper's blind father. He knows that his son consents to, indeed profits from, the use of his rooms for adultery and fornication, but he is anxious that Romont not think badly of his son because of this (*GW,* 335).

It is much more difficult to arrive at any certain conclusions about the play's representation of conjugal love. The reader or viewer gains most of his knowledge from Charolais's and Desirée's speeches in act V, after the action has already taken its tragic turn. Otherwise, except for the brief scene of contented family life in act IV, we are given few indications of what these two feel for each other. This is especially true of Desirée. In the scene just mentioned, stage directions such as *"in zufriedenem Glück über Desirée gebeugt"* and *"zärtlich leicht Desirées Haar streichelnd"* [*"bent over Desirée in contented happiness"* and *"tenderly stroking Desirée's hair"*] make it clear that Charolais loves his wife deeply. Whether she returns his love is very much an open question. We already know that the judge, not Desirée, selected Charolais to be her husband; it is possible that she has married him out of obedience to her father. Her ambivalent behavior during the seduction scene tends to support this possibility: she is strangely reluctant to answer Philipp when he asks if she loves Charolais. Pressed for an answer, she finally says, "Ich liebe meinen Mann und lieb' mein Kind!" ["I love my husband and my child!"], to which the perceptive Philipp replies: "Halt! Misch das nicht! Du weichst mir aus!" ["Stop! Don't mix the two! You're evading me!"]. Perhaps Philipp is simply refusing to believe what he does not want to hear, but the audience, too, is left with the impression of Desirée's evasiveness, a notion that does not derive from her spoken lines alone. Once again the stage directions are important indicators: in this scene Desirée speaks her lines *"with rising indignation,"* *"in increasing haste,"* *"flaring up,"* and so on. Her bearing and manner are perhaps meant to convey only offended pride and a secret sense of shame, however unwarranted. She confesses to such a feeling:

Fragst du, was du getan?!
Genommen mir die Sicherheit, mich tief
Gedemütigt, dass ich es nicht verwinde!
Ich war nicht blind, ich sah die Welt, ich wusste,
Dass jeden, täglich, eine gelbe Flut
Von Hässlichem und Niedrigem umbrandet!
Doch ich, so dacht' ich, durfte sicher schreiten!
Den Saum nicht einmal konnt' es mir bespülen—
So stolz war ich!—ich bin's nicht mehr! Denn etwas,
Es muss etwas in mir gewesen sein,
Das Mut dir gab!   (*GW,* 420)

[You ask what you have done?!
Robbed me of security, humiliated
Me so deeply that I cannot overcome it!
I was not blind, I saw the world, I knew
That daily a yellow tide of
Ugliness and baseness surges about everyone!
But I, so I thought, could walk securely!
It could not even wash against my hem—
So proud was I!—I am no longer! For something,
There must have been something in me
That encouraged you!]

Desirée's realization that for her, as for all human beings, there is no "certain step" recalls Charolais's words in act I, and also represents a foreshadowing of his bitter recognition of life's uncertainty in act V.

The injured pride expressed in this passage does not, however, seem sufficient explanation for Desirée's behavior; too many puzzling questions are left unanswered—the reader wonders, for example, why she does not simply call one of the servants (as she threatens repeatedly to do). Apparently, Beer-Hofmann sketched an ambiguous relationship between Desirée and Charolais, intending her to be seen at this point in the drama as a woman who does not know her own heart and mind. This certainly gives the problem an additional psychological dimension, to say nothing of an element of irony. Philipp says to her: "Du! Ihn lieben: (*verächtlich*) Du weisst ja gar nicht, weisst nicht, was es heisst" (*GW,* 422). ["You! Love him: (*contemptuously*) You don't know at all, don't even know what it means."] Only after her infidelity does Desirée seem to know her own feelings and speak them with conviction. In the final scene of the play, she defends Charolais to her father:

Begreif ihn, Vater!
Er ist nicht hart—er wehrt sich seines Lebens!
Sonst nichts! Er liebt mich, und er meint, er könnte
Nicht weiter leben ohne diese Liebe;

Sie will er retten—wär's durch meinen Tod!
... Ich versteh ihn gut! Er will mich tot,
um wieder mich zu lieben.   (*GW,* 462)

                                    [Understand him, Father!
He is not hard—he's fighting for his life!
Nothing else! He loves me, and thinks he could not
Go on living without this love;
He wants to save it—even if it means my death!
... I understand him well! He wants me dead,
in order to love me again.]

To Charolais she says: "Ich hab' dich lieb! Sonst niemand, so wie dich!
/ Jetzt mehr als je!" (*GW,* 462). ["I love you! No one else, as I love
you! / Now more than ever!"]

There has been some discussion of the character of Philipp already;
he speaks of his erotic conquests—indeed of all the human beings he
encounters—as "conquered provinces." Desirée is certainly on a different plane than "the girls at windows, swiftly greeted, with glances that
untie their bodice strings," but Philipp's attitude is essentially the
same: in describing to Desirée his dreams of her, he uses metaphors of
the hunt and the chase, such as calling his thoughts "eine lechzende
Meute" ["a panting pack"] (*GW,* 424). The difference is only one of
degree: Philipp has to expend much greater effort and be far more
subtle in order to seduce Desirée. Charolais regards him as a contempt-
ible degenerate, but Philipp's eroticism is no less an attempted answer
to death than the conjugal union of which Charolais speaks.

The love between friends is shown primarily through Romont. There
are no speeches on friendship *per se,* but "my friend" is one of Charolais's final utterances as the play ends. This type of love is also implicit
in the allegiance and faithfulness to Charolais that mark Romont's
behavior throughout the drama. He remains with him when Charolais
has been forsaken by everyone else, attempting to shield him and ease
the pain of the loss of his father (acts I–III). Charolais's devotion and
respect for Romont are indicated by the latter's continued presence
(acts IV–V) as his trusted friend and confidant. Only once is there a
slight suggestion that Romont's devotion to Charolais has been shaken;
in act V, immediately after Desirée's death, Charolais, *"as if calling for
help,"* says: "Romont! Was siehst du zu Boden? (*Romont blickt auf.*) Du
weinst?" (*GW,* 464). ["Romont! Why do you look at the ground?
(*Romont looks up.*) You weep?"] As the closing lines of the drama show,
however, his loyalty overrides his grief.

Charolais depicts human love as the only thing that makes life meaningful, or even tolerable. Early in the play Charolais says:

> Romont! was hab' denn ich? wer hat mich lieb?
> Um wen soll ich mich sorgen? Woran kann ich
> Mein Leben knüpfen, dass es mir nicht schwerlos,
> Unwichtig, leer, entrollt? Gib mir den Menschen—
> Das Ding—das Tier! Nur etwas—ich ertrag's nicht,
> So arm zu sein—an allen arm! . . .   (*GW*, 361)

> [Romont! What do I have? Who feels for me?
> For whom shall I care? To what can I
> Attach my life, so that it will not glide away,
> Weightless, unimportant, empty? Give me a person—
> A thing—an animal! Something—I cannot bear
> To be so poor—so destitute of everything! . . .]

Love, in one form or another, is the only thing that can alleviate the terrible loneliness of the individual and give substance to his life.

To say that *Charolais* also deals with the question of love of God perhaps states the case too narrowly; the drama, in fact, explores the whole nature of the God-man relationship. This is especially true of act V, though the theme is also treated earlier. The judge, an upright man throughout his life, also becomes devout—through the experience of fatherhood. He says to his secretary:

> . . . Nicht aus Sturm, Gewittern und
> Gestirnter Himmelspracht, und Schöpfungswundern,
> Sprach Gott zu mir—im Lallen meines Kindes
> Vernahm ich ihn—fromm ward ich durch mein Kind.   (*GW*, 381)

> [Not through tempest, storm,
> Heaven's starry splendor, and wonders of creation
> Did God speak to me—in the babbling of my child
> I heard Him—through my child I became devout.]

He is convinced that Desirée, who nearly died at birth, was allowed to live because God heard his anguished supplication:

> . . . und ich rang
> Die Hände auf zum Himmel, und ich rief:
> "Mein Lebtag hab' ich doch an dich geglaubt,
> Soll ich denn jetzt an dir verzweifeln? Lass
> Mir Weib und Kind!" Dann horcht' ich auf, als müsste

Mir Antwort kommen; keine kam. Da warf ich
Mich auf mein Antlitz, drückte meine Stirn auf
Den harten, spitzen Kies, und schrie: "Du d a r f s t nicht
Mir alles nehmen! Wenn nicht beides—lass
Mir E i n e s doch—ich bin ein alter Mann—
Lass mir mein Kind!" . . .
. . . da stand ich
Vom Boden auf, und in mir fühlte ich's:
Ich war erhört von Gott . . .
Von G o t t, so denk' ich.   (*GW,* 380–81)

          [. . . And I wrung
My hands to heaven and I cried:
"All my life I have believed in You,
Shall I now despair of You? Leave
Me wife and child!" I listened then, as though
An answer had to come; none came. I threw
Myself upon my face, pressed my brow on the
Hard sharp stones and cried: "You *may* not
Take everything from me! If not both—then leave
Me *one* at least—I am an old man—
Leave me my child!" . . .
. . . I arose then
From the earth, and sensed within myself:
I had been heard by God . . .
By *God,* that's what I think.]

The image evoked here is that of a merciful, benevolent God. In sharp
contrast is the image in act V, where God is presented as a being whose
capriciousness is as cruel as it is incomprehensible:

CHAROLAIS: Auch Gnade ist bei Gott allein! Gerecht,
Und gnädig! Beides ist nur er—nur er!
Lobpreise seinen Namen!
PRÄSIDENT: Höhnst du Gott?
CHAROLAIS: (*erst mit gespieltem Erstaunen, dann die Maske fallen
lassend, mit tiefster Bitterkeit*)
Höhnt ihn, wer ihn gerecht und gnädig nennt?!
Lernst, Alter, du in dieser Stunde um,
Was deine Weisheit war durch achzig Jahre?!
Weil, fromm, ich meinen toten Vater ehrte,
Gabst du dein Kind mir—sieh, damit begann's!   (*GW,* 461)

[CHAROLAIS: Mercy, too, is God's alone! Just
And merciful! Only He is both—only He!

Sing praise unto His name!
PRÄSIDENT: Are you mocking God?
CHAROLAIS: (*first with feigned astonishment, then, dropping his mask, with profound bitterness*)
Does he mock, who calls Him just and merciful?!
Are you learning in this hour, old man, to change
What was your wise belief for eighty years?
Because, devout, I honored my dead father,
You gave me your child—it began with that!]

The catastrophic destruction of his marital happiness is Charolais's "reward" for having revered God, and the judge's "reward" is the shame and dishonor of his daughter:

CHAROLAIS: Weil fromm ich war—darum muss ich heut leiden,
Für deine Güte—dies dein Lohn! Gerecht!
Du batest ihn um eines Kindes Leben—
Er hat's gewährt! Freu dich an deinem Kind!
Liess dich zu selten hohen Jahren kommen,
D i e s zu erleben!
(*Als stimme er ein Lobgesang an*)
Gnädig! Gnädig! Gnädig!
Verstehst du ihn?
(*Sich vorneigend, als vertraue er ihm ein Geheimnis an, leise*)
Er scherzt mit uns! Er scherzt!
Und scherzt der Herr—was bleibt uns Knechten übrig,
Als g u t den Scherz zu finden—und zu lachen!   (*GW*, 461)

[CHAROLAIS: Because I was devout—today I have to suffer,
For your goodness—this your reward! Just!
You begged Him for the life of a child—
He granted it! Rejoice in your child!
He let you reach a rare old age,
To experience *this!*
(*as though striking up a song of praise*)
Merciful! Merciful! Merciful!
Do you understand Him?
(*bending forward, as though to confide a secret, softly*)
He jests with us! He jests!
And if the master jests—what can we servants do,
But view the jest as *good*—and laugh!]

Charolais's bitter words to the innkeeper likewise emphasize the apparent capriciousness of God: "Sangst du sein Lob? Und nahm er dir die Stimme? / (*Er weist auf den Präsidenten*) Der dort—pries ihn!

Ihm liess er sie—zu stöhnen!" (*GW*, 466). ["You sang His praise? And He robbed you of your voice? / (*Pointing to the judge*) That one praised Him! And him He left a voice—that he might moan!"] The concluding lines of this speech summarize Beer-Hofmann's view of the nature of God:

> Es scheint, er liebt es nicht, wenn man zu viel
> Von ihm spricht—sei's mit Beten oder Fluchen!
> Zu Sichres hasst er—und ein allzusehr
> Auf ihn vertrauen——nennt Er: Ihn versuchen!   (*GW*, 466)

> [It seems He does not like it, if one speaks
> Too much of Him—be it with prayer or curse!
> Too much certainty He hates—and trusting in Him
> All too much—He calls: tempting Him!][12]

The theme of justice remains to be discussed. Its major representatives are, of course, Charolais and the judge. That Charolais is a just man is apparent from the outset. There is, however, a certain discrepancy in his sense of justice that might be considered a flaw in Beer-Hofmann's characterization, an inconsistency which detracts more from the play's unity than the two "plots" to which so many critics objected. In the first three acts of the play, Charolais's strong sense of justice is tempered by humaneness and mercy; he clearly represents the spirit rather than the letter of the law. Realizing that his father's creditors are fully within their rights, according to the strict letter of the law, he believes that a grave injustice will be done in a higher sense if his father's body is not released. The rigidity, then, of his sense of justice in acts IV and V is very difficult to reconcile with his earlier attitude. This inflexible element first emerges at the beginning of act IV, when Charolais refuses to allow the innkeeper to continue as agent for the sale of the harvest. Later, Charolais's humaneness prevails and he changes his mind, saying, "Im Grund tut er mir leid!" (*GW*, 416). ["At bottom I'm sorry for him!"] In act V, however, there is no such return to humaneness; Charolais's sense of justice is marked by a complete and final absence of compassion and mercy. He is inexorable in his insistence that sentence be passed on Desirée: "Mein Degen und mein Recht sind mir geblieben— / Die beiden nur! Gebt mir mein Recht!" (*GW*, 451). ["My sword and justice remain to me— / Only those two things! Give me justice!"]

In all likelihood, Beer-Hofmann characterized Charolais in this way to achieve a complete reversal of roles between him and the judge.

One of the play's bitterest ironies, this exchange of roles lies not only in the external fact that the judge of act III becomes the defendant in act V and Charolais, earlier the supplicant, becomes the prosecutor. Charolais's transition is from humaneness to complete relentlessness, while the judge's is precisely the opposite. Numerous speeches in acts II, III, and IV place the judge unequivocally in the stern, unyielding tradition of Old Testament justice. He makes the strongest such statement in act II:

> Gnade! Lasst doch
> Das Wort, ich mag es nicht! Wer Recht hat, kommt
> Mit seinem Rechte aus! Wer Unrecht hat,
> Braucht Gnade.   (*GW*, 378).

> [Mercy! Leave off with
> That word, I do not like it! He whose cause is just
> Finds justice sufficient! Only who is not in the right
> Needs mercy.]

In act V he tears his judicial robe from his shoulders and says to Charolais:

> Hier lieg ich vor dir, wie ich nur vor Gott lag
> . . . Ein Mensch in tiefster Not! Und ist auch dies
> Zu viel des Hochmuts noch—die letzte Würde,
> Ich tu sie ab—kein Mensch, ein Tier, gehetzt,
> Gemartert, windet sich vor dir am Boden,
> Und schreit und winselt um sein Junges! Gib ihm's!
> Sei gnädig du! Hab Mitleid! Übe Gnade!   (*GW*, 460–61)

> [Here I lie before you, as I lay only before God
> . . . A man in deepest need! And if even this
> Is too much arrogance still—the final dignity,
> I cast it off—no more a man, a harried animal,
> Tormented, writhes on the ground before you,
> And whimpers for its young! Give it to him!
> Be merciful! Have pity! Practice mercy!]

The play's ending leaves no doubt that the view of a just world order expressed in the final pages of *Der Tod Georgs* had undergone some modification by the time Beer-Hofmann wrote *Der Graf von Charolais*. It could be argued that the injustices presented in the drama constitute his renunciation of the earlier view of God. An examination of *Charolais* within the context of Beer-Hofmann's total production suggests, however, that the play is not a negation of his earlier position, but a modification to this extent: if God's ways are just, then only in a sense that far transcends human comprehension. Seen in this light, *Charolais* is the artistic expression of its author's agonizing struggle to reconcile his conception of God and the universal order with the suffering, ugliness, and injustice he saw in the world. As early as 1893 (in *Das Kind*) Beer-Hofmann had expressed the idea of doubt as a means to faith; his development from *Der Tod Georgs* to the *Historie von König David*—by way of *Der Graf von Charolais*—is evidence of this process at work in his own life.

Upon examining the language, style, and dramatic techniques Beer-Hofmann uses in *Charolais,* one has first of all the impression of very powerful dramatic effects. They stem primarily from the language of the play itself, but also from the playwright's attention to such details as timing, dynamics, gestures, even stage properties. Robert Musil observed in his review of *Charolais* that the effects are achieved very naturally—they do not strike the audience as cheap theatrical tricks. "There are passages in which virtue rides upon a high horse, preceded by a trumpeter . . . and other passages that aim for an effect very naively, in a way that only complete purity can permit itself. . . . They [the effects] arise quite naturally, that is to say, from a nature that takes pleasure in this, and not from one which merely knows that in the theatre one gives pleasure to others and garners their applause with such effects. Thus there is something tart and free of ulterior motives in the tender passages of this play, where another would be mawkish."[13]

Charolais is written in blank verse and, with few exceptions, the language is very elevated. At least one critic objected to this language on the grounds that it was inconsistent with the place and time in which the drama was set.[14] Actually, one is tempted to ask if people of any time or place ever talked to each other as Charolais does to Romont (*GW*, 361) or to Desirée (*GW*, 414), or as the judge speaks to his secretary (*GW*, 380–82). A more important question—with respect to Beer-Hofmann's purposes and his success or failure in achieving them— is whether the language and verse form are not inconsistent with the place and time in which the drama was written and performed. The playwright's use of the verse form was undoubtedly a reaction to Naturalist drama, a desire to avoid the language and style of "social realism." (He must have had very mixed emotions indeed at sharing the Schiller Prize with—of all people—Gerhart and Carl Hauptmann.) One of Beer-Hofmann's purposes was to revitalize a dramatic form that had once been compelling and meaningful, but no longer seemed relevant to many. It cannot be said that he enjoyed more than partial success, though this is not altogether an indictment of him or a denial of his talent. It is doubtful that anyone in our century could have performed this feat, which was probably an impossibility, and perhaps also a mistake: "As we enter the twentieth century, the old shadows and stale ideals again crowd upon us . . . the entire baggage of dusty theory is again invoked, long after Ibsen and Chekhov have shown that it is irrelevant to the modern spirit. . . . The [old] image of the theatre . . . is a noble phantom. . . . But it should never have been summoned back to the electric light, where it stands naked and inept. The verse tragedies produced by modern . . . poets are . . . attempts to blow fire into cold ash. It cannot be done."[15] Verse drama, in short, was already something of an anachronism in the early years of this century. The reason, as Steiner notes, is that "the contact between verse of a dramatic and musical order and the everyday world has grown ever more precarious and infrequent. . . . Verse no longer stands at the center of communicative discourse. . . . This does not signify that modern poetry is any the less compelling or important to the survival of literacy and sensuous apprehension. But it does mean that the distance between verse and the realities of common action with which drama must deal is greater than ever before."[16]

One of the fundamental characteristics of the verse form is that it lends formality to the dialogue, establishing a certain distance between the characters and the audience. This distance is increased in *Charolais* by the hyperbolic nature of the language itself. There are a few passages in which the language is prosaic, and some in which it is vulgar;[17] there are not many such passages, however, and their function is usually to provide a measure of relief from the almost unbearable intensity and feverish pitch of the other passages. Beer-Hofmann clearly recognized that such relief is occasionally necessary. He writes in the letter of 1933 to Erich Kahler: "And *this* is how I see the matter for the reader: precisely because I attempt to intensify the word to its highest precision and power of penetration—a complementary, retarding, epic element is necessary that reduces the supra-sharp and gives me the possibility of controlling the dosages. This epic element is meant to *compel* the reader to rest, if necessary even to *cast him out of the mood*—when I deem that appropriate" (*GW,* 878). Here Beer-Hofmann speaks specifically of stage directions as a temporary means of lessening the dramatic tension; this, of course, would apply only for the reader. For the spectator, the alternation in the language itself, from the feverishly intense or sublime to the prosaic, achieves the necessary relief. Thus, Charolais's impassioned courtroom speeches are offset by the judge's dry, measured legal admonitions and the creditors' matter-of-fact statements; the highly-charged scene between Charolais and Red Ike is followed by an initially prosaic conversation between Charolais and Romont about their financial straits; and the language of the scene in which the innkeeper suddenly achieves stature and eloquently defends himself to Charolais and the judge returns to the mundane level when the innkeeper says, *"returning to his everyday tone"*: "Die Kundschaft hab' ich mir jetzt ganz verscherzt, / Ich weiss (*er zuckt die Achseln*), so hab' ich wenigstens einmal / Mir ordentlich mein Maul doch ausgeleert!" (*GW,* 412). ["Now I've lost the account for good, / I know (*he shrugs his shoulders*), but at least for once / I've given you an honest piece of my mind!"]

Corresponding to the alternating language of the play are changes in tone, tempo, and dynamics. Beer-Hofmann also mentions these in the letter to Erich Kahler: "My work . . . does not live at a 'forest and meadow tempo' of dramatic speech and counter-speech. Who at times rides at such a tempo as I, who attempts to whip the word to such feverish pitches . . . also needs *for that* the corrective of epic insertions, must be able to reduce temperatures, according to the needs of the moment, suddenly or gradually" (*GW,* 879).

In analyzing the pronounced influence of modern psychology on *Charolais,* one finds, paradoxically, that it both strengthens and weakens the play. The psychological elements give the play its interest and relevance for the twentieth-century audience, but their introduction also created some serious problems that the playwright could not entirely overcome. One of them is a discrepancy between the play's reflection of modern psychological ideas and attitudes, and the reaction of Charolais to his wife's infidelity. Especially when contrasted with the judge, the Charolais of the first four acts is not unlike the modern man whose attitudes have been "enlightened" by the findings of psychological research. Nowhere in act V, however, does he pose a single question "about the psychic event that was the cause, or about the psychic condition that is now reality. . . . One thing never occurs to him: to consider whether this woman is really 'fallen' in the inner sense. He does not see her soul at all."[18] This contention is substantiated by Charolais's reaction in act V when Desirée defends him to her father:

> Wie klug sie ihre Worte setzt! Die Hand erst—
> Und Tränen—und auf meine Tränen lauern—
> . . . den Mund dann—und zuletzt
> Versöhnung! Drin steht schon das Bett bereit!

Der Zorn hat eingeheizt—dein Vater setzt sich
Hin vor die Tür, gibt acht, dass niemand stört—
Und freut sich der versöhnten Kinder! Was?
So denkst du dir's! . . . D a s willst du!

[How cleverly she speaks! First her hand—
And tears—and watching for my tears—
. . . Then her mouth—and finally
Reconciliation! The bed stands ready inside!
Rage has fired me up—your father seats himself
Before the door, makes sure that none disturb us—
And rejoices in the reconciliation of his children! Eh?
That's how you imagine it! . . . *That* is what you want!]

Desirée answers sorrowfully: "Kennst du mich so?" (*GW*, 462). ["Is that how you know me?"]

The introduction of modern psychology created other problems of characterization and motivation for the playwright; before they are discussed, however, it needs to be said—and illustrated—that Beer-Hofmann's skill at characterization is very impressive indeed. His figures are not rough sketches; he fills in every detail with infinite care, and in the process subjects the character to scrutiny from a variety of angles, so that the focal point of our attention is first one facet of character and then another. All are gradually woven together to produce a colorful, vigorous personality.

Another of Beer-Hofmann's techniques is to make his minor characters appear merely as supporting figures for a time and then to thrust them suddenly into the limelight, giving them an unexpected importance. This causes the reader to realize that, in a sense, the play has no "minor" characters at all. Almost all of the drama's lesser figures—and especially Red Ike and the innkeeper—are given such moments.

Initially, Red Ike appears as a distasteful moneylender, whose only importance derives from the distress he is causing the hero. When he speaks of the fate of his father and of Israel, however, he suddenly becomes a commanding presence, the playwright's vehicle for the introduction of an important motif:

CHAROLAIS: Von dir hängt alles ab, du bist ein Jud zwar—
Du bist ja aber auch ein Mensch, wie wir—
ITZIG: (*Blickt misstrauisch auf. Befremdet. Leise.*)
Ein Mensch? Wie Ihr? Seit wann bin ich e Mensch?
Mei Lebtag hat man mich's nicht fühlen lassen,
Dass ich e Mensch bin; h e u t grad soll ich's sein?

Weil's Euch so passt? Und für die fünf Minuten,
Die's Euch g'rad passt? Nein, heute will i c h nicht!
(*Unnahbar. Stark, aber nicht zu laut*) Nein!
E Jud bin ich! Was wollts Ihr von dem Juden!
—Denn etwas wollts Ihr doch, wenn Ihr mir so kommts!   (*GW,* 354)

[CHAROLAIS: All depends on you. You're a Jew, of course,
But you're also a human being, like us—
ITZIG: (*Looks up distrustfully. Surprised. Softly.*)
A human being? Like you? Since when?
All my life people have not made me feel
That I'm a human being; just *today* I'm to be one?
Because it suits you? And just for the five minutes
That it suits you? No, today *I* don't want to!
(*Unapproachable. Firmly, but not too loud*) No!
I am a Jew! What do you want from the Jew?
—For you must want something, if you approach me thus!]

The lines with which Ike ends this scene are even more forceful:

Und wenn Ihr alles das getan, Herr Graf—
Und ich dann noch lebendig bin—dann will ich
Mit Euch so reden, wie e Mensch—ich mein'
E g u t e r Mensch—soll zu e Menschen reden!
—Bis dahin lassts mich sein, was ich für Euch—
—Und wenn ich wär', ich weiss nicht was—d o c h bleib:
E J u d', e J u d', e ganz gemeiner J u d'!   (*GW,* 359)

[And when you've done all that, Count—
And I am still alive—then I will
Speak with you as one human being—I mean
As one *good* man—should speak to another!
—'Til then let me be what I'd remain for you,
No matter what I was:
A *Jew,* a *Jew,* a common, vulgar *Jew!*]

With these lines, the theme of brotherhood as one aspect of the unity of all life is effectively treated in terms of its absence among men. It is reintroduced and stated affirmatively in act II when the judge recalls his early admonition to his daughter:

. . . Sie werden's dich
Genug noch lehren, dass er Mann und Weib
Sie schuf—du halte fest: er schuf den M e n s c h e n!
. . . "Den Menschen"—und noch einmal, leise—fast
Wie Ehrfurcht klang's: "Den Menschen, Kind, den Menschen!"
                                                        (*GW,* 386)

[. . . They will teach you
Often enough that He made them male and female
—You hold fast to this: He created the *human being*!
. . . "the human being"—and again, softly—sounding
Almost like reverence: "the human being, child, the human being!"]

The innkeeper's moment comes at the start of act IV, when he suddenly ceases to be a disreputable, shabby profiteer and a procuror who has aroused the reader's distaste and contempt. Quite unexpectedly he achieves compelling human dignity:

> . . . Wie bin ich denn? Was wisst Ihr,
> Wie ich bin? (*Tieftraurig*) Weiss ich's selber denn? Ich weiss
> Nur, wie ich war! . . .
> Herr, ich war gut! Nicht stolz . . .
> Nicht geizig, Herr! Mit vollen Händen gab ich!
> Kein Spötter! Gläubig sang im Dom ich mit
> Das Lob des Herrn, der mir Gesang verliehen—
> (*mit bittrem Lachen*)
> Es blies ein Wind, ein Frühlingswind und nahm
> Die Stimme mir—und mit ihr alles! . . .
> (*Nicht ohne Grösse*)
> Wie Ihr, hatt' ich auch Ekel vor Gemeinem—
> Und alles dies zerblies ein Wind in nichts!—
> Wie bin ich? Wie seid Ihr? Wisst Ihr's? . . . Seid Ihr
> So sicher, dass kein Wind Euch Lügen straft?   (*GW*, 411–12)

[. . . How am I then? What do you know of
How I am? (*with deep sadness*) Do I know myself?
I know only how I was . . .
Sir, I was good! Not proud! . . .
Not stingy, sir! With full hands I gave!
Not a mocker! Believing, I sang in the cathedral
The praise of Him who gave me song—
(*with a bitter laugh*)
There blew a wind, the wind of spring, and took
My voice away—and with it everything! . . .
(*not without stature*)
Like you, I felt disgust for all things mean—
And a wind blew all of that away!—
How am I? How are you? Do you know? Are you
So certain that no wind will give the lie to you?]

Beer-Hofmann discusses the application of this technique in the prose fragment, "Nebenfiguren" ["Secondary Figures"], written May 22, 1927: "The fates of the minor characters must be sharply outlined in the drama—even where that *appears* to be superfluous. In the drama a figure becomes the 'main character' for the couple of hours I concern myself with him, because I am speaking of his fate—in those hours the others are 'minor figures.' Were I to place the focus upon them, they could be 'main characters' and the former 'main character' would be a 'minor figure' in their fate. One always has to sense that somehow . . . because one must always have a presentiment of the eternal poetic justice that—like the divine—does not distinguish between major and minor characters" (*GW,* 625–26).

In making modern psychology a decisive factor in the play—that is to say, in presenting its figures as guiltless and free of tragic flaws—Beer-Hofmann created problems of characterization that he did not entirely succeed in overcoming. This is especially true in Desirée's case. Even if one concedes the subtle psychological refinements and enormous persuasiveness of Philipp's performance as a seducer, it is extremely difficult to reconcile Desirée's capitulation with her character as it has been presented up to that point; this tends to weaken the play's climax or turning point. Of those who voiced this criticism, Rudolf Kassner stated the case most emphatically. Discussing peripeteia in general, he refers to the play's "unsuccessful, indeed thoroughly wretched seduction scene, which at the same time signals the turning point in the drama," and adds: "At that time I wrote the poet, to whom, as a person, I was very devoted and whose understanding in matters of art was admirable, that for me his play would always remain a fragment, that is, that I could read it with enjoyment only up to the aforementioned scene, which I found intolerable. He didn't quite see it, and took refuge behind psychology. But one does not achieve the turning point of dramatic action with psychology alone."[19] Karl Frenzel likewise focused his objection on Desirée's surrender to Philipp: "If it is a wild upsurge of the blood, a sudden outbreak of sensuality, then it should have been suggested to us earlier that there were such bottomless depths in Desirée's character and temperament."[20]

These critical objections are justified with regard to a weakening of the play's turning point, but they overlook the crucial fact that the playwright does not *intend* that we search within Desirée's character for the answer. Beer-Hofmann spoke of her, indeed of all the play's characters, as guiltless;[21] he expects us simply to accept the fact that "it happened."

This leads to the larger question, then, of whether *Charolais* is really a tragedy. The play does contain some elements traditionally associated with that genre: the characters are obviously exposed to destructive forces that lie "outside the governance of reason or justice." Like classical tragedy, *Charolais* tells us that "things are as they are, unrelenting and absurd," and we cannot hope to understand them or explain them in rational terms.[22]

There are important differences, however, between the characters of *Charolais* and those of classical tragedy. To be sure: tragic figures are frequently punished far in excess of their guilt, but they are not represented as being entirely free of flaws. They are not merely the helpless victims of irrational and cruelly capricious forces from without; to some degree, at least, they are morally responsible for their own downfall. As Steiner says: ". . . tragedy embodies the notion of moral responsibility. There is a concordance between the moral character of the tragic personage and his destiny. This concordance is, at times, difficult to make out. The sufferings of Oedipus or Lear are far greater than their vices. But even in these puzzling instances we assume some measure of causal . . . dependence between the character of the man and the quality of the event. The tragic hero is responsible. His downfall is related to the presence in him of moral infirmity or active vice. The agonies of an innocent or virtuous man are, as Aristotle observed, pathetic but not tragic."[23] The characters of *Charolais,* by contrast, are not morally responsible for the catastrophe that befalls them; we are asked to believe that they have no guilt at all.

Heroic struggle is another fundamental element of tragedy that is missing from *Charolais.* The Count is not a "non-hero" in the manner of a Willy Loman, but neither is he a tragic hero in the traditional sense. Kraft observed, "Precisely fate, against which the tragic hero struggles heroically, is here eroded and reduced to a mechanical, psychoanalytical 'it,' which allows room only for marionettes who no longer struggle at all."[24] In classical tragedy the hero's suffering and struggle, however futile, have a strangely ennobling effect: the audience feels shock and sorrow at his fall, but also something approaching exaltation at his demonstration of the heights to which the human spirit can rise. There is no such fusion of joy and sorrow at the end of *Charolais;* no sense of exaltation offsets the reader's shock and dismay.

Tragedy, finally, is irreparable. "Where the causes of disaster are temporal, where the conflict can be resolved through technical or social means, we may have serious drama, but not tragedy."[25] The catastrophe in *Charolais* is certainly irreparable (the hero drives his wife to suicide), but one feels that it was not necessary. Alfred Kerr suggested this: "Several have asked whether he [Beer-Hofmann] is the 'great tragic poet' we need. But we don't need one at all. Nowadays there is nothing tragic . . . that would not seem ridiculous within a foreseeable period of time. That is just the point. That is exactly why we become uneasy at this ending: when the husband insists on the destruction of the faithless wife; when the just father says everything but this one thing: 'don't be heroic, be reasonable!' "[26] This, to be sure, is not so much a criticism of the playwright as a commentary on the nature of the times in which we live.

Steiner argues convincingly that tragedy is entirely alien to the Judaic view of the world:

> The book of Job is always cited as an instance of tragic vision. But . . . God made good the havoc wrought upon his servant; he . . . compensated Job for his agonies. [Job 42:12.] But where there is compensation, there is justice, not tragedy. This demand for justice is the pride and burden of the Judaic tradition. . . . Often the balance of retribution or reward seems fearfully awry, or the proceedings of God appear unendurably slow. But over the sum of time, there can be no doubt that the ways of God to man are just . . . they are [also] rational. The Judaic spirit is vehement in its conviction that the order of the universe and of man's estate is accessible to reason.[27]

This insistence upon justice is very pronounced in *Charolais,* culminating in the count's inexorable demand for "compensation." In this connection, Beer-Hofmann's Jewish heritage was probably an important influence on the play. The influence of modern psychology, however, was just as strong. Largely because of its findings, people no longer believed in the finality or absoluteness of evil; indeed, they thought more in terms of sickness or mental aberration. Increasingly, they attributed a man's wrongdoing not to flaws in his character but to his environment, his education, and all the other circumstances and forces that had shaped him as a person. Implicit in this essentially optimistic view is the belief that sick people can be healed, criminals rehabilitated, education and social conditions improved. Tragedy becomes impossible in such a climate; that Beer-Hofmann was aware of this is evident in his statement that with *Der Graf von Charolais* he had written an end to tragedy. Despite its flaws, the play is a superb piece of literature; it is also "excellent theatre."

Das goldene Pferd[28]

Beer-Hofmann returned in 1921 to a genre that had attracted him thirty years before: his interest in pantomime was a natural offshoot of his extraordinary preoccupation with visual theatrical effects (not only in *Das goldene Pferd*—where it does not strike one as unusual—but also in the *David* cycle, the scenes are called "pictures"). This is reflected in Beer-Hofmann's introduction to *Das goldene Pferd*: "The pantomime . . .was a tempting effort for once to give up the word, to invent a course of events in structure and direction—in such a way that it would be understandable and captivating through action, gesture, mimicry, the play of beautiful, well-trained bodies, light, color, and music" (*GW*, 467). Beer-Hofmann's attraction to pantomime was undoubtedly also influenced by his acute awareness of the ultimate limitations of the word and by his conviction that the most basic human experiences occur outside the realm of language. He expressed this conviction in the prose fragment, "Ur-Zeit des Wortes" ["The Primeval Period of the Word"], written in 1943: "It is natural for man's most decisive affairs to be conducted *wordlessly*—from eating, which stops up his mouth, to siring, conceiving, giving birth, dying, slaying. The full, undiverted strength of the person has to flow into every action—every breach of silence weakens that strength, opens up a path through which it can escape—all important action is instinctively sealed against the word" (*GW*, 632). This view is also implicit in the prose fragment, "Stumme Szenen" ["Silent Scenes"], undated, but probably written in 1927: " . . . the more the silent execution of situations is incorporated into the drama, i.e., the pantomimic element flows into the drama to a stronger degree, the more the universal intelligibility of the drama will increase, the circle to which drama can speak be widened. . . .The genuine gesture born of feeling does not become archaic; styles of speech do. Thus the penetration of the mimic element will become a substitute for much that was previously spoken—in addition to untold other advantages, it will also prevent the exclusivity of [literary] art, prevent art from becoming overly subtle, something to which the word often entices" (*GW*, 625).[29]

Das goldene Pferd, a pantomime in six scenes, is a fairy tale in the manner of *A Thousand and One Nights*. Late in life, it will be recalled, Beer-Hofmann remarked that what impressed him most about *A Thousand and One Nights* was its manifold linking of fates, and this is one of the most striking features of *Das goldene Pferd,* announced in the prologue by the "Märchenerzähler" ["Narrator of the Fairy Tale"]:

> Ich grüsse Euch!—I c h bins, dem sonst man lauscht
> In hellbestirnten lauen Sommernächten,
> Denn Märchen weiss ich, drinnen sich Geschicke
> Zu Wundern—seltsam, unerhört—verflechten.   (*GW*, 467)

[I greet you!—it is *I*, to whom one listens
On mild and starry summer nights,
For I know fairy tales, in which fates
Are woven into wonders—strange, unheard-of.]

The motif of the mysterious workings of fate is also reinforced by the blind minstrel's song, which, coming at the beginning and the end of the pantomime, has the effect of a motto. It reaffirms the author's belief in the ultimate justice and wisdom of God's ways, however little we may understand them:

Misst du denn, wozu dein Leben
Gott in seinem Planen braucht?
Dünkt dirs klein und niedrig? Gott dünkt
Gross vielleicht es und erlaucht!   (*GW*, 474)

[Can you measure then for what
God needs your life in His great plan?
Does it strike you as small and lowly?
To Him perhaps it is great and noble!]

The last strophe of the song concludes the poet's affirmation:

Erz, das dir verliehen, schmiede,
Stark und stolz, zu e i g n e m Los!
Reines Ringen wird zum Segen
Gott dir wenden—Gott ist gross!   (*GW*, 474)

[Metal that is given you, forge,
Strong and proud, into your *own* fate!
The struggle, pure, God will
Turn to blessing—God is great!]

These lines also express Beer-Hofmann's belief that the sovereignty of fate does not absolve the individual of the responsibility to act.

The dream motif is also dominant: Tarkah's lines in the epilogue show that Beer-Hofmann was just as strongly drawn to this theme in 1921 as he had been when he wrote *Der Tod Georgs*. Like the early novel, the pantomime presents the dream as the anticipator, if not the manipulator, of the events of real life:

Was—gebändigt—tief sonst schlummert,
Wacht im Traum gebietend auf.
Taten, Träume—und ein Ahnen
Lenken jedes Lebens Lauf!   (*GW*, 518)

[What otherwise—restrained—sleeps deeply,
Awakes, commanding, in the dream.
Deeds, dreams—and a presentiment
Direct the course of every life!]

The dreamer is characterized by an absence of restraints and inhibitions; the dream is represented as the realm in which the true self emerges:

Zeigt im Traum euch euer Antlitz,
Was euch tief befremden mag—
Fragt euch ob im T r a u m ihr Maske,
Oder Maske tragt am Tag!   (GW, 518)

[If in the dream your face reveals
What may seem deeply strange to you—
Ask yourself whether you wear a mask
In *dreams* or during the day!][30]

In all likelihood the avoidance of tragedy was still another reason why Beer-Hofmann was drawn to the dream motif: Bahádur (together with all the other principals) comes to a bloody end, but the reactions of pity and terror are displaced by relief when he wakes at the farm to find that the entire experience had been a dream.

The dream motif places *Das goldene Pferd* in a tradition that dates much farther back than Grillparzer, of course, but there are some marked similarities between the characters of Rustan and Bahádur, and their respective dream adventures (including exposure to a world previously unknown to them, the experiences of sexual love, guilt, suffering and death, and the insight derived from them). Like Grillparzer's *Traum ein Leben,* Beer-Hofmann's pantomime also represents the simple life, close to the earth, as that most likely to bring one happiness and "des Innern stillen Frieden" [Grillparzer's famous "quiet inner peace"].[31]

Most of the motifs already familiar to the reader from Beer-Hofmann's earlier works re-emerge in *Das goldene Pferd.* Especially the king exemplifies the transitoriness of life and the ultimate purposelessness of worldly power and wealth. His expression and gestures reveal that Tarkah has guessed his innermost thoughts and feelings when she sings to him:

Schlaflose Stunden vor Tag hörst du's hämmern
Rastlos, hart, ohne Ruh:
Länder—Triumphe—und Schätze—und Frauen—!
W o z u noch taugt dirs—w o z u?   (*GW*, 493)

[In sleepless pre-dawn hours you hear it hammering
Restless, hard, without peace:
Lands—triumphs—and treasures—and women—!
Of what value is all this to you now?]

In the same song she briefly treats the motif of posterity as an answer to death:

Jugend verflog!—Was hoffst du noch? Fühle,
Wie dir dein Leben entrinnt!
Leichter trügst du das Grauen, umspielte
Deine Knie ein Kind!   (*GW*, 493)

[Youth fled swiftly—what hope do you have? Feel
How your life trickles away!
The horror you feel would be less heavy to bear,
If a child played about your knees!]

The fear of death and the loneliness of the individual are dealt with even more fully in the following lines:

Frauen im silbernen Käfig, sie teilen
L u s t mit dir—w a n n du's verlangst—
Doch in schlaflosem Dunkel—wer teilt da,
Wer—mit dir deine Angst?   (*GW*, 494)

[Women in silver cages share
Lust with you—*when* you command—
But in the sleepless dark—who shares
With you, there, your fear?]

The closing lines of the song are a recapitulation of the theme of loneliness and ultimate isolation:

Einsamer! M e i n Herz gedrängt an das d e i n e—
Fühle, es pulset dir zu:
Was dich umschmiegt—das sehnet und leidet,
Bangt—und stirbt einsam—wie du!   (*GW*, 494)

[Lonely one! *My* heart pressed to *yours*—
Feel, it pulses to you:
What embraces you—yearns and suffers,
Is fearful—and dies alone—like you!]

Having chosen an opulent Middle Eastern setting for *Das goldene Pferd* and justified to some extent by the absence of the spoken word, Beer-Hofmann could give completely free rein to his love of splendor and pageantry. One senses that it gave him enormous pleasure to do so.[32] The stage directions are even more detailed than usual, and the painstaking attention to costuming—especially to the dress and regalia of the emir, the king and queen mother, and the members of the court— convinces one that Rudolf Kassner did not exaggerate when remarking that Beer-Hofmann could talk for hours about exactly where on Lady Macbeth's robe a ruby should be placed.[33]

The characters of *Das goldene Pferd* are decidedly lurid—justified to some extent by the fact that the work is a pantomime. Each character represents a pronounced type or indeed, in Tarkah's case, an arche- type. As the Märchenerzähler introduces the characters to the audi- ence, he typecasts each one: Bilal is the good and contented man of the soil, his own master on his own farm; his daughter Halimah por- trays ideal maidenhood—gentle, beautiful, and virtuous; and Bahádur is vigorous young manhood, longing to experience life and the world: "Er liebt sie—doch Liebe, sie hält / Ihn gekettet an Heimat und Scholle und Haus— / Und die Welt lockt draussen—die Welt!" (*GW*, 469). ["He loves her—yet love holds him / Chained to home, house and soil— / And the world entices beyond!"] The king is typecast as the jaded older man, disillusioned by worldly power and wealth; and Tarkah, the femme fatale, embodies all fleshly lust, evil, and death.[34]

Music plays a prominent role in *Das goldene Pferd*, serving at many points as a substitute for the word. Each character has his own leit- motif, which the viewer comes to associate with his entrances and exits and to expect in scenes which he dominates. Thus, the oboe motif (which in the first scene was associated with the boy who led the blind minstrel) is reintroduced in the fourth scene when the boy, leading the minstrel and followed by the emir, Bilal, and Halimah, re-enters the picture and the pantomime approaches its climax.

Although no musical score was composed specifically for *Das goldene Pferd*, it is clear that Beer-Hofmann had a definite conception of what the music should be. The stage directions describe the music in great detail; it is highly romantic, expressly so in the entr'acte between the first and second scenes. Here the Märchenerzähler sings a ballad, "Ritt durch die Nacht" ["Ride Through the Night"], and the musical accompaniment is described thus: *"Über dem immer gleichen Trabmotiv der Bässe und gedämpften Pauken flimmernd die Stimmung der Mondnacht. Ritt durch den Wald. Ritt längs des Flusses. Aus dem nächtlichen mondhellen Weben hebt sich immer deutlicher ein balladenhafter Satz"* (*GW*, 476). [*"Above the unvarying trot-motif of the bass viols and muted drums, the glittering mood of the moonlit night. Ride through the forest. Ride along the river. From the nocturnal, moonbright texture of the whole, a balladesque theme rises more and more clearly."*] At other points the music is not only romantic, but distinctly Wagnerian. In one such passage (scene 2), the stage directions call for music that is *"nicht hell, heiter—eher dunkel, werbend und lockend, ihre Elemente aus dem Liebeslied Tarkahs . . . schöpfend. . . . Jeder Ansatz, zu lösen, zu entspannen, wird von dumpf vibrierenden gewitternden Paukenwirbeln verschlungen, schwillt zu neuer, fast schmerzlicher Spannung, um endlich, beseligt zu veratmen"* (*GW*, 482). [*"not bright, serene—but dark, wooing and enticing . . . drawing its elements from Tarkah's love song. . . . Every onset of a resolution or relaxation is swallowed up by the muffled thunder of vibrating drum rolls, then swells to new, almost painful tension, finally to die away enraptured."*]

As Beer-Hofmann acknowledges in his introduction to *Das goldene Pferd*, he does not depose the word entirely. Whatever the limitations of the word, he would have been hard-pressed without it to make the action entirely clear to the viewer. He solves this problem by allowing spoken lines in the prologue, the two entr'actes (between scenes 1 and 2, 3 and 4), and the epilogue. In this scheme of things the Märchenerzähler functions on more than one level: he is one of the figures in the work, but also the intermediary between the audience and the characters and action on the stage. In the prologue his functions are to set the scene, introduce the characters, and indicate the mood in which the audience is expected to receive the story. In the first entr'acte his task is to provide answers to questions which have inevitably arisen in the viewer's mind and which were not clarified by the pantomimic first scene: Who is the emir? What brought him to Bilal's farm? Where is Bahádur going, now that he has exchanged places with the emir? The fairy tale atmosphere of the work is not seriously challenged by these interruptions, because the Märchenerzähler provides his information in ballad form. His function in the second entr'acte, however, is somewhat different. Because the preceding scene (3) consisted of actions that spoke for themselves, the Märchenerzähler does not have to clarify any obscure or puzzling points. Instead he gives a brief recapitulation (again in ballad form) of the forces and events that have led to

Bahádur's accession to the throne and of the situation in which he consequently finds himself. Since the pantomimic action of scene 3 does not require explanation, Beer-Hofmann probably included this entr'acte for the sake of balance, but also to ease the dramatic tension: in scene 3 Tarkah has offered herself to the king and then killed him, and Bahádur stands guilty with her by maintaining the silence of assent. In the epilogue the characters parade before the curtain to take their bows, and Tarkah speaks directly to the audience about herself and the other characters, concluding with some general observations about the nature of dreams and the figures who people them—all of which serves to return the audience from the fairy tale realm of the pantomime to the present "real" world.

In all of these passages, the spoken lines are in verse with musical accompaniment. The verses are usually rhymed, as are the songs in the pantomime scenes. The blind minstrel's song is set in regular four-foot trochees—a metre that corresponds to the solemn, measured character of the song—with regularly alternating rhyme (lines 2 and 4, 6 and 8, 10 and 12). Alliteration, with its very sensuous effect, is kept to a minimum in this song; in most of the others the alliteration is pronounced, especially in the song which introduces Tarkah:

> Es lockt ihre Laute, ihr Lied und ihr Leib,
> Bis die Glut zur Flamme hoch loht!
> Sie lockt über Lügen und Leichen und Leid,
> Zu Lust und Taumel und Tod!   (*GW,* 469–70)

> [Her lute, her song, and her body entice
> 'Til the smouldering embers flame high!
> She entices through lies and corpses and grief
> To lust and frenzy and death!

In the original the sensuous impression is drastically heightened by the use—in the short space of four lines—of no fewer than twelve alliterative l-sounds.

One's reaction to such passages is that the author is surely ironizing a poetic form. This is not irony in the ordinary sense, however, for there is a complete absence of ridicule or sarcasm. It is the playful irony of a writer indulging his own inordinate delight in the sensuous quality of words. In fact, the pantomime as a whole is dominated by this kind of play. Of course, the author is quite serious about the motifs he deals with, and the reader is meant to take them seriously, too; but otherwise *Das goldene Pferd* is the product of the same sheer delight in sensuous, dramatic effects that Robert Musil identifies in *Der Graf von Charolais*. Stylistically, the principal difference between the two works stems from the fairy tale nature of *Das goldene Pferd*. Because Beer-Hofmann was concerned in the pantomime with the fantastic, rather than with "the realities of common action," he was able to abandon the restraints he usually imposed on himself, and most of the scenes do not suffer as a result.[35] He advises the audience at the outset: "Gebt willig euch hin! Nehmt schwerer es nicht, / Als ein Märchen, ein Spiel—einen Traum!" (*GW*, 470). ["Submit willingly! Take it no more seriously, / Than a fairy tale, a game—a dream!"] If one follows his advice, *Das goldene Pferd* becomes an entertaining piece of reading.

Die Historie von König David

Beer-Hofmann unquestionably regarded the *David* cycle as his major literary work. Not all of his notes on the *Historie* are dated, but we know that he considered a series of Biblical dramas as early as 1898, and the last dated item of the *Historie* (a scenario of *Davids Tod*) was completed April 4, 1937. Thus Beer-Hofmann was occupied with the *Historie* for most of his adult life, although his work on it by no means proceeded uninterruptedly during that period.[36] Having consented (reluctantly) to the publication of *Jaákobs Traum* before the entire cycle was completed, Beer-Hofmann subsequently allowed the separate publication of various other parts of the cycle. The entire work (all that he completed) did not appear as a whole until his collected works were published in 1963.

Beer-Hofmann changed his mind more than once about the structure of the work and also about the Biblical characters who should figure most prominently in it. According to the plan he ultimately decided upon, the *Historie* was to consist of: (1) *Jaákobs Traum. Ein Vorspiel,* (2) *Der junge David,* (3) "Vorspiel auf dem Theater zu *König David,*" (4) *König David,* and (5) *Davids Tod.* Of these, only *Jaákobs Traum, Der junge David,* and the "Vorspiel auf dem Theater zu *König David*" exist in finished form. Regardless of changes in the cast of characters and the material to be included, Beer-Hofmann's conception of the *Historie* was of epic proportions almost from the beginning. In addition to the Old Testament,[37] Beer-Hofmann used many secondary works (a list of them apears in *GW*, 894), and his voluminous notes on the *Historie* attest to "an interest in the minutia of the Biblical world that goes far beyond the specific needs of the dramatist."[38] Against this rich and carefully detailed background, the themes of the young Beer-Hofmann, the ideas he conceived in his early manhood as tentative possibilities, are presented in the final stages of their development.

Jaákobs Traum

Although written as a prologue to provide the ancient historical or mythological background of the David story, *Jaákobs Traum* is a complete dramatic work in its own right.[39] The play is very simply structured, consisting of two parts. The first, which is much shorter than the second and provides a background for the action of Part II, is set at Isaac's farm. The second part, which presents the main action of the play (i.e., the vision itself), is set at Beth-El. Despite this structural division, Beer-Hofmann actually deals with three distinct episodes: (1) Jacob's theft of the blessing, (2) the reconciliation of Jacob and Esau, and (3) Jacob's vision and fateful decision at Beth-El.

The drama is overwhelmingly dominated by the motif of suffering—suffering and doubt as a means to faith, and suffering as the decidedly preponderant element of *Auserwähltsein*. Jacob is not a sceptic who leaves open the question of God's existence, neither affirming nor denying it. There is obviously no doubt in his mind that God exists: "Gross ist der Gott! Und ist mit uns!" ["Great is God! And is with us!"], he says to Idnibaál (*GW,* 41). Jacob's doubts and questions, causing him profound spiritual anguish, stem from his bitter struggle to understand the contradictory nature of God. Even before the vision, there are indications of the doubts that torment Jacob, beginning with his thoughtful but still noncommital question, "Und es schützten / Die Götter ihren Diener nicht?" (*GW,* 37). ["And the gods / Protected not their servant?"] He expresses his feelings more heatedly as he and Idnibaál discuss the myths associated with Mount Moriah, the site of Abraham's near-sacrifice of Isaac. To Idnibaál's remark, "—Und dein Vater / Ward nicht geopfert!" ["—And your father / Was not sacrificed!"], Jacob bitterly replies:

> Ward er's w i r k l i c h nicht?
> Was dort des Kindes Augen—schreckgeweitet—
> Einmal gesehn—glaubst du—vergisst sich das?!
> . . . Wem Gott—als Kind—Vertrauen so zertrat—
> W o darf der trauen noch und sicher fühlen?!   (*GW,* 40)

> [Was he *really* not?
> What the eyes of a child—wide with fear—
> Once saw—do you think—can be forgotten?!

> ... A child whose trust God trampled thus—
> *How* can it still feel trusting and secure?!]

He is clearly dissatisfied with the traditional explanation of this horrifying incident; when Idnibaál reminds him that the people regard it as God's supreme test of Abraham's loyalty, Jacob says accusingly: "Gott / Ist alle Antwort! Muss ein Gott erst fragen?" ["God / Is all answer! Must a God first ask?"] (*GW*, 40).

In the vision itself, Beer-Hofmann expresses doubt and its attendant suffering primarily through Samáel, and it cannot be overemphasized that this outcast is not represented as a blasphemer.[40] To the accusations of the archangels, he says:

> Ich lästre n i c h t! Ich k a n n nur nicht lobsingen,
> Gleich euch, die ihr euch sonnt in Seinem Strahl!
> Doch euren Sang mit Cymbeln und Posaunen,
> Ihn ü b e rtönt furchtbar der Schrei der Qual,
> Der a u fsteigt, ewig aufsteigt, niemals endend
> Aus Seiner Welt! Ich neide sie Ihm n i c h t!   (*GW*, 70–71)

> [I blaspheme not! I simply *cannot* praise
> Like you who sun yourselves in His bright light!
> But your song with cymbals and trumpets
> Is drowned out *dread*fully by the cry of torment
> That *rises,* ever rises, never ending,
> From His world! I do *not* envy Him that world!]

Then Samáel poses the ancient question about the existence of suffering in the world:

> Ist Leid nur Strafe? Sagt—was tat das Tier,
> Das unter Martern stumm am Weg verendet?
> Ihr ewig Seligen! Die Schuld nennt mir,
> Um die Er Neugeborenes ins Leben,
> Geschmückt mit Wunden, giftigen Beulen sendet?
> Lobsinget Seiner Güte, Seiner Stärke—
> Mir—graut vor Ihm! Ich fass' Ihn nicht! Hat Er's
> Gekonnt nicht anders? Anders nicht gewollt?
> Greift Ihn Entsetzen nicht vor Seinem Werke?
> Schuf Er zur L u s t Sich diesen Ball? Nun rollt
> Er taumelnd hin—entglitten Seinen Händen—
> Hin durch die Zeit—ich frag: Zu welchem Enden?   (*GW*, 71)

[Is suffering only punishment? Tell me—what did the beast
That dies in silent agony along the way?
You ever blissful ones! *Name* me the guilt
For which He sends newborn to life
Adorned with wounds and venomous sores?
Praise His goodness, praise His power—
I shudder before Him! I understand Him not!
Could He not do otherwise? Would He not?
Is He not seized by horror at His handiwork?
Created He this sphere for *pleasure?* Now
—Slipped from His hands—it rolls dizzily
Through time—I ask you: to what end?]

Jacob obviously feels a much greater kinship to Samáel than to the archangels; the questions Samáel raises here are the very ones Jacob has wrestled with so bitterly. For him, as for Samáel, God is a painful wound: the more they probe it, the more intolerably it hurts, but they cannot leave it alone. Samáel urges Jacob with all the persuasiveness he can muster: "Lass ab von Ihm!" ["Leave off from Him!"], but Jacob answers:

> Ich k a n n nicht von Ihm lassen!
> Du Leid-Erfüllter—lässt denn du von Ihm?
> Und—näher Seinem Throne steht dein Hassen—
> Als a l l e Liebe Seiner Cherubim!   (*GW,* 80)

> [I *cannot* cease with Him!
> You suffering one—do you leave off from Him?
> And—nearer His throne your hatred stands—
> Than *all* the love of his cherubim!]

Samáel and Jacob also have the same attitude toward the archangels. When Raphaél asks, "Was drängst du zwischen uns dich und den Knaben?" ["How dare you force yourself between us and the lad?"], Samáel retorts, "Was drängtet ihr euch zwischen mich und Gott!" (*GW,* 70). ["How dare you force yourselves between God and me!"] In language which reflects not only a complete lack of envy, but even contempt for the three, he cries:

> Verworfen—n i c h t!
> V e r s t o s s e n—Und verstossen noch, geeint
> Im Tiefsten euerm Herrn—nicht euch, den Dienern,
> Den immer jubelnden, den selig satten!   (*GW,* 72)

[*Not*—rejected!
Only *cast out!*—And outcast, still united
In the deepest sense with your Master—not with you servants,
The ever rejoicing, blissfully sated!]

Jacob, initially awed by the radiance that emanates from the archangels, says essentially the same to them in a later passage:

Ein Wurm bin ich! Und weise d o c h zurück euch
In euer dienend Amt: (*Gebietend*) Von Ihm zu mir—
Von mir zu Ihm—seid Boten ihr—n u r B o t e n!
. . . Wand seid ihr zwischen mir und Gott!   (*GW,* 76)

[A worm am I! And *yet* I send you back
To your servants' place: (*imperiously*) from Him to me—
From me to Him—you are messengers—*only messengers!*
. . . A wall between God and me!][41]

The theme of the suffering of *Auserwähltsein* is similarly introduced, as Jacob attempts to fathom this God who promises endless blessing, gives Abraham the son he has yearned for, and then directs him to kill the child and offer him up as a sacrifice. Shuddering, Jacob questions: "Zu n a h umweht uns dieser Gott—was will Er? / Was w i l l Er—dass er also uns umdrängt?!" ["Too *closely* wafts this God about us—what does He want? / What does He *want*—that He presses thus upon us?!"] To Idnibaál's reminder, "Sie sagen, Herr . . . Er habe— / Aus allen Völkern—e u c h für sich erwählt!" ["They say, my lord . . . He has / Chosen *you*—from among all peoples—for Himself!"], Jacob replies, starting up in pain, anger, and accusation: "Was wählt Er uns—und fragt nicht, ob wir w o l l e n?!" (*GW,* 42). ["How dare He choose us— without asking whether we *will*?!"]

During the dialogue with Esau, Jacob's speeches express the poet's belief that the destiny of the elect is to be the *exculpator dei,* and that this entails so much suffering and anguish of spirit that one may well ask whether *Auserwähltsein* is not more curse than blessing. Bitterly, Jacob says:

So heisst "erwählt": Traumlosen Schlaf nicht kennen,
Gesichte nachts—und Stimmen ringsum tags!
Bin ich erwählt? D a z u erwählt, dass alles,
Dem Leid geschieht, mich ruft, mich heischt, mir klagt?
Dass selbst der Blick des Tiers, das stumm verendet,
Mich fragt: "Warum?!" . . .
Wie will Er, dass ich Antwort a l s o gebe,

Als wär' ich—Er, der mich und alles schuf?
Wie k a n n ich das?
(*Mit finsterem Aufblick, stark*)
Wählst Du—Du Gott da droben—
D a z u mich aus? Dann k o m m zu mir und raune
Ins Ohr mir, wie ich Rede stehen, w i e ich—
Ich—Dein Geschöpf—Dich Gott entschulden soll!   (*GW*, 58–59)

[So "chosen" means: Not to know a dreamless sleep,
Phantoms by night—and voices round about by day!
Chosen am I? Chosen *for this,* that everything
Which suffers calls me, demands of me, laments to me?
That even the glance of a beast that mutely dies
Asks me: "Why?!" . . .
How does He intend that I answer,
As though I were He—who made me and all things?
How *can* I do that?
(*With a dark upward glance, emphatically*)
You choose me—you God above—
For *that*? Then *come* to me and whisper
In my ear, how I shall give answer, *how* I—
I—Your creature—shall exculpate you, God!]

During the vision, the suffering of *Auserwähltsein* is depicted in terrible detail by Samáel, whose lines either quote Old Testament passages exactly or closely paraphrase them:

"Du wirst!" M i c h höre—was du wirst!
Sie lügen n i c h t! W o h l neigt man deinem Wort sich—
Doch blutig schlägt den Mund man, der es sprach!
W o h l darfst du wandern! Aber rasten? Heimat?
Sie wird dir Wort—du sinnst ihm ewig nach!
Volk wirst du, d'raus sich alle Beute holen—
An dir zu freveln? Wem wär's n i c h t erlaubt?
Die Erde eisern unter deinen Sohlen,
Ehern der Himmel über deinem Haupt . . .
Dein Sinn, dein Leib, wird allen Abscheu, Ekel—
Man s p e i t ins Antlitz dir . . .
Man tut es! Jedes Volk, dran du dich schmiegest,
Es brennt dich aus, wie eitriges Geschwür . . .
Du Liebling Gottes, wirst der Welt verhasster,
Als Pest—als giftiges Kraut—als tolles Tier! . . .
So—segnet Er!   (*GW*, 78–79)

["You shall be!" *Hear*—what you shall be!
They do *not* lie! One *will* incline to your word—
But bloodily beat the mouth that uttered it!
Indeed may you wander! But rest? Homeland?
It will become a word you ponder evermore!
A people you'll become, from which all fetch their booty—
To sin against you? To whom will it *not* be allowed?
Iron the earth beneath your soles,
Brass the sky above your head . . .
Your spirit, your body repugnant to all—
They will *spit* in your face . . .
They will do it! Every people you espouse
Will burn you out, like a festering cyst . . .
You favorite of God the world will despise more
Than pestilence—poisonous weed—rabid animal! . . .
Thus—he blesses!][42]

Jacob's development is from the reluctant object of God's election to a free and independent individual. God has singled him out, but only he can make the decision to accept or reject the covenant God offers. Far different from the stereotype of the humble servant, Jacob is characterized by fierce pride and independence: "Gott wählt mich aus—Gott will mich frei! / . . . Gott will mich stolz und wahr!"["God chooses me—God wants me free! / . . . God wants me proud and true!"]. Indeed, Jacob has boundless self-assurance, if not audacity, and even makes—to the consternation of the archangels—the sovereign gesture of releasing God from His oath to Jacob's ancestors (*GW*, 76).

In reaching his decision, Jacob is not at all influenced by the glittering promises of the archangels, to whom he says with deeply offended pride:

> Wählt Er, nur um zu schenken,
> Dass er uns Gut und Macht und Glanz verspricht?
> Taugt Ihm mein Blut zu mehr nicht, als zu Königen?
> Ich will nicht Herrschaft! Weiss Er denn das nicht?
> Mizrajim, Babel und des Meerlands Fürsten—
> Wie—glaubt Er wirklich sie von mir beneidet?
> N i c h t s neid ich—euch nicht eure Seligkeit . . .   (*GW*, 75)

> [Does he elect, only to give gifts,
> Promising us goods and power and splendor?
> Does he think my blood fit for nothing more than kingship?
> I want no dominion! Doesn't He know that?
> The princes of Mizraim, Babylon and the coast—
> Does He really think I envy them?
> I covet *nothing*—not even your bliss . . .]

His own conception of *Auserwähltsein* is completely different; his description of it is a poetic expression of Beer-Hofmann's statements on the role of the *exculpator dei* as well as a poetic treatment of the motif of the unity of all life:

> K ö n n t' ich denn selig sein, wenn alles leidet?
> Alles mir naht, am Tag naht, nachts in Träumen,
> Mensch, Tier, und Kraut der Erde, und Gestein—
> Klagt, Antwort heischt, mit stummen Augen fordert—
> M i c h fragt—und alle Antwort ist doch S e i n! . . .
> So wählt m e i n Blut Er aus zum stolzen Reise—
> In alle Zeiten spriessend, nie verdorrt—
> Dass m e i n e m Mund—von neuem immer wieder—
> Entstürze Seines ewigen Willens Wort!
> Und zwischen mir und sorglos jungem Blühen
> Brach d a r u m Brücke Er entzwei und Steg—
> Dass e w i g ich, mit Menschenschritt, hiernieden
> Mitschreite Seinen fernen Gottesweg,
> Und—Leid mit S e i n e m Worte lösend—hier
> Sein ewiger Mund und ewiger Anwalt werde . . .   (*GW*, 75)

> [*Could* I be blissful, when all things suffer?
> Approach me by day and at night in dreams?
> Man, beast, plants of the earth and rocks
> Lament, seek answer, demand with silent eyes—
> Ask *me*—and yet all answer belongs to *Him!*
> So chooses He *my* blood for a proud shoot—
> Sprouting for all time, never withered—
> That from *my* mouth—ever and ever anew—
> May pour the word of His eternal will!
> *For this* he cut off bridge and narrow path
> Between me and all carefree, youthful flowering—
> That I *eternally,* with human step, on earth
> Tread with Him His divine and distant way,
> And—easing suffering with His word—here
> Become His eternal mouth and advocate . . .]

Jacob's decision to enter into the covenant is an affirmation of God despite His incomprehensible and contradictory ways: "Ich lieb' Ihn— wie Er ist! Grausam und gnädig, / Lauteres Licht—und Abgrund, finster, tief!" (*GW*, 80). ["I love Him—as He is! Cruel and merciful, / Pure light—and chasm dark and deep!"][43] This certainly does not mean, however, that Jacob's doubts are forever laid to rest. His past suffering and doubt have led him to "the ultimate serenity, which we can only bear when it is born of the last bitterness and deepest torment"; but the battle will be fought many times over, and Jacob knows it:

> Hör mich, mein Gott! Es schweigen Deine Boten—
> Du, der mich wählt—Du, den ich wähle—sprich!
> Sag ihnen, dass wir—zweifelnd—zürnend—hadernd—
> Doch aneinander hängen, ewig—D u und i c h!   (GW, 80)

> [Hear me, my God! Your messengers fall silent—
> You, who elect me—You, whom I elect—Speak!
> Tell them that we—doubting—quarreling angrily—
> Cling nevertheless to each other forever— *You* and *I!*]

The basis of Jacob's newly won serenity is trust, and herein, despite their many similarities, lies the difference between Jacob and Samáel, to whom he says: "Sieh: Tief in mir—wohin Wort nicht mehr dringt, / Schläft—was dir fremd ward: Seliges Vertrauen!" (GW, 80). ["See: deep in me—where words no longer penetrate, / Slumbers—what became alien to you: blissful trust!"]

Just as Jacob is not tempted by the promises of the archangels, he is equally unmoved by the agony that Samáel so vividly prophesies for him and his descendants. As the drama ends, Jacob promises: "Herr! Was Dein Wille mir auch auferlege . . . / Wie K r o n e will ich's tragen—nicht wie Joch!" (GW, 83). ["Lord! Whatever Your will may lay upon me . . . / Like a *crown* will I wear it—not a yoke!][44] He declares his willingness to assume the burden of God's guilt, with all that that implies:

> Du w i l l s t ja schenken! Sei dies Deine Gnade:
> Hin durch mein Blut lass ewig fluten Deine
> Drei heiligen Ströme—Herr: Kraft—Stolz—Geduld!
> Und . . . t r ä g s t Du Schuld—will m i t ich tragen—
> . . . L a d e
> Du Gott—auf meine Schultern Deine Schuld!   (GW, 80)

> [You *want* to give! May this be Your gift of grace:
> Let flow forever through my blood Your
> Three sacred streams, Lord: strength—pride—patience!
> And . . . *If* You bear guilt—I will carry it *with* You—
> . . . *Place,*
> God—on my shoulders Your guilt!]

This underscores one of the most interesting ideas that Beer-Hofmann advances in *Jaákobs Traum*—namely, that God needs man just as
much as man needs God. Significantly, it is through Samael that Beer-
Hofmann develops this idea most fully. The archangels have nothing
but rapturous praise for the Almighty, and in their eagerness to win
Jacob they are sometimes less than honest, but Samáel never fails to
speak the truth, however bitter it may be. God himself confirms this:
when Samáel describes the future suffering of Israel, declaring that
God will permit it and show no sign of mercy, the archangels passionately call him a liar, but God resolves the dispute with the words,
"Wahr ist Samáels Wort! (*GW*, 81). ["True is Samáel's word!] God's
ensuing explanation of His lack of mercy to Israel is a poetic statement
of the very foundation of Judaism—that is, the Law:

> Wenn andre, knieend, zum Erbarmer flehen,
> Ü b ich Erbarmen—wie der Herr am Knecht!
> Doch d u—sollst aufrecht vor dem Vater stehen,
> Erbarmen—weig're ich! Fordere du—dein R e c h t!   (*GW*, 81)

> [When others, kneeling, plead for mercy,
> I *practice* mercy—as master to serf!
> But *you*—shall stand upright before the Father,
> Mercy—I refuse! You demand—your *right!]*

The question of God's need of man is pursued throughout the drama.
In the earlier passages it is implicit in Jacob's efforts to understand the
nature of God, in his questions about what God wants from him and
why He will not leave him alone. It is treated more specifically during
the vision. Pondering the question of why God wants the covenant
with Jacob, Samáel asks: "Bangt denn dem Einzigen—fühlt er sich
allein?" (*GW*, 77). ["Is the Supreme One fearful?—does He feel alone?"]
The answer Samáel ultimately gives is that God needs Israel not only
for the preservation of His divine image as a just God, but, in fact, for
His very existence:

> Du Tor! Von Gott erkorener Prügelknabe!
> An d e i n e m Dulderleibe peitscht Er ewig
> Sein Gotttum allen andern Völkern ein!
> Ihn schaudert vor der Qual, die Er erschaffen,
> Dich braucht Er, dass du—gläubig durch die Zeit
> Dich schleppend—allen Völkern rings verkündest,
> Schuldlos sei Er—und Strafe alles Leid!
> Dich o p f e r t Er! Du taugst ihm nur als Zeuge,

Als unbestochener, auf den er weist;
Wer zweifelt noch, wenn d u—von Ihm zertreten,
Verblutend—deinen Gott, g e r e c h t, noch preist!   (*GW,* 79)

[You fool! God's chosen whipping boy!
On *your* long-suffering body he whips
Into all other peoples the belief in His divinity!
He shudders at the torment He created,
He needs you—dragging yourself, faithful,
Through all time—proclaiming to all peoples
That He is innocent—and all suffering punishment!
He *sacrifices* you! He values you only as a witness,
An incorruptible one to whom He points;
Who will doubt, if *you*—trodden by Him,
Bleeding—still praise your God as *just!*]

An interesting aspect of God's need of Jacob is the status Jacob acquires through this need and the relationship to which it leads. It is no exaggeration to say that because of God's need of him, Jacob in a sense becomes a god himself.[46] The text contains many indications of this; one of the earliest is Jacob's seemingly innocent question, "Wie will Er, dass ich Antwort also geb, / Als wär' ich—Er, der mich und alles schuf?"(*GW,* 59). ["How does He intend that I answer, / As if I were—He, who created me and all things?"] Jacob here acknowleges God as the creator of all things, but he and all men share this attribute with God and are participants in creation. The archangels describe creation not as an isolated event of the remote past, but rather as a perpetual, never-ending process:

. . . Er s c h u f . . . nicht—Er s c h a ff t!
. . . Und hat uns alle . . .
Aufgerufen,
Mit Ihm zu schaffen . . .
Und stummer Tiere dumpfer starker Wille—
Und unser Lobgesang—und a u c h dein Neid—
Du Dunkler dort [Samáel], begreif' es, schaffen—schaffen
An Seiner Welt, mit Ihm . . .
. . . in E w i g k e i t!   (*GW,* 71–72)

[. . . He *created* not—He *creates!*
. . . and has called upon us all . . .
To create with Him . . .
The dull, dark will of silent beasts—
And our song of praise—and *even* your envy—

You dark one [Samáel], grasp, are co-creators
With Him, of this world . . .
. . . in all *eternity!*]

Despite such lines as "Ein Wurm bin ich!" ["A worm am I!"] and the reaffirmation of God's sovereignty in the closing monologue, Jacob addresses God essentially as an equal, and God expresses His acceptance and approval of Jacob's stance with the words He speaks directly to him (rather than through the archangels). By God's own statement, their relationship is not that of master and servant; they are partners, equal in the sense that each is a voluntary party to the covenant and, more importantly, each is indispensable to the other, and knows it.

Most of the other themes that preoccupied Beer-Hofmann from the time he was a young man are also treated in *Jaákobs Traum*. The familiar motif of posterity as an answer to death is introduced during Jacob's conversation with Idnibaál. Having granted this slave his freedom, Jacob envisions Idnibaál's return to his homeland and the life he will have there, concluding:

> Glaub' mir, es steigt
> Für dich, Idnibaál, herauf ein Morgen—
> Da ruht zum erstenmal in deinen Händen
> Dein Kind—und, in den neuen Leib gerettet,
> Durchrollt ihn, jung und mutig nun—dein Blut!   (*GW,* 50)

> [Believe me, there dawns
> For you, Idnibaál, a morning
> When your child rests in your hands
> —And saved in this new body,
> Your blood courses through him, young and brave!]

The concept of continued life through one's seed, expanded to encompass an entire race, is also implicit in Jacob's reference to his blood, "in alle Zeiten spriessend, nie verdorrt" ["sprouting for all time, never withered"], and in the jubilant proclamation of the archangels:

> Was hoch jetzt ragt an Völkern, wird zerrieben
> Zu Staub! Wie Staub lässt es der Herr verwehn!
> Nur d u darfst dauern! Tausend Tode sterben—
> Und tausendmal aus Toden auferstehn!   (*GW,* 77)

> [Peoples which now prevail will be ground to dust!
> Like dust the Lord will let them be blown away!

Only *you* may last! Die a thousand deaths—
And a thousand time be resurrected!]

Sometimes dominating our attention and at other times receding temporarily into the background, the fate motif pervades the entire drama. Sealed by Jacob's covenant with God, Israel's destiny is to be God's witness, the *exculpator dei*. The blessing this represents is expressed by the archangels in speeches which either closely parallel or quote verbatim the prophecies of the Old Testament;[47] the contrasting speeches by Samáel (which provide other Old Testament prophecies with equal exactness) supply ample evidence that this destiny is also a curse.[48] Jacob, fully aware of this, voluntarily assumes both the pride and the burden of his destiny, asking only that his descendants not be allowed to forget the purpose of their election:

> Lass Deiner heiligen Wahl—Herr—n i e vergessen,
> Was fern und spät noch meinem Blut entstammt!—
> Doch w e n n sie es vergessen—müde sinken
> Am Weg—Lass sie in Kleinmut nicht vergehen,
> Herr—rufe, r u f e—und aus meinem Blute
> Wird immer wieder einer dann erstehen,
> . . . Und ihnen sagen—s a g e n—s a g e n . . .
> W o z u sie Gott—in alle Zeit—erwählt.   (*GW*, 83–84)

> [Lord—let my issue, even the most distant,
> *Never* forget Your sacred election!—
> But *if* they forget it—sink wearily
> Upon the way—let them not perish despondent,
> Lord—*call*—and one of my blood will always arise,
> . . . and tell—*tell*—*tell* them . . .
> *What* God chose them for—throughout all time.]

The theme of the unity of all life is reflected in Jacob's love of nature; throughout the drama he shows great sensitivity to the natural phenomena that surround him. As he remarks more than once, they speak to him: the vision, for example, is introduced by the talking spring and rocks of Beth-El.[49] This sense of oneness with all life again is not confined to the present or even to the span of one's own lifetime; it encompasses the remotest past and also the future. Jacob has a keen awareness of his ancestors, who are literally a part of him as a person; the same will be true of his descendants. A suggestion of this is found in the angel Gabriel's last words to Jacob:

Wenn du mit dir—mit Fremdem ringst—
(*Mahnend*) G e d e n k e:
Mit G o t t d e m H e r r e n rangest heute du!
In deinem Samen schau're immer wieder
Erinnern dieser Nacht—s o sein Befehl!   (*GW*, 82)

[When you wrestle with yourself—and with strange things—
(*admonishing*) *Remember:*
Today you wrestled with *God the Lord!*
May remembrance of this night ever shudder
In your seed!—*Thus* His command!]

It is worth emphasizing that the word used here is *Erinnern:* the fact
that the playwright does not mean a dim, subconscious awareness of
one's heritage, but a very live and active process, is underscored by
his use of the verb form instead of the substantive, *Erinnerung.*

The motif of the unity of all life is closely interwoven with the theme
of brotherly strife and reconciliation in the drama, notably in the scene
between Jacob and Esau. Their brotherhood, originally an accident of
birth, is renewed voluntarily during the reconciliation scene, as symbolized by their blood pact (which is not part of the Biblical myth).
Raising Esau's arm and linking it in his own, Jacob says:

So—schneid' ich in euch ein, heilige Zeichen!
Feindlicher Bruder, du, vom Mutterleib her—
Aus freier Wahl sei mir von neuem Bruder!
Ström'—ström' entzweites Blut zur Erde nieder
Und mische dich—und werde wieder eins!   (*GW*, 61)

[Thus into these arms I cut holy marks!
Brother hostile to me from the womb—
By free choice be my brother anew!
Stream, separated blood, to earth
And mingle—and be one again!]

Jacob, moreover, emphatically rejects the idea that their inherent differences make him superior to Esau, to whom he says:

Fühlst du
Den Duft, der dort von meinem Lager quillt?
Kein einzeln Kraut gibt ihn so süss und stark,
Von vielerlei der Duft muss sich vermählen!
Ein jedes Kraut haucht andern—Blatt und Blüte
Am selben Stamm den gleichen nicht—glaubst du,
Eins dünke vor dem andern sich gering?

... Gott braucht mich so—und a n d e r s dich! Nur weil
Du, Edom bist—darf ich, Jaákob sein!   (*GW,* 62)

> [Do you sense
> The fragrance that rises from my bed?
> No single herb emits it, sweet and strong.
> From the union of many the fragrance comes!
> Each herb breathes others ...
> ... Do you believe
> One considers itself inferior to another?
> ... God needs me thus—and you *differently!* Only because
> You are Esau—may I be Jacob!]

Esau's differentness is not equated with inferiority here; instead there is the contention that each person is as God needs and wants him to be, and the suggestion that the nature and character of each individual contributes in some way to a grand design, however ill-equipped we may be to understand it.

The discussion of characterization in *Jaákobs Traum* is best begun with a comparison of the play and the Jacob myth as related in the Pentateuch. Since the writer, in creating a work of literature, must do what he deems best with the material he has selected (no matter how well-known a myth that material may be),[50] such a comparison has no particular value for its own sake. It is, however, a necessary basis for any attempt to ascertain why Beer-Hofmann exercised the license he did. It has been said that in writing the *Historie* he "contented himself with filling in the gaps of narrative and with motivating the behavior of the men and women paticipating in the ... events. ... ."[51] Granted that some passages of *Jaákobs Traum* are exact quotations from the Old Testament, this contention nevertheless implies a faithfulness to the Biblical text that is not borne out by a comparison of the play and the Old Testament myth that served as the playwright's primary source. The spirit and the underlying message of *Jaákobs Traum* do not differ in any significant respect from those of the Biblical account, but in his treatment of this material Beer-Hofmann was far more of a creator than many critics have recognized.

Jaákobs Traum is actually a fusion of two separate episodes in the Biblical Jacob story. The experience at Beth-El (Jacob's vision during the flight to Haran of a ladder extending from earth to heaven, with angels upon it and God at the top) is recounted in Genesis 28:10–22; the experience of wrestling with God, told in Genesis 32:24–30, did not take place until twenty years later and not at Beth-El, but at a

place which Jacob named "Peniel" [Hebrew for "The face of God"],
"for I have seen God face to face, and my life is preserved."[52]

Beer-Hofmann likewise altered the time sequence of the reconciliation of Jacob and Esau. In *Jaákobs Traum* Esau overtakes his brother
at Beth-El, within hours of his theft of the blessing. According to the
Biblical account, Esau did not succeed in intercepting his fleeing
brother at all; Jacob safely made his escape, and the reconciliation did
not occur until twenty years later, when Jacob returned from Haran
(Gen. 33:1–15).

These changes are important to this discussion insofar as they shed
light on Beer-Hofmann's artistic intentions; they show that he combined these two Biblical episodes and altered the time sequence in
order to enhance his characterization of the play's protagonist.

Jacob certainly does not appear in a heroic light at the beginning of
the play. With sly and deliberate deceit, abetted by his doting mother,
he has taken advantage of a blind and helpless father, and stolen the
blessing which rightfully belonged to his brother.[53] He is a thief, and it
is inevitable that one's sympathies lie initially with the brother whom
he has wronged. Thus the playwright was confronted at the outset by
the problem of justifying Jacob and winning the audience's sympathy
for him. Beer-Hofmann solved this problem by several means. Before
Jacob makes his initial entrance in Part II, the groundwork for his
justification has already been laid by Rebekah, whose lines express the
conviction that she and Jacob bear no active burden of guilt because
things happen as they must:

> Jaákob s p r a c h—und aus den Tiefen hob's sich
> Und straffte Jizchaks Leib und warf ihn aufrecht,
> Und Segen brach aus ihm, und Jizchaks Antlitz
> War wie ein Schleier nur, dahinter Térachs,
> Náchors, A b r á h a m s Antlitz atmend glomm!
> Des rechten Erben Stimme rief die Ahnen—
> Die segneten—und die belog ich n i c h t!   (*GW*, 27–28)

> [Jacob *spoke*—and from the depths it rose
> And tautened Isaac's body, threw him upright,
> And blessing burst from him, and his face
> Was like a veil, behind which Terah's,
> Nachor's, *Abraham's* countenance, breathing, glowed!
> The true heir's voice called to the ancestors—
> They blessed—and them I did *not* deceive!]

Several of Beer-Hofmann's favorite themes are interwoven in this
passage: the mysterious and unfathomable workings of fate, the con-

cept of our ancestors living in us with an active will of their own, and the power of the word, independent of its user.

When Jacob first appears, what he has done to Esau recedes almost completely from the audience's mind, so appealingly does Beer-Hofmann present him. His sensitivity to nature; his feeling of oneness with all life, and especially with all who suffer; his compassion and gentleness toward the lamb (for the death of whose mother he feels responsible); his kindness to Idnibaál and his sensitive understanding of the slave's feelings—all these combine to make Jacob what he initially was not: an appealing protagonist with whom we can sympathize.

Beer-Hofmann did not choose to make Jacob more attractive by undermining Esau, although there would have been some Scriptural basis for doing so: even before the theft of the blessing, Esau had sold his birthright to Jacob for "bread and pottage of lentils."[54] The playwright had at least two reasons for omitting all mention of this episode: (1) in it Jacob himself does not appear in a favorable light—he takes advantage of the famished condition in which Esau returns from the hunt, refusing to give him food unless he may buy the birthright; and (2) focusing attention on unfavorable aspects of Esau's character would have undermined one of the main points that Beer-Hofmann wanted to make in the reconciliation scene—namely, that each individual is as God wants and needs him to be. The fact that Esau differs from Jacob in every conceivable way does not mean that he is inferior to him (see Jacob's previously quoted lines, *GW,* 62).

Despite the reader's growing sympathy for Jacob, the troublesome fact of his theft of the blessing remains; in order to strengthen the main part of the drama (the vision itself), Beer-Hofmann first had to solve this problem. The best way to resolve any nagging doubts about Jacob was clearly through Esau himself. If he, the injured party, were reconciled to his brother, how could the reader refuse to be? Hence, Beer-Hofmann decided to alter the chronological sequence of these events and place the reconciliation before the vision.

It is equally probable that problems of characterization led Beer-Hofmann to decide on a fusion of the two Biblical episodes. The Jacob he wanted to (and did) present is strong, unafraid of suffering, incorruptible, and intensely proud; these characteristics and Jacob's partner-like relationship with God have already been discussed. This, however, is not the image of Jacob one derives from the Biblical account of his vision at Beth-El. In the Genesis narrative, he appears as a totally passive figure; there is no indication that he says a single word. Only God speaks, making the famous promise, "And thy seed shall be as the dust of the earth . . . and in thee and in thy seed shall

all the families of the earth be blessed. And, behold, I am with thee, and will keep thee in all places whither thou goest, and will bring thee again into this land . . ." (Gen. 28:14–15). More specific evidence emerges in the verses that describe Jacob's reaction to the vision: "And Jacob awaked out of his sleep, and he said, Surely the Lord is in this place; and I knew it not. And he was afraid, and said, How dreadful is this place . . ." (Gen. 28:16–17). Beer-Hofmann's Jacob, moreover, is not merely indifferent to the archangels' attempts to bribe him with promises of material wealth and worldly power and security; rather, he bitterly resents their efforts to do so. This is not true of the Biblical Jacob, who clearly expects security and a measure of material well-being in return for his faithfulness. He says so with engaging candor in the vow he makes the morning after his vision: "If God will be with me, and will keep me in this way that I go, and will give me bread to eat, and raiment to put on, so that I come again to my father's house in peace; then shall the Lord be my God . . ." (Gen. 28:20–21). The hero of *Jaákobs Traum* also "negotiates" with God, but not on the material level.

The Biblical account of Jacob's wrestling with God, by contrast, provides precisely the image of Jacob that Beer-Hofmann wanted to project. Here we encounter the proud, courageous man who stubbornly continues to wrestle with his adversary even after his thigh is out of joint, the man who says, "I will not let thee go, except thou bless me" (Gen. 32:26). God's emissary confirms this image of Jacob with the words, "Thy name shall be called no more Jacob, but Israel [Hebrew for "a prince of God"]: for as a prince hast thou power with God and with men, and hast prevailed" (Gen. 32:28).

Beer-Hofmann—unwilling to relinquish the motif of the dream as the prophetic shaper of life, yet wanting to characterize Jacob as he appears at Peniel—solved the problem by combining the two episodes. Employing a system of creative selectivity, he discarded those elements of both episodes that did not suit his purposes and retained those that would enhance and strengthen the literary work he had conceived.

While *Jaákobs Traum* is a dramatic re-creation of an ancient myth whose motifs (centering as they do upon the God/man relationship) are religious in nature, the play is unquestionably also an allegory of the poet and his calling. Beer-Hofmann's ambivalent attitude toward the poet was discussed in chapter 1. Like Jacob, the poet is God's elect; the purpose of his election, like Israel's, is to be the *exculpator dei*. Like Jacob, the poet lives in a state of grace, but this is a mixed blessing at best, as Beer-Hofmann suggests in the fragment, "Ultra Posse" (written December 24, 1930): " 'Ultra posse nemo tenetur.'—To achieve beyond one's strength, one's ability, one's possibilities can be required of no one. Except the poet. Woe to him for that!—Happy is he for that!" (*GW,* 626). Infinitely more receptive, more sensitive than most people to every aspect and phenomenon of life, the poet experiences its joys to a correspondingly greater degree. His sensitivity, however, makes him equally conscious of life's suffering and ugliness. His unique blessing is offset by so great a measure of anguish, doubt, and spiritual suffering that the state of grace is as much curse as blessing. As the biographical material of chapter 1 indicated, Beer-Hofmann frequently found the burden of *Auserwähltsein* so heavy that he despaired of being able to carry it. Ample evidence of the dual nature of *Auserwähltsein* is also found in many of his prose fragments. In "Die Beschenkten" ["The Gifted"], written on July 13, 1933, he says: "God's elect receive a bitter, hopeless world and—to turn the knife in the wound—God grants them a deeper knowledge of the world's woe than others—and calmly, as though it were His due—God receives from them, these eternally unrewarded laborers of love, these eternally unpaid exculpators of God, a world in which woe appears only as an austerity of sweetness—suffering as a way, perhaps, to bliss—death as the breaking open of a gate to . . . life—a poet's world—in spite of all—full of hope, for which in this, His, world there is not much room. Not much!" (*GW,* 629).

In Beer-Hofmann's view, the poet's calling, like Jacob's, is a religious one. This is implicit in all the statements quoted above and expressed with unmistakable clarity in the fragment, "Vorspiel im Himmel" ["Prologue in Heaven"] written in the summer of 1941: "Every great and true work of literature has—like 'Faust'—its 'Prologue in Heaven'—written or unwritten, but unmistakably secured at the center of the work like a shining core. It will always be a matter of how man and God, igniting themselves on each other, stand each other's tests" (*GW,* 631). In this view of the poet and what he creates, the encounter with a work of literature is likewise a religious experience. Before this idea is discussed, however, Beer-Hofmann's concept of the word, mentioned briefly in the preceding chapters, needs to be examined more closely.

For Beer-Hofmann the word has an existence of its own, independent of the use to which it is put, and strange, indeed mysterious properties, including a unique power that can transcend the will and purpose of its user. Nowhere does this concept of the word find stronger artistic expression than in *Jaákobs Traum.* Isaac certainly did not intend to give Jacob the blessing that was the right of Esau, his firstborn, but the words poured from his mouth as though impelled by a force other than his own (see Rebekah's lines, *GW*, 27–28). The word, moreover, is irrevocable. The fact that Isaac *unwittingly* uttered it to the wrong person does not alter the word's force and validity in the slightest. Oholíbamah's argument that the blessing is invalid because Isaac meant it for Esau is refuted with scornful finality by Esau's other wife, Basmath:

> Er g i l t! Versuch's, Oholíbamah.
> Versag' dich Edom Nacht um Nacht, und wenn dann
> Lust, Sehnsucht, Trotz in ihm zu einer Flamme
> Aufschlägt, die n u r nach d i r . . . lechzt,
> Dann schieb ihm nachts—ihm, der's nicht merkt—statt deiner
> Die Sklavin unter, dass er sie beschläft.—
> Und sie empfängt, wird fruchtbar und gebiert
> Ein Kind, das Edoms Lust und Trotz und Sehnsucht,
> Die d i r galt, nun in i h r e m Blute trägt . . .
> Dann lach', Oholíbamah, sprich zum Kinde:
> "Du giltst nicht, Kind—denn m i r war's zugedacht!"   (*GW*, 20).

> [It is *valid*. Try it, Oholíbamah.
> Deny yourself to Esau night for night, and then
> When lust, longing, spite rise to a
> Flame that pants *only* for *you* . . .
> Then push under him, unnoticing, in your stead,
> The handmaiden, so that he lies with her.—
> And she conceives, is fruitful, and bears
> A child that carries in *her* blood
> The lust and longing and spite Esau meant for *you* . . .
> Then laugh, Oholíbamah, say to the child:
> "You're invalid, child—for it was meant for *me*!]

When Esau implores Rebekah, "Mach's ungeschehen, Mutter!" ["Mother, undo it!"], she replies: "Ich kann es nicht! K e i n Bronnen strömt zurück!" (*GW*, 25). ["I can't! *No* spring flows backward!"] The following exchange between Esau and Rebekah also alludes to the mysterious irrevocability of the word, once it has been uttered:

> EDOM: Ich sagt' euch's doch—ein Eid ist auf mir!
> REBEKAH: (*mit verhaltenem Atem*) Was—
> W a s schwurst du?
> EDOM: . . . Des Feld's verworfnes Unkraut meine Speise!
> Mein Trank die Pfütze und der Stein mein Bett!
> Kein Weib mir nah—und F l u c h mir, wenn ich's breche,
> Eh' ich . . .

REBEKAH: (*beschwörend*) Schweig! Schweig!
EDOM: . . . Jaákobs Blut . . .
REBEKAH: (*auf ihn losstürzend, als wollte sie mit ihren Händen ihm den Mund schliessen*)
Sprich's n i c h t aus!   (*GW*, 25–26)

[ESAU: I told you—I am under an oath!
REBEKAH: (*holding her breath*) What—
What did you swear?
ESAU: . . . The field's abandoned weeds my food!
My drink the slough, the stone my bed!
No woman near me—and a *curse*
Upon me if I break this oath
Before I . . .
REBEKAH: (*imploring*) Be silent! Be silent! . . .
(*throwing herself upon him, as if to close his mouth with her hands*)
Do *not* utter it!]

Beer-Hofmann elaborates on this view of the word in the undated prose fragment, "Der Freund der Worte" ["The Friend of Words"], ascribing to it not only an existence of its own, but even the ability to feel: "The word is always older and wiser than the person who uses it. It has experienced more. It also tells—trembling with inner life at every moment—what it has experienced—but so few have ears to hear it. So many who, as scientists, struggle diligently with the word . . . report on words like anatomists and viewers of the dead. The word— and the marvelous cellular states of the word that we call works of literature—lie like corpses on the dissecting table. And what is reported about them in the end can only be the findings of a post-mortem examination. Only the poet—friend and companion of the word—lives its life with it. For that reason words love the poet" (*GW*, 638–39).

Elsewhere, Beer-Hofmann's concept of the word and the poet's use of it shows a marked similarity to ideas that Rilke expresses in the *Duino Elegies*.[55] This is especially true of the fragment, "Form-Chaos" (written September 17, 1932), in which Beer-Hofmann says: "Because form is the act of naming, something daemonic still clings to it, as to *every* name. Each thing exists for us only when it is named. To be a poet means: to christen all things. To re-christen them, to remove from them the burden of names that have become mute. Only he who gives them new names that cause people to pick up their ears and concur with a sense of release, as though things had only now received their *true* names, is really a creator" (*GW*, 628).

For Beer-Hofmann the encounter with literature, like the process of creating it, is a religious experience. Implied by many of his aphorisms and other prose fragments, this view is stated unambiguously (and expressed in religious metaphors) in the fragment, "Von einer Dichtung reden" ["To Speak of a Work of Literature"], written on July 31, 1938: "The emotional upheaval of the religious experience is never triggered by 'insight,' but by a feeling of confrontation, of standing eye to eye, of being in closest proximity to something that is not merely bigger than we are, but that stands beyond all conception of 'big' and 'small'—removed from all earthly measurement. This terrifying and bliss-causing shock is the elusive moment of a communion in which the word really seeks to become flesh." The poet, as the instrument of this effect, fulfills the same function as that of the priest in religion. His task is "to erect weightless bridges from the small, anxious world of understanding to the infinite, bold world of presentiment." The closing lines of the fragment emphasize Beer-Hofmann's conviction that if the poet does any less than this, he betrays his high calling: "Only *this* can justify the poet's near-sinful activity, which otherwise would be worthless foolishness—or a repugnant game that takes delight in itself" (*GW*, 630–31).[56] This fragment was written in 1938, when Beer-Hofmann was seventy-two years old; that it also expresses the younger Beer-Hofmann's concept of the poet and the word is demonstrated by *Jaákobs Traum*, the allegory of the poet and his calling.

Der junge David

Beer-Hofmann's affirmation of the universal order, despite God's unfathomable and apparently contradictory ways, has been traced from *Der Tod Georgs* to *Jaákobs Traum*. In *Der junge David* the playwright, as before, presents the bitter suffering and doubt which precede such an affirmation and frequently assail it once it is made. As before, he deals with *Auserwähltsein* as both a state of grace and an agonizing burden, but he carries his treatment of these themes a step further than he had in the earlier works: by far the most important motif of *Der junge David* is *Treue* [faithfulness]. Once the resolution has been made to accept the universal order and to assume that God's ways are somehow ultimately just, then the logical consequence is this faithfulness. When Achitophel, the very embodiment of self-interest, asks David why he feels obliged to keep his oath to the Philistines, David says: "Weil Treu und Glauben sein muss" ["Because faithfulness and trust must be"]. Achitophel replies airily: "Treu—Glauben! Nehmts nicht schwer!—Auch nur zwei Worte!" ["Faithfulness—trust! Don't take it so hard! They're just two words!"], and David answers, "Ja—

zwei nur!—doch auf ihnen steht die W e l t" (GW, 238). ["Yes—just two!—but on them rests the *world*!"] In a later passage he remarks: "Dass Treue auf der Welt ist, / Lässt leichter leben uns—mag sein, auch leichter sterben!" (GW, 292). ["That faithfulness is in the world / Lets us live more easily—perhaps die more easily, too!"]

Beer-Hofmann's treatment of this motif is by no means limited to man's faithfulness to God. On the contrary, he presents almost endless variations on the theme. By the time the drama ends, he has dealt with virtually every kind of human faithfulness, as well as the faithfulness of God, who (no less than human beings) is bound by the universal laws He himself has established.

The motif is already introduced in the prologue, which relates the story of Ruth and her faithfulness to Naomi, her marriage to Boaz, and her genealogical relationship to David. In scene 1 the playwright focuses on the faithfulness of God. To Abjathar's question, "Kann Gott nicht alles?" ["Can't God do everything?"], Timnah answers, "Wohl! Doch dem Gesetz, / Das Gott sich selbst schuf, muss Gott Treue halten! / Hielt er nicht Treue—stürzte seine Welt!" (GW, 100). ["Indeed! But with the law / That God himself created, He must keep faith! / If he did not—His world would collapse!"] In scene 2, which is dominated by King Saul, the motif emerges in various forms, beginning with Saul's conviction that David is both hostile and disloyal to him. Saul is suspicious of the members of his own family, believing that Dóeg is more faithful to him than any of them:

> Da—Dóeg—seht ihn:
> Aus Edom, das mir feind—und hält zu mir!
> Ein Knecht! Verdingt! Um w a s? Um Speis und Trank,
> Um ein paar goldne Spangen, die ihn freuen!
> Ihr hasst ihn! Sterb ich—tötet ihr ihn noch
> Am selben Tag! Das weiss er—darf zurück—
> Ich gab ihn frei—in seine Heimat, und
> Er b l e i b t! Und was mein Sohn mir tut—er, Dóeg,
> Hätts n i e getan! Ein Knecht! Bezahlt! Und m e h r
> (*Auf Jehónathan weisend*)
> Als dort—mein eigen Blut—mir treu!   (GW, 153)

> [There—Dóeg—look at him:
> From Edom, a land hostile to me—and yet he holds to me!
> A servant! Hired out! For *what*? For food and drink,
> And a few golden bracelets that give him pleasure!
> You hate him! If I die—you'll kill him
> On the same day! He knows that—may return—

I freed him—to his homeland, and
He *stays*! And what my son does to me—he, Dóeg,
Would never have done! A servant! Paid! And
(*Pointing to Jonathan*)
More faithful to me than my own blood!]

The motif receives its most moving treatment in scene 2 through the fourteen-year-old Uriah—the same Uriah the Hittite who was to have reappeared in *König David*, the second drama of the cycle, as one of David's captains and the husband of Bathsheba. More dead than alive from the tortures he has endured, the boy remains unshakable in his loyalty to David, despite Saul's desperate efforts to win him over:

> Ich weiss, unwürdig, schamlos ist mein Betteln—
> Doch sieh: ich liebe deine Treue—bleib!
> Zum Wunderzeichen hab ichs mir gesetzt:
> Kann ich, von—jenem weg, zu mir herüber
> Dich reissen an mein Herz, Uriah—dann
> Ist noch nicht alles aus für mich—Uriah!   (*GW*, 159)

> [I know: unworthy, shameless is my begging—
> But you see: I love your loyalty—please stay!
> I've set myself this as a miraculous sign:
> If I can win you over from him,
> Uriah, draw you to my heart—then
> It's not all over for me—Uriah!]

Love for and loyalty to David are characteristics shared by all the figures in scene 3. Toward the end of this scene, the *Treue* motif also takes on political implications when David, whose period of service and oath of allegiance to the King of Gath are still in force, must choose between breaking his oath and going to war against his own people. This aspect of faithfulness is further developed in scene 4, culminating in David's decision to be true to his oath, although in all likelihood it will mean his death. Still another variation on the theme is developed at this point in the play: the faithfulness of husband and wife (David and Maácha). This type of *Treue* re-emerges in scene 5 when Achinoam, the wife of Saul, remains with his body after he has been killed by the Philistines and ultimately takes her own life. Similar faithfulness is shown by Jonathan, who accompanies his father into battle, and dying,

> ...warf er
> Mit letzter Kraft den Kopf noch in den Nacken
> Und schrie hinauf zur Felswand: "Vater! Hör mich!
> Wir alle liebten dich—wir alle—immer, Vater!"   (*GW*, 258)

> [...he threw
> Back his head with his last strength
> And cried out toward the rocky cliff: "Father! Hear me!
> We loved you—all of us—always, Father!"]

In all of these instances the willingness to self-sacrifice is presented as one of the primary elements of faithfulness.

The severest test of David's faithfulness comes in the seventh (final) scene of the drama, when he learns of Maácha's death. His acceptance of the crown in spite of his personal grief and pain underscores the self-sacrificing nature of faithfulness. This is confirmed by Ruth, who, addressing God, says:

> Er ist "erwählt"!—so wird er einmal klagen:
> "Wo blieb der S e g e n—welches G l ü c k ward mein?!"
> Lass dann ihn ahnen: Ü b e r allen Segen
> Thront n o c h ein Segen: a n d e r n Segen sein!   (*GW*, 304)

> [He is "elected"!—thus will he someday lament:
> "Where is the *blessing*? What *happiness* became mine?!"
> Let him then sense: *Above* all blessings
> Reigns *another* one: being a blessing to *others*!]

Respect for tradition and concern for its preservation is still another type of faithfulness Beer-Hofmann presents in *Der junge David*. In scene 1 this concern has prompted the elders of Jabesh to make their long journey, "... auf dass endlich / Der Dienst des Herren wieder so geschehe, / Wie unser Ahnherr Aharon ihn übte!" (*GW*, 107). [" ... so that at last / The service of the Lord may occur / As our ancestor Aaron practiced it!"] The passage reflects not only reverence for traditional rites of worship, but also reverence for and faithfulness to the ancestors who instituted them. The respect for tradition is demonstrated in scene 2 by Saul's servant, Ziba, who says to his reluctant helper, Akub:

> Mein Lieber: Unter diesem Baum hier sass man
> Seit Vätertagen zu Gericht, und seit er
> Die Krone trägt, hält hier einmal im Mond
> Schaúl Hof und Gericht! Weil du zu faul bist, wird man
> Den Brauch n i c h t ändern!   (*GW*, 126)

[My dear fellow: since the days of our fathers one has
Sat in judgment under this tree, and ever since
He has worn the crown has Saul held court here
Once a month! Just because of your laziness
The custom will *not* be changed!]

The most compelling example of this kind of faithfulness is in the seventh scene of the drama. Having learned of Maácha's death only minutes before the sacred rites are to begin, David cries: "Jubelt nicht!" ["Do not rejoice!"]. Zadok, the officiating priest, answers him: "Wir feiern heilgen Brauch!" (*GW,* 297). ["We celebrate a holy custom!"] The priest, not David, prevails in the ensuing contest of wills, and the celebration continues.

Interwoven with the theme of faithfulness are all the other motifs which the reader has come to associate with Beer-Hofmann's view of life and the world. The struggle to fathom the nature of God and the anguish of doubt are represented in scene 1 by the thirteen-year-old Abjathar, who tries desperately to understand why God tolerated the massacre of his entire family:

War Vater, Mutter, unser ganzes Haus
Geheim verrucht und tief getaucht in Sünde,
Die d u nur weisst—und du hast streng gerichtet?
(*Unerbittlich*) N e n n mir die Schuld! Du weisst sie—m u s s t sie wissen—
(*Mit irrsuchendem Blick*) Weisst du sie nicht—
. . . dann—lastet furchtbar
B l u t s c h u l d—mein Gott—auf deinem heilgen Haupt!   (*GW,* 103)

[Was father, mother, our whole house
Secretly vile and deeply dipped in sin,
That only *You* knew of?—and You passed stern judgment?
(*Inexorably*) *Name* me their guilt! You know it—*have* to know it—
(*With a wildly searching glance*) If You know it not—
. . .then—*murder*
Weighs terribly—my God—upon Your holy head!]

Timnah's response to these words is reminiscent of the archangels' reactions to similar lines by Jacob in *Jaákobs Traum:* "So d a r f s t du nicht zu deinem Gotte reden!" ["You *may* not speak thus to your God!"]. Abjathar, however, is not blaspheming. His answer to Timnah reflects the poet's view of the worthiness of doubt: "So m u s s ich,

Timnah—denn ich hab ihn lieb!" (*GW*, 103). ["So *must* I speak, Timnah—for I love Him!"]

Jaákobs Traum contained the suggestion that the way of doubt is
perhaps worthier than the way of unquestioning faith. Treatment of
this motif in *Der junge David* indicates that the playwright's attitude
had perhaps undergone some modification. There are no passages
which explicitly state this, but it is clear that the way of doubt is not
necessarily right for everyone; the doubt of Abjathar is balanced by
the unquestioning attitude of Timnah. When he asks her if God will
give him an answer, she says, her voice "filled with grief": "Frag
nicht! Da Gott mich schlug, had ich den Nacken / Ihm hingehalten und
hab n i c h t gefragt!" (*GW*, 103). ["Ask not! When God struck me, I
proffered / Him my neck and did *not* ask!"] The stage directions for
these lines suggest that the unquestioning attitude entails as much
spiritual suffering as does doubt. Timnah states with conviction that
God does answer, "Doch Gottes Tage s i n d nicht / Der Menschen
Tage! Gott misst ander Maß!" (*GW*, 104). ["But God's days *are* not /
The days of men! God measures differently!"] When Abjathar protests,
she adds,

> Ich weich nicht aus!
> (*In schmerzlichem Lächeln*) Ich such nur
> Demütig Unterschlupf in Sturm und Wettern,
> Darin—mein Kind—wir Menschen a l l e leben!"   (*GW*, 104)

> [I'm not evading!
> (*Smiling painfully*) I only seek
> Humbly a shelter in the storm
> In which—my child—*all* human beings live!]

In later scenes the suffering and doubt of David are balanced in the
same way by the calm and unquestioning faith of his great-grand-
mother, Ruth.

When David first appears in scene 3, his bitterly resigned words on
the nature of God are reminiscent of the statements of Charolais.
Asked by Abjathar what he had done to deserve being orphaned, poor,
and homeless, David answers bitterly:

> D a s willst du mich fragen?
> . . . Früh schon
> Fragst du die alte Frage, Kind! Merk auf—
> Ich sprech zu dir, als spräch ich mit mir selber:
> . . . Frag n i c h t!—Es k o m m t nicht Antwort! D i r nicht— K e i n e m!

Der droben spricht—doch nie, wenn wir ihn fragen!   (*GW,* 188)

[You want to ask me *that*?
. . . Very early, child,
You ask the ancient question! Give heed—
I speak to you as I would to myself:
. . . Ask *not!*—No answer *comes!* Not to *you*—nor *anyone!*
. . . That one up there does speak—but never when we ask!]

Jacob, one recalls, characterized God as both cruel and merciful; David also sees Him in both lights. He believes God's grace extricates him from the apparently hopeless dilemma that resulted from his oath to the King of Gath (*GW,* 248), but he is confronted repeatedly by evidence of God's cruelty or toleration of evil and suffering: the death of Maácha, the massacre of the House of Ahimelech, the torture and mutilation of the slave in scene 4.

For David the most crushing of these experiences is the loss of Maácha. His reaction is not an outright renunciation of God, but an attempt to withdraw from life and the world. At this point, when David refuses the crown, saying, " . . . steht auf—ich k a n n / Nicht euer König sein" ["stand up—I *cannot* / Be your king'"], the fate motif again comes to the fore. David is destined to be king, and he cannot evade his destiny. He wonders what shall become of him, and the immovable Ruth answers:

Was aus uns a l l e n einst wird: Dung der Erde!—
. . . Vielleicht ein Lied—
. . . auch d i e s e s bald verweht!
(*Ruhig, aber bestimmt*) Und doch: bis dahin—ewiger nicht, und nicht
Vergänglicher als SEINE Sterne—musst du,
Wie sie, vollenden—David!—deine Bahn!   (*GW,* 303)

[What once shall become of us all: dung of the earth—
. . . Perhaps a song—
. . . even *that* soon wafted away!
(*Calmly but firmly*) And yet: 'til then—no more eternal and no more
Transitory than HIS stars—must you,
Like them—David—complete your course!]

Der junge David provides ample evidence that the problem of death was still very much in the playwright's mind. Ruth's attitude toward death, as expressed in the lines just quoted, is one of calm and matter-of-fact acceptance. She has reconciled herself to the inevitable. The exchange between David and his brother Eliab, however, indicates that for Beer-Hofmann, this calm and resigned attitude was achieved at great cost and maintained only with the greatest effort:

> DAVID: Du wirfst dein L e b e n hin in meinen Brand—
> Ich—f r e v l e, dass ichs dulde! Leb doch auch
> Dein e i g n e s Leben—denk doch auch an dich!
> ELIAB: Es lohnt nicht—
> DAVID: (*seinen Blick suchend. Leise*) Was?
> ELIAB: Und tut nicht gut, an sich
> Zu denken—an dies Bündel Fleisch und Knochen—
> Kurz blühend, langsam welkend: bald verwest!
> DAVID: (*In leichtem Aufseufzen, Sichfügen . . .*)
> Des Menschen Los!—Man d a r f nicht daran denken!   (*GW*, 195)

> [DAVID: You throw your *life* into my fire—
> I—*sin*, to tolerate it! Live also
> Your *own* life—think also of yourself!
> ELIAB: It doesn't pay—
> DAVID: (*seeking his glance, softly*) What?
> ELIAB: And is not good, to think of
> Oneself—this bundle of flesh and bone—
> Briefly flowering, slowly wilting, soon decayed!
> DAVID: (*with a gentle sigh, resignedly*)
> The fate of man! One *dares* not think of it!]

Also touched upon in this passage is the theme of self-sacrifice and the life for others. It is reintroduced with great emphasis in scene 7; in addition to Ruth's already quoted lines, the motif is represented by the old man who implores David to accept the crown:

> Hier k n i e n hundert Jahre Bangen, Hoffen—
> Jagst du sie fort—weil heut dir Weh geschah?!—
> Horch, w i e viel Weh, hervorgebrochen aus
> Gilboas Schluchten, durch die Nacht heut stöhnt!
> Und du—willst geizig deinen Schmerz dir hüten?!
> Sei königlich!
> (*Innig. Flehend*) Dein Weh—verschenks, vergeud es,
> W i r f s in die F l u t von Leid, die uns umspült—
> S e i königlich!   (*GW*, 300–301)

> [Here *kneel* a hundred years of fear and hope—
> Will you chase them away—because you suffered hurt today?!—
> Hark, *how* much woe, erupting from
> The canyons of Gilboa, moans through this night!

And you—like a miser—will hoard your pain?!—
Be kingly!
(*Fervently pleading*) Your woe—make a gift of it, squander it,
Throw it in the *flood* of suffering that washes round us—
Be kingly!]

Here and elsewhere the life of self-sacrifice is closely linked to the motif of community. The playwright's most obvious treatment of this theme, of course, is the Jewish community, which he presents as a relationship of blood. Just as in *Jaákobs Traum* Jacob and Esau pledged brotherhood in a sense that transcended their actual blood relationship, community in a wider sense is treated in *Der junge David*. Significantly, this community reveals itself in suffering or in sensitivity to the suffering of others: at the sight of the mutilated slave in scene 4, David says to Sil-Bel; *"in a desperately pained and sobbing cry"*: "Ein M e n s c h— ein B r u d e r—Antlitz wars—und wie / Hat mans geschändet!"(*GW*, 249). ["A *human being*—a *brother's* countenance it was—and how / Have they defiled it!"]

The theme of *Auserwähltsein* receives expanded treatment in *Der junge David*. On one level, as before, the hero's election symbolizes the *Auserwähltsein* of the poet. How heavy a burden this is, is suggested as early as scene 1, when Timnah describes the prophet Samuel as a mouth through which God spoke, adding, in answer to Abjathar's question, that this does not make a person happy (*GW*, 96–97). Another passage which indicates that the playwright had the poet and his suffering in mind is that in which David says of the mute shepherd boy, Nebajoth:

Wie gut ers hat!

Er liebt sein Tagwerk, muss nicht Worte machen—
Das hält ihn rein—, und ist ihm wie ums Herz,
Spielt er ein wortlos Lied!   (*GW*, 181)

[How well off he is!

He loves his daily work, does not need to talk—
That keeps him pure—and if his heart dictates,
He plays a wordless song!]

Beer-Hofmann's own frequent despair and sense of inadequacy are reflected in David's words to Maácha:

Hätt ich doch Kraft, mein Wort e m p o r
Zu schleudern—dass es an des Himmels Wölbung

Aufschlüge, feuersprühend, und dort strahlte:
Leuchtendes neues nächtiges Gestirn—
Allen nach uns zu ewigem Gedenken.   (GW, 230)

> [Had I only the power to hurl my word
> *On high*—that it might break against the dome
> Of heaven, showering sparks, and shine there:
> A gleaming, new, nocturnal star—
> As an eternal remembrance for all who come after us.]

Many of David's followers have a naively false impression of *Auserwähltsein*, particularly with respect to the Jews as a chosen people. They think in terms of: " 'Die Grenzen weiten' und 'Tribut' erpressen— / 'Fuss auf den Nacken setzen'—'starker Herr sein'— / Am Prunk besaufen sich . . ."(*GW*, 198). [" 'Extending the borders' and exacting 'tribute'— / 'Placing a foot on the neck of others'—'being a mighty lord'— / Becoming drunk on splendor. . . ."] David rebukes them passionately, and in his exchange with Abischai he outlines the true naure of *Auserwähltsein* as Beer-Hofmann understood it:

DAVID: Ich will es anders! Und nicht viel erbitt ich:
Ein wenig Frieden—eine Spanne Zeit—
Die Saat zu werfen nur, dass ein Geschlecht
Aufgehe—n i c h t uns gleichend—besser, r e i n e r!
Eins, das nicht f r o h wird, wenn es Q u a l ringsum weiss—
Nicht a t m e n kann, wenn F r o n daneben keucht—
Das nicht nach Herrschaft giert—sich nicht verwirft
An G l a n z und M a c h t—
ABISCHAI: (*zornig dreinfahrend*)
W a r u m nicht Glanz und Macht?!
Der Herr hat doch mit eigner Hand die Kinder
Jisróels aus Mizrajim ausgeführt—
DAVID: Und hat mit e i g n e r Hand die Kinder Arams
Aus Kir geführt—aus Kaphtor die Pelischtim—
(*in unerbittlicher Abweisung, Abischai anherrschend*)
Wie—sie—n i c h t a n d e r s gelten wir vor Gott!
ABISCHAI: (*hartnäckig*) Wir sind e r w ä h l t!
DAVID: (*in Zorn und Hohn auflachend*)
B i s t dus?—Narr!
(*Drohend und warnend*) N u r, solang du
Zu tausend schweren Pflichten s e l b s t dich wählst—
Bereit, dich hinzugeben, wenn es ruft—
So—l a n g: "E r w ä h l t"—
(*Allen Anspruch erbarmungslos hinwegfegend*)
—und k e i n e n Atem länger!   (GW, 200)

[DAVID: I intend it otherwise! And I ask not much:
A little peace—a span of time—
To cast the seed, that a race might
Arise—*not* like us—better, *purer!*
One that is not *glad* to know of torment round about—
That cannot *breathe*, when men in bondage gasp—
That covets no dominion—and does not throw itself away
On *magnificence* and *power*—
ABISCHAI: (*interrupting angrily*)
Why not magnificence and power?
The Lord, after all, with His own hand
Led the children of Israel out of Egypt—
DAVID: And with *His own* hand led Syria's children
Out of Kir—the Philistines out of Caphtor—
(*in immovable refusal, addressing Abischai imperiously*)
Before God we have the same value as they—*no more!*
ABISCHAI: (*stubbornly*) We are the *elect!*
DAVID: (*laughing in anger and scorn*)
Are you?—Fool!
(*warningly, threateningly*)
Only as long as you elect
Yourself for a thousand heavy tasks—
Ready to sacrifice yourself at the call—
Only *that* long are you *"elect"*—
(*ruthlessly sweeping aside all demands*)
And *not a* moment longer!]

This voluntary assumption of the heavy burden of *Auserwähltsein* is symbolized in scene 7 by David's placement of the crown upon his own head. The passage also shows that while part of the playwright's purpose was to bring "the past to life and to enshrine the destiny of a people," the play is "innocent of chauvinism. It envisages the destiny of Israel not as dominion but as service. . . ."[57] David's representation of God to Abischai as more than the tribal deity of the Israelites also recalls Paul's ultimate image of God in *Der Tod Georgs*. Finally, *Auserwähltsein* emerges in this passage as a matter of self-sacrifice. David's later words indicate, moreover, that this applies to a people as much as to an individual: "Eliab! Ewiger Bruder—sag es ihnen: / Auch für ein Volk—'l o h n t s   n i c h t,' bloss sich zu leben!" (*GW*, 201). ["Eliab! Eternal brother — tell them: / Also for a people —'*it doesn't pay*' to live merely for oneself!"]

David does more than tell his followers what the purpose of their election is *not*; his impassioned speech is at once a statement of the purpose of Israel's election and a fusion of man's destiny with the destiny of the word:

E r f a s s t es doch: Zu Euch
Kam Wort, das über aller Tage Tun
Und über aller Nächte Traum—ein Drittes—
Ein wunderbares seliges Ahnen wölbt—
(*Silbe um Silbe stark und rasch vor sich hintürmend*)
U n—e i n—n e h m—b a r ist Wort!
(*Die geballte Faust vor sich hinwerfend*)
D a r a n will ich euch schmieden—
Lebt, e i n s mit ihm, und—soll auch dies einst enden—
Nun—(*in letzter stolzer Opferbereitschaft*)
—Sterbt mit ihm auch einstens seinen Tod! . . .
Wort strahlte e u c h—und will nun a l l e n leuchten—
Wort—ausgesandt zu froher Botschaft allem Elend—
Wort—neuen Himmel schaffend, neue Erde—,
Licht fernsten Inseln, fernster Zeit gewährt—
Flammt, lodert m i t i h m—und v e r g e s s t zu fragen,
Ob ihr im Brand nicht auch euch selbst verzehrt!
Nicht kalt, nicht sicher seid, nicht weltzufrieden—
Bangt, ringt, lasst immer neu h i n e i n euch reissen,
In Gottes Braus—sein heilges Sturmeswehen . . .   (*GW,* 201)

[But *grasp* this: to you
Came the word, that stretches
Above all days' activity
And above all nightly dreams a third thing:
A marvelous blissful presentiment—
(*Firmly and rapidly building up syllable for syllable*)
In - vul - ne - rable is the word!
(*Throwing out his clenched fist*)
To that I want to weld you—
Live, *one* with it, and—should this too end one day—
Well—(*in final, proud self-surrender*)
—Then also *die* with it its death! . . .
The word glowed for *you*—and now wants to shine for *all*—
The word—sent out as joyous message to all in misery—
The word—creating new heaven and new earth—
Light granted to the most distant times and places—
Flame, blaze *with it*—and forget to ask
If in its fire you too shall be consumed!
Be not cold and sure, not content with the world—
Be fearful, wrestle, let yourselves be drawn ever anew
Into God's tumult—the pain of His holy storm. . . .][58]

This is an impassioned plea for involvement in life; it is also a representation of the identity, the life and death of the human race, as unalterably linked to the life and death of the word.

The irrevocable nature of the word is also treated in scene 4. Maácha, sensing that David is going to his death, says:

> W e n n unabwendbar über uns jetzt einer
> Die eisigen schweren schwarzen Flügel schlägt—
> W e n n jetzt ein Opfer sein muss—
> (*Den Kranz sich vom Kopf reissend und zur Seite schleudernd,*
> *den Kopf in den Nacken geworfen, sich darbietend*)
> H i e r— sei i c h es—Nicht er!   (*GW*, 231)

> [If unavoidably above us
> The icy, heavy black wings beat—
> *If* now a sacrifice must be—
> (*tearing the wreath from her head and hurling it aside, throwing*
> *back her head, offering herself*)
> *Here!* May it be I—Not he!]

David cries, "N e i n! Nimms zurück!" ["*No!* Take it back!"], but just as Isaac could not retract his blessing from Jacob, Maácha cannot withdraw her offer of literal self-sacrifice, and the irrevocability of the word is subsequently confirmed by her death.

The playwright's ambivalent attitude toward the word is given forceful expression in scenes 3 and 4. In the earlier scene, David says to Serujah, who has told him that his description of Maácha is beautiful:

> "Schön?"—"Schamlos!"—übel schmeckts nun auf der Zunge!
> Nein—nein! Man s o l l aus seiner Heimlichkeit
> Nichts reissen—und verkaufen und verraten
> An Worte: "schöne!"
> (*Auf Nebajoths Weise horchend. Aufseufzend*) H a t ers gut—Nebajoth!
> Stumm sein—und quillt das Herz schon einmal über—
> Mags dann verströmen als ein w o r t l o s Lied!   (*GW*, 193)

> ["Beautiful?"—"shameless!"—it leaves a bad taste in my mouth!
> No! No! One *should* not tear anything from its
> Secrecy—and sell and betray it
> To words: "beautiful" ones!
> (*Listening to Nebajoth's song, sighing*) *How* well off he is!—Nebajoth!
> To be mute—and if his heart overflows—
> It can stream forth as a *wordless* song!]

In scene 4 Maácha protests, *"interrupting forcefully"*: "Geheimes ruft man / Mit Namen nicht! Nicht Gott—nicht seine Liebe! / Schweig—sprichs nicht aus—man solls nicht hören!" ["Secret things one does not call / By name! Not even God!—not His love! / Be silent—utter it not—one should not hear it!"]. This time David takes the opposite position, saying "D o c h! Man s o l l s!"(*GW*, 230). [" *Yes!* One *should!*"]

The idea of one's ancestors within one—not as an amorphous composite of inherited factors, but as living entities whose wills can mysteriously assert themselves over that of the descendants they inhabit—was introduced in *Jaákobs Traum* and reappears in *Der junge David.*[59] Throughout the play the characters' (and most notably Ruth's) reverential attitudes toward all of their ancestors suggests this view of the living, active nature of one's ancestral heritage. The theme is dealt with more explicitly in the final scene of the drama. When David dismisses the old man who is imploring him to take the crown, he replies: "Ich d a r f nicht gehen!—Steh i c h denn hier?! / Hier stehen hundert Jahre deines Volkes . . . "(*GW*, 300). ["I *dare* not go!—Stand *I* then here?! / Here stand a hundred years of your people. . . ."] Herein lies the old man's identity; he *is* his people and all that comprises his past and theirs.

This concept of one's ancestors leads naturally to the discussion of characterization in *Der junge David* and the entire question of identity. The problem is particularly interesting in David's case because he is a myth in his own lifetime. Thus he has two identities: David as a private person—the image he has of himself—and David the mythical hero of his people. The image of the mythical David is introduced in scene 3 before David himself appears. "Wie sieht er aus?" ["What does he look like?"] Elischeba asks.

> Man sagt: Oft war ein kindlich Staunen noch
> In seinem Blick—
> . . . Sein Haar—
> Wie Gold, drin Kupfer schmolz, und immer leicht
> Bewegt, als streichle flüchtig es ein Wind. . . .   (*GW*, 177)

> [They say: there is often still a childlike wonder
> In his glance—
> . . . his hair—
> Like gold, with molten copper in it, and always in
> Gentle motion, as though caressed by a breeze. . . .]

Later in this scene David shows deep resentment of his mythical image:

Serujah! Manchmal trag ichs nicht! Sie machen
Sich was zurecht—und nennens "David"!
(*Zornig den Platz durchmessend*) Malen
Die Wangen ihm, bestreuen mit Gold das Haar,
Besalben ihn mit dem, was ihnen duftet,
Behangen ihn mit Lappen, Putz und Flitter—
(*Ausbrechend*)
Ich b r a u c h das nicht! Ich w e i s s schon, wer ich bin!
(*Durch die Bescheidenheit der Worte bricht
stärkstes Bewusstsein seiner Kraft und Sendung*)
J e m a n d—der viel zu tun hat, bin ich! J e m a n d—
(*Mit kurzem Blick nach oben*) Dem aufgeladen ward!
der selbst sich auflädt und—
Den euer lächerlicher Prunk nur widert!   (*GW,* 184)

[Serujah! Sometimes I cannot bear it! They put
Something together—and call it "David!"
(*Pacing angrily*) Paint
His cheeks, sprinkle his hair with gold,
Annoint him with their fragrances,
Bedeck him with cloths, ornaments, and finery—
(*explosively*)
I do not *need* that! I *know* who I am
(*A strong consciousness of his strength and mission breaks
through the modesty of his words*)
Someone—who has much to do, am I! *Someone*—
(*With a quick upward glance*) given a burden!
Who places burdens on himself and —
Who is only repelled by your ridiculous pomp!]

David sees his true identity as a person in his love for Maácha and
his union with her. He tells her in scene 4:

L i e b e—stark wie d i e—
W u c h s noch nicht—nie! Dies ist mein Ich—mein wahres!
In dich hinein—Maácha—warf ichs—h ü t es—
Bewahrs—und lächle wenn die andern meinen—
Ich wär nicht mehr!   (*GW,* 230)

[*Love*—as strong as *this*—
Never *grew* before—never! This is my self—my true self!
I hurled it into you, Maácha—*protect* it—
Preserve it—and smile when the others think—
I am no longer here!]

David is referring here not only to his seed. He himself lives in Maácha through their union:

> Hör, wie dein Herz schlägt, und—noch e h du fragst—
> Kommt Antwort von mir—n i e bist du a l l e i n!
> T r ä g s t mich in dir, bist—wie mit mir gesegnet!
> Trank—Duft, der dich erquickt, ein Frohsein—Anteil
> Ist mir an alldem—fühls wie du! Und d a r u m
> Darfst du nie traurig sein . . .   (*GW,* 231)

> ["Hark, how your heart beats, and—even *before* you ask—
> Answer comes from me—*never* are you *alone*!
> You *carry* me in you, you are blessed with me!
> Drink, fragrance that refresh you, your times of joy—I have
> A part in all of it—feel it with you! And *therefore*
> You must never be sad . . .]

Whether he likes it or not, David's mythical identity is equally valid. Moreover, it derives from essentially the same source: just as his personal identity lies in his submersion of self in the union with Maácha, so is his submersion of self in the people the source of his mythical identity. The old man of scene 7 says to him: "Du b i s t nicht d e i n!— ein Volk hat dich erträumt! / Erschaffen aus der Sehnsucht von Geschlechtern, / Steigst du aus ihrem T r a u m—gehst ein in ihre S a g e !"(*GW,* 301). ["You *are* not your *own*!—a *people* has dreamed you! / Created from the yearning of generations, / You arise from their *dream*—enter into their *saga*!"] Like the old man, David *is* the people, their past, their aspirations and their longings. His resentment of his mythical image in scene 3 shows that initially he does not understand this himself, but his assumption of the crown in scene 7 symbolizes both his acceptance of the life for others and his acknowledgment of the mythical identity as valid.

Without meeting a single time in the course of the drama, David and Saul are a superb study in the contrasts of youth and age, vigor and decline, the self-assurance of young manhood and the fears and self-doubt of old age. Saul was also one of the annointed, but he has betrayed his election and is no longer worthy of it. On the surface there appears to be a contradiction between the concept of the irrevocable word and the assertion in scene 1 (*GW,* 119) that Saul's head is no longer consecrated. (The symbolic ritual of annointment is not unlike that of the blessing; once done, can anything undo it?) One must keep in mind, however, that the assertion comes from Jerigoth, a man consumed by hate, who is later sharply rebuked by the prophet Gad with the words, "Nie noch / Sprach Gott durch eines Hassers Mund!" (*GW*, 287). ["Never yet / Did God speak through the mouth of a hater!"] The behavior of the people after Saul's death substantiates that the annointment, like the blessing, cannot be retracted. Despite the widespread fear and hatred of Saul in the last years of his life, the people, at no little danger to themselves, bring home his mutilated body and honor him in death; there is no hypocrisy in what they do—for better or worse, he was God's annointed and their king. This attitude is reflected in the words of the woman who explains to her child why a circle of fire surrounds the crown:

> Und das Feuer rings ist,
> Dass keiner nah ihr kommt! Der Sklave aus Amálek,
> Der sie vom Haupt des toten Königs stahl,
> S t a r b, weil er sie berührt! Das darf nur, wer
> Gesalbt ward, sie zu tragen!   (*GW*, 279)

> [And the fire is around it
> So that no one comes close to the crown! The slave from Amalech,
> Who stole it from the dead king's head,
> *Died* because he touched it! Only he may do that
> Who has been annointed to wear it!]

Beer-Hofmann makes no attempt to conceal the unfavorable aspects of Saul's character—his ruthlessness, his cruelty, his neurotic suspicions—but he does not make him out a villain. Indeed, he evokes in the reader neither contempt nor even dislike, but rather a compassion tinged with sadness. To sympathize with Saul is not difficult, for the reality he represents is a universal one. The problems that beset him are those of a man who knows he is declining and who suffers acutely from that knowledge. With his profound sensitivity to the suffering of others, David is aware of this as his followers are not. In lines which reveal his own compassionate nature (and which recall the perceptive treatment of the problem of old age in *Der Tod Georgs*), David comes to Saul's defense:

> Was w i l l s t du denn?—Er herrscht—
> Er trägt ein Leben lang Jisróels Krone—
> Und da auf ihn des Abends eisige Schatten
> Sich senken—wirft das Schicksal mich—den jungen—
> Quer über seinen Weg! Und m e i n wird alles:
> Das Herz des Sohns, der Tochter—, und die Menge

Vergisst, was e r getan, und jauchzt nur m i r zu—
Hart—h a r t geschieht dem alten Mann—er meint,
Er stirbt an m i r—soll er mich da noch l i e b e n?!   (*GW*, 190)

[What do you *want?*—he rules—
He wears throughout his life the crown of Israel—
And when the icy shadows of evening sink
Upon him—fate tosses me—the young man—
Directly in his path! And all becomes mine:
The heart of his son, his daughter—and the multitude
Forgets what *he* has done, cries jubilantly for *me*—
What is happening to this old man is hard, *hard*—he thinks
He is dying of *me*—and shall he then still *love* me?!]

Der junge David has a huge cast of characters, but there are only two major female figures—Ruth and Maácha—and Paula Beer-Hofmann was undoubtedly the model for both of them. Paula's most obvious similarity to Ruth is the espousal of a people, a religion, and a cultural heritage not originally her own; Ruth's declaration, "Thy people shall be my people, and thy God my God," must have had very special significance for Beer-Hofmann. Like Paula, Ruth represents a kind of faithfulness that transcends the ancestral ties of blood; she is of this people not by accident of birth, but by volition. Beyond this, Beer-Hofmann's characterization of Ruth as a woman of beauty, quiet poise and serenity, and a certain indomitable quality corresponds in many respects to his descriptions of his wife in *Paula, ein Fragment*. The stubbornness Ruth shows in refusing to leave Naomi, for example, has its parallel in the unexpected strength and independence with which Paula met her brothers' opposition to her marriage to Beer-Hofmann: "Sie haben 'die Kleine', die mit ihnen zusammen lebt, gern, warnen sie, wollen sie vor mir schützen, sie 'retten', und fassen es nicht, woher ihr mit einem Mal die Kraft kommt, Widerstand zu leisten, alles Eingreifen jäh abzuwehren, jedes Rechenschaftgeben stolz zu verweigern—entschlossen, frei, unbekümmert den Weg zu gehen, den zu gehen es sie heisst" (*GW*, 788). ["They love the 'little one,' who lives with them, warn her, want to protect her against me, 'rescue' her, and they cannot understand where she suddenly acquired the strength to resist, to ward off all interference, to refuse, proudly, to justify herself—determined, free, unconcerned she goes the way fate bids her go."][60] Beer-Hofmann's characterization of Ruth is strikingly similar to the physical appearance and bearing of his wife, as seen in the following description of Paula:

Ein h e i l i g e s Antlitz—aber nichts in ihm von demütig gehorsamer, zum Himmel flehend aufblickender . . . Heiligkeit—eher, als wären ihre Züge noch eine letzte zarte Schleier-Hülle über ihrem wahren, nur zu ahnenden Antlitz, das schweigend verschlossen, geheimnishütend, von Menschenblicken nie betastbar, darunter ruht: Gottes geliebtes heiliges Werk, aus S e i n e m Wunsch e i n m a l geworden, immer, still atmend, I h m nah. . . . (*GW*, 857–58)

[A *holy* countenance—but nothing in it of the humbly obedient, devoutly pious holiness that looks heavenward . . . it is rather as if her features were a delicate veil over her true . . . countenance, which lies beneath, silent, reserved, guarding secrets, never touchable by human glances: God's beloved, holy work, created from *His* wish . . . breathing quietly, close to *Him*. . . .]

Scene 4, which presents the meeting of David and Maácha, is likewise the playwright's objectified, fictionalized representation of his relationship with Paula. Many statements in *Paula, ein Fragment* reflect Beer-Hofmann's belief that a love like theirs was something very few people experience. David expresses the same belief: "Maácha—hör: Wies zwischen uns ist—so— / E i n - m a l i n t a u s e n d Jahren darf vielleicht / Dies Wunder blühn!" (*GW*, 229). ["Maácha —listen to me: what is between us— / *Once*, perhaps, in *a thousand* years may / Such a miracle flower!"] The peace and security Beer-Hofmann felt in this union are also expressed in *Paula:* ". . . und ich fühle, was für uns auch kommen mag, wenn wir auch in die Fremde müssen—solange meine Hand in ihrer ruhen darf, bin ich geborgen—nichts kann mir geschehen" (*GW*, 855). [". . . and I feel that whatever may come for us, even if we have to go into exile—as long as my hand may rest in hers I am safe—nothing can happen to me."] In *Der junge David*, David voices the same feelings to Maácha: "Ich b a r g mich nur in dich—" ["I *sheltered* myself in you—"] (*GW*, 230). Earlier in the scene he had told her: "Du nimmst nur meine Hand—und schon / Ist rings gebannt ein Kreis—Vergängliches / Der Welt weicht weit . . ." (*GW*, 229). ["You have only to take my hand—and immediately / A circle is proscribed about us—the transitory / Things of the world recede. . . ."] The lines that follow reflect not only David's and Maácha's sense of oneness with each other, but also their feeling of unity with all life and the phenomena of nature: ". . . wir schreiten Hand in Hand— / Geschwister—und doch ahnenlos—wir beide— / Am ersten Schöpfungstag" (*GW*, 229). ["We walk hand in hand— / Siblings. . . we two— / On the first day of creation."] This passage also has its parallel in *Paula:* "Und wir beide sind Kinder geblieben, die Welt bestaunend, immer neu sie entdeckend. Alles ist uns Genosse und Gespiele—nie reisst die Gemein-schaft, die uns mit Tieren, Pflanzen, Gestein, dem Rauschen der Ströme und dem lautlosen Zug der Wolken verbindet . . ." (*GW*, 855–56). ["And we two have remained children, looking at the world with astonishment, discovering it ever anew. Everything is a companion and playmate to us—the communion is never broken that binds us to animals, plants, rocks, the murmur of streams and the silent march of clouds. . . ."]

Beer-Hofmann's first glimpse of Paula and the welter of emotions he felt (as described in *Paula, ein Fragment*) have already been discussed, and the passages in question need not be quoted again. David's descrip-tion to Serujah of his first glimpse of Maácha is undoubtedly a poetic representation of Beer-Hofmann's own experience:

> . . . zusammen zog sich
> Mein Herz, stieg schluchzend in mir auf—im Atem
> Entwichs aus mir—schwang schwerlos sich zu ihr—
> Und liess zurück mich, leer—in Schwäche—Schwärze—
> Vergehn—"nun sterb ich"—dacht ich—und die Lider
> Z w a n g ich noch einmal auf—und da—
> Da k a m ihr Blick zu mir—er kam—und m i t ihm
> K a m mir zurück mein Herz—schwoll—schlug und schlug—
> Lebendges Leben—jubelnd—E i n s nur—E i n e s:
> "Dies dorten und dies hier—m u s s zueinander!"
> H i e r—muss ichs halten, bergen, hüten dürfen
> Vor Leid—und kann mein Leben tragen n u r—
> Wenn d i e s e Augen segnend auf mir ruhn!   (*GW*, 191)

> [. . . my heart contracted,
> Rose sobbing in me—and in that breath
> Escaped from me—swung weightlessly to her—
> And left me behind, empty—in black weakness—
> "I am dying," I thought—and forced my
> Eyes open one last time—and then—
> Her glance *came* to me—it came—and with it
> My heart returned—swelled—beating hard—
> Jubilant life—*one* thought—only *one*:
> "These two—*must* join each other!"
> *Here*—must I be allowed to hold and shelter her
> From pain—and can endure my own life *only*—
> If *those* eyes rest with blessing upon me!]

David's description of Maácha's physical appearance is also reminis-cent of Paula: "Fast noch ein Kind . . . ich schied / Die Züge kaum—

den Blick nur—, über mich / Hinaus—ging ruhig er in grosse Ferne!"
["Almost still a child . . . I scarcely / Distinguished the features—only
her glance—which / Calmly travelled beyond me—into great dis-
tances!"]. In *Paula, ein Fragment* the poet describes his wife's unusual
gaze in almost identical terms: "Ihr Blick kommt von weither, er steigt
aus einer Tiefe auf, die nichts von sich verrät, er trifft, und gleitet
durch mich weiter, zu etwas, hinter mir, über mir, das nur sie allein
sieht, von dem nur *sie* weiss, und das vielleicht mein Schicksal heisst"
(*GW,* 856). ["Her glance comes from afar, arises from a depth that
betrays nothing of itself, it rests on me, passes through me to something behind me, above me—which only she can see, of which only *she*
knows, and which is perhaps my fate."]

It is interesting to note that Beer-Hofmann chose to develop his
characterization of David without using any of the more famous Biblical legends about his youth—e.g., the humble shepherd boy with his
harp, the slaying of Goliath with a slingshot. These events have already
taken place when the drama begins, and there is virtually no reference
to them. These episodes in the story of David are so well known that
Beer-Hofmann undoubtedly felt justified in assuming the reader's
familiarity with them, but his selection and organization of the Old
Testament material was also dictated by artistic purpose. He clearly
had no intention of functioning merely as the editor of an already
famous myth, but rather selected those elements of the story that
would enable him to dramatize creatively the themes that comprised
his view of life and the world. Liptzin was quite right to note that Beer-
Hofmann "is most eloquent when his model does not overawe him
with too many details."[61]

In the David-Maácha relationship, for example, Beer-Hofmann
wanted to give an artistic re-creation of his own experience of love, but
this would have been impossible on the basis of the Biblical narrative
alone. The Old Testament gives only the most meager information
about Maácha: the daughter of Talmai, King of Geshur, she was one
of at least five wives David had while he was in Hebron and she was
the mother of Absalom (II Sam. 3:3). In *Der junge David* Maácha
becomes the great love of David's life. The love scene between the two
and the account in scene 7 of Maácha's death and royal entombment
in Geshur are, in fact, the poet's creation; none of this is mentioned in
the Biblical narrative.

Der junge David also suggests that Maácha bore David's first son and
male heir:

> "Gehst d u zum König—melde: Gott befand

Michal u n w e r t von D a v i d zu empfangen!
Maácha, einziges Kind des Thalamái,
Des Königs von Geschúr, gebar dem David
Nach einer Tochter—nun auch noch den E r b e n!
A b s c h á l o m heisst er. . . .   (*GW,* 113–14)

[Go *you* to the king—and announce: God found
Michal *unworthy* to conceive from *David!*
Maácha, only child of Talmai,
King of Geshur, has born David
After a daughter—now also an *heir!*
His name is *Absalom*. . . .]

This also represents a deviation from the Biblical account: "And unto David were sons born in Hebron: and his first-born was Amnon, of Ahinoam the Jezreelitess; And his second, Chileab [Daniel], of Abigail the wife [widow] of Nabal the Carmelite; and the third, Absalom the son of Maacah . . ." (II Sam. 3:2–3). The artistic reason for this deviation was probably Beer-Hofmann's plan for the second drama in the cycle, *König David,* in which Absalom was to win the hearts of the people from David, as David earlier had won them from Saul. Making Absalom David's heir and favorite son by his beloved wife would certainly have deepened the irony of this situation.

There is also nothing in the Biblical account to suggest that Saul's wife, Ahinoam, accompanied him into battle against the Philistines, stayed with him as he died, and then took her own life (see I Sam. 31:1–6). This addition to the story, however, enabled Beer-Hofmann to present still another variation on the theme of faithfulness, the drama's major motif.

As he did in *Jaákobs Traum,* Beer-Hofmann found it necessary to take certain liberties with respect to time. In *Der junge David* these changes are largely a matter of condensation, dictated by the very nature of the dramatic genre: it would have been impossible to maintain the necessary dramatic tension while conforming to the time sequence of the lengthy narrative in the first and second books of Samuel. *Which* episodes and time periods to omit, however, was surely dictated less by the need to preserve dramatic tension than by problems of characterization and the treatment of themes that were important to Beer-Hofmann. In the drama, David's coronation at Hebron (scene 7) follows closely upon Saul's death and thus suggests that David immediately succeeded Saul as king. According to the Biblical narrative, this was not the case: Saul's only surviving son, Ish-Bosheth, became King of Israel, and only the tribe of Judah acknowledged David as its ruler (II Sam. 2:4, 8–11). Seven and one-half years elapsed before David was crowned king of all Israel (II Sam. 5:1–5), and during that period he continually warred against the house of Saul (II Sam., chapters 3 and 4). The Old Testament narrative gives every indication of a power struggle—including the defection of Abner, Ish-Bosheth's captain, and his subsequent secret negotiations with the elders of Israel to persuade them to make David their king. David emerges from this account not as a man who reluctantly allows himself to be drafted by the people, but as a man of strong ambition who *wants* the crown. None of this conformed to the image of David that Beer-Hofmann wanted to develop: that of a man who sees his election as a state of profound suffering and a burden almost too heavy to be borne, a man who has to be persuaded to ascend the throne. Thus the events of this period were omitted entirely. This part of the Biblical account was perhaps also omitted because it deals with a period of strife and division in Israel: to include this would have undermined the theme of a unified people and, by extension, the unity of all life.

Der junge David undeniably has only limited appeal to a twentieth-century audience, but not, as some critics have claimed, because the themes and ideas developed in it are no longer topical.[62] Beer-Hofmann was never in the vanguard of any specific movement for political or social change, but he was not indifferent to the events of his time. His many statements on the nature and purpose of art, his repeated renunciation of art as an esoteric, self-serving phenomenon, and his view of the poet as one called by God all clearly refute any suggestion that the *David* cycle represents an idle escape into the past. Beer-Hofmann's preoccupation with the history of Israel certainly stemmed from personal pride and interest in his Jewish heritage, but as an artist he undoubtedly also believed that a dramatization of Jewish history, as he understood and interpreted it, had much to tell modern man about himself and his life in the world.

Der junge David, as a dramatic work of literature, does suffer from what Sheirich has called the playwright's "interest in the minutia of the Biblical world that goes far beyond the specific needs of the dramatist." However fascinating these details of dress, social customs, religious rites, etc., may be as subjects for historical or anthropological study (or in an epic prose work like Thomas Mann's Joseph novels), they do not enhance the *dramatic* re-creation of history if they are allowed to be obtrusive. This is sometimes the case in *Der junge David:* lengthy stage directions regarding regal dress and priestly raiment, allusions to obscure customs, to the legendary characteristics of the various tribes, and other such details too often slow the central action and distract one's attention from it.

In addition, the playwright assumes a far more intimate knowledge of the Old Testament than most present-day readers actually possess. Without such knowledge, however, the reader is not likely to grasp the full significance of some of the play's lines. The emphasis, for example, with which Timnah says at the close of scene 1 that her home is at Endor alerts the reader to the fact that this information has some special import; one needs more than a passing acquaintance with the Old Testament, however, to realize that she is the seeress of Endor to whom Saul later went secretly by night.[63] The full significance of Saul's praise of Dóeg in scene 2 can likewise only be appreciated by someone who recalls that he was the servant who carried out the massacre of the House of Ahimelech when Saul's other servants refused (I Sam. 22:17–19). This problem is largely solved for the reader by the Biblical references Beer-Hofmann appended to the drama; to solve the problem for a theatre audience, the appendix would have to be converted into extensive program notes.

The artistic organization and structure of *Der junge David* remain to be discussed. One of the immediate difficulties is that the traditional nomenclature of literary genre is inadequate. The work is usually referred to as drama, and it may properly be regarded as such, but in a sense that requires some qualification. Beer-Hofmann disregarded the conventional division of dramatic material into acts, creating instead seven scenes which he called "Bilder" ["Pictures"]: "Strasse bei Rahels Grab" ["Road Near Rachel's Grave"]; "Königszelt in Gibea" ["Royal Tent in Gibea"]; "Alter Burgplatz in Bethlehem" ["Old Fortress Court- yard in Bethlehem"]; "Höhle und Lager am Jordan" ["Cave and Camp on the Jordan"]; "Schlucht in Gilboas Bergen" ["Ravine in Gilboa's Mountains"]; "Lager am Bach Besor" ["Camp By Besor Creek"]; and "Auf den Wällen von Hebron" ["On the Ramparts of Hebron"]. The word "pictures" is of the utmost importance, because it underscores what Beer-Hofmann was attempting in *Der junge David:* to fuse the customary elements of drama, particularly action, with those of the pageant and the tableau. This means that although there is a central thread of action running throughout the entire work, it is accompanied in every scene by a vivid picture that provides considerably more than mere background. None of these scenes is a "still life," but rather a "moving picture" full of kaleidoscopic color and motion. In scene 3, for example, the central action develops amidst a bustle of diverse activities which depict the life of David's family and friends in Bethle- hem; the action of Scene 7 is set against the lively and colorful picture of the excited, jostling crowds who have arrived in Hebron for the religious observances and festivities.

Beer-Hofmann's observations on some of the weaknesses of conventional drama, expressed in the letter of 1933 to Erich Kahler, provide an explanation of why he was intent on achieving this kind of fusion:

> What passes for drama . . . all too often lives on gelatinous neutral ground . . . is all too often the dramatic dialogue of big, hypertrophied mouths saturated with intellect, at best with feeling, sometimes also with fantasy—mouths from which stunted bodies, *figures* dangle. What the viewer or reader is given is an easy-to-play piano arrangement for two hands, usually conceived as a piano piece, thought up and written down at the keyboard. Scarcely any recognition is to be found of the fact that one must try to capture the complete musical score of life in the fullness of its mute and speaking voices. . . . Epic features—action—the element of language want to penetrate the drama in a different, freer blend than before. (*GW,* 877–78)[64]

The effort to fuse these elements is more successful in some scenes of *Der junge David* than in others. At times the action and the tableau balance and complement each other, and are indeed so skillfully blended that they become a unified whole. In some scenes, however, they vie with each other to the detriment of both. This happens in scene 3, at least up to the point of David's conversation with Serujah, and in the first part of scene 7, where the minutely detailed "picture" becomes rather wearisome before the thread of the central action is taken up again.[65]

One of the finest scenes of *Der junge David*, by contrast, is "Königs-zelt in Gibea" (scene 2). It, too, includes a tableau—which the playwright has ingeniously contrived to erect before our eyes through the servants who ready the tent for Saul's court session—but the elements of pageantry enhance rather than compete with the spoken lines, so that the action and the characterization of Saul and his family proceed at a vigorous pace which forestalls any decline in the reader's interest. The same is true of the brief but excellent sixth scene, in which the news of Saul's death and David's swift departure for Hebron are skillfully complemented by a vignette of the camp life of the soldier. In general, then, Beer-Hofmann is most successful in the application of his theories when his pictures of "life in all its fullness" are not so detailed or so extended that they threaten to obscure the drama's central action.

"Vorspiel auf dem Theater zu *König David*"

Beer-Hofmann left no better statement of his aesthetic theories and artistic purposes than the prologue "Vorspiel auf dem Theater zu *König David*," whose external purpose is to bridge the twenty-five-year period between *Der junge David* and *König David*. The prologue outlines what has happened to David and the other characters of *Der junge David* in these intervening years: David's battles and conquests, the building of the palace at Jerusalem, the pomp and splendor of court life, etc. The most important point made in this part of the prologue is that David as king has become less and less like David the young man of lofty dreams and ideals for himself and his people, and more and more like the bitterly disillusioned Saul, whose waning vitality was matched by his declining political power. Beer-Hofmann emphasizes this change by giving King David a certain physical resemblance to his predecessor:

Und David?—
Gleicht er noch dem, den man gekrönt in Chebron sah?
Da hielt der Kronreif winddurchwogtes goldnes Haar—
Nun ists zu feierlicher Locken Prunk erstarrt—
Die Schläfen
(*zögernd, als sage er es nur ungern*)—weiss.
Der Kronreif—hohe Tiara—
Ein Rest von Anmut noch umspielt den Mund—doch hart,
Zu Sturm geballt die Stirn—
(*unwillkürlich die Stimme dämpfend*) wie die Schaúls einst war.
                                                        (*GW*, 308–09)

[And David?—
Does he still resemble him whom one saw crowned in Hebron?
There the simple crown held windblown golden hair—
Now stiffened into ostentatious locks of splendor—
The temples (*hesitating, as though saying this unwillingly*)—white.
The crown—a high tiara—
A trace of charm still plays about the mouth—but hard,
Storm-furrowed is the brow—
(*involuntarily lowering his voice*) as was the brow of Saul.]

Implicit in these lines is the playwright's recognition and resigned acceptance of the fact that man's active involvement in life, however desirable, inevitably robs him of the purity and innocence of his youth. One of Beer-Hofmann's numbered (59) but undated notes on *König David* says: "One should grasp that absolute purity is not possible for him who acts. As king, and even more strongly as an old man, David yearns for that lost purity."[66]

Beer-Hofmann, however, makes short shrift of David and the events that transpired in the first twenty-five years after his coronation, and proceeds with dispatch to what one senses is the real purpose of this prologue: his *apologia* of himself as a poet. Initially, he speaks in the guise of "Der Prolog," but before the prologue ends he has abandoned even this transparent disguise. His lines have an intense earnestness, unquestionably expressing his deepest feelings and convictions about the nature and purpose of art, about the poet and his task, and about his relationship to the word. He avoids pomposity, however, and gives this part of the prologue both charm and humor by having his wife appear (initially as "Frau des Prologs," but when his mask falls, hers of course does, too), and by engaging in a verbal exchange with the audience.[67] The outspoken, highly critical comments which come from Beer-Hofmann's audience indicate that as a writer he fully understood the viewpoint of the reader or spectator. This part of the prologue also shows that while Beer-Hofmann was deeply serious about the convictions he expresses here, he did not take *himself* more seriously than he should.

The opening lines of the playwright's conversation with the boy in the audience touch upon the use of tableau elements in the drama:

> KNABE: . . . sag, kannst du, als Prolog,
> Vom Dichter nicht verlangen, dass er uns doch mehr
> In Bildern zeigt? Ja—ist denn das so schwer?
> PROLOG: Nicht schwer!—ich brauch nur zu befehlen,
> Und Lampen leuchten milde Mondesnacht,
> Und strahlen blendend grellen Sonnenschein,
> Aus Holzgerüst und trügerischer Leinwand–Pracht
> Ragt Haus, Palast, türmt Berg sich, buscht sich Hain!
>
> (*GW*, 311–12)

> [BOY: . . . say, can't you, as the prologue,
> Demand of the playwright that he show us
> More in pictures? Is that so difficult?
> PROLOGUE: No!—I need only to command,
> And lamps glow forth a moonlit night,
> Or bright sunshine's blinding rays,
> From wooden frame and deceptive canvas splendor

Arise a house, a palace, towering
Mountain and sylvan grove!]

By providing this behind-the-scenes glimpse of the technical process
of creating stage properties, the playwright deliberately destroys theatrical illusion. He does this to emphasize that the writer must never
succumb to the danger of allowing even such "pictures" to dominate
the word itself:

Aus Wort—aus Wort allein—muss ausgehn alle Kraft,
Die Wolke, Wetter, Licht und Finster schafft!
Wort muss euch zwingen, selber Fels zu türmen,
Meer zu erschaun, Flut, Wogen, Branden, Stürmen—
Wort mit euch ganz allein, in tiefer Einsamkeit
Spricht: "Werde!"—und um euch wird Raum, wird Zeit!
Neimanden brauchend, nackt, auf sich allein gestellt,
Muss Wort neu schaffen Schein des Scheines dieser Welt!

(GW, 312)

[From the word—the word alone—must emanate the power
That creates cloud, weather, light and darkness!
The word must compel you to imagine towering cliff—
To view the sea, flood, waves, surf and storm—
Alone with you, in deep isolation, the word
Speaks: "Let there be!"—and around you is created space and time!
Needing no one, naked, relying only on itself,
The word must create anew the appearance of this world!]

In acknowledging the playwright's debt to the actor, Beer-Hofmann
again refers to his concept of the life and power of the word, independent of its user:

Versteht mich recht: mir kommt nicht in den Sinn,
Erst euer Tun zu nützen, und hochmütig dann
Zu prahlen, dass ich euer nicht bedürfend bin!
Dankbar erkenn ichs: Helfer seid ihr jedem Werke,
Und Wortes Macht wächst hoch, durch eure Macht gemehrt!—
Doch glaubt: Nur was sein Leben lebt aus e i g n e r Stärke—
Was e u c h nicht braucht—erst das ist eures Dienens wert! (GW, 312)

[Understand me rightly: I do not think to
Use your activity, then haughtily
To boast that I had no need of you!
I acknowledge gratefully: You are helpers of every work,
And the word's power grows high, increased by yours!—
But believe: only what lives through its *own* strength—
Only what does not need *you*—is worthy of your service!]

"Service" is used here in reference to the actor. It later emerges as the very essence of the writer's calling. Urged by the boy to ask the audience what *its* wishes are, the playwright says in brusque rejection: "Nach ihren Wünschen hab ich nicht gelernt zu fragen!" (*GW*, 313). ["About their wishes I have not learned to ask!"] At this, an angry spectator cries (in lines which show that Beer-Hofmann was well aware of the criticism directed at him by some of his contemporaries):

> . . . Euch kenn ich schon! Umbraust von Jubel sein—
> Das passt euch—doch: entgegenkommen?—Nein!
> Kein Quentchen opfert man von seinem Eigensinn—
> Man sagt: (*nachspottend*)
> "Ihr müsst mich nehmen, wie ich bin!"
> (*zornig abfertigend*)
> Das geht nicht!—Wollt ihr unsern Beifall—nun—
> Dann hat gefügig uns zu dienen euer Tun!   (*GW*, 313-14)

> [. . . I know you! To be greeted by thundering applause—
> That suits you well enough—but: meet us half-way?—No!
> Not a jot of your obstinacy will you give up—
> You say: (*in mocking imitation*)
> "You must take me as I am!"
> (*in angry dismissal*)
> That won't do!—If you want our applause—well—
> Then your activity must accommodate our wishes, serve us!]

The playwright's reply is an emphatic rejection of art for its own sake, but also an unequivocal statement of Beer-Hofmann's firm belief that the writer's true service to men lies in uncompromising service to the word. If he engages in calculated efforts to win applause, he prostitutes his art and betrays his calling:

> Euch dient mein Tun—und mehr als ihr es fasst,
> Euch dient es—doch verwehrt ward mir zu fragen,
> Ob es euch so gefällt, ob es euch recht!

Herr bin ich, der als Herr dient—nicht als Knecht!
Mein Wort ist nichts als meines Herzens Schlagen,
Und euer Herz zu gleichem Puls zu zwingen—
Ist Amt—ist Dienst—
(*in ernstem, unerbittlichem Abweisen*)
Doch nie von euch mir aufgetragen!   (*GW*, 314)

[My activity serves you—and more than you know,
It serves you—but I am forbidden to ask
Whether it pleases you thus, or suits you!
A master am I, who serves as master—not as slave!
My word is nothing but my own heartbeat,
And to compel your heart to the same pulse—
Is an office—is service—
(*in earnest, inexorable refusal*)
—but not one placed upon me by you!]

The playwright's reply to the spectators who have accused him of
arrogance, pride, and scorn reveals his awareness of his own shortcom-
ings, and also expresses his view of the creation of literature and man's
encounter with it as religious experiences:

Kein Höhnen—nein!—
Ein Mensch bin ich, voll Fehler, sehr gering—
Nur ward—zeit meines Lebens—mir verliehn zu tönen,
Wenn rauschend Gottes Sturm durch meine Wipfel ging!
Doch ist SEIN Stürmen über euch wie über mir!
So steh ich hier—
Und suche nicht nach Gunst in euern Mienen—
Doch, wollt ihr, sei geteilt mit euch mein Opferbrot—
Mein Wort und euer Lauschen—beide dienen
An gleichem Altar, drauf—Allen—die Flamme loht! (*GW*, 315-16)

[Not scoffing—no!—
A man am I, insignificant, full of flaws—
But—all my life—it was given me to resound,
When God's storm, rustling, through my treetops passed!
But HIS storm is over you as well as me!
So stand I here—
And seek not favor in your faces—
But if you will, share my sacrificial bread with me—
My word and your attentive ear—both are service
At the same altar, on which—for all—the flame flares high!]

Whether the reader or viewer actually has this experience depends, of course, on the degree of his receptivity, and the playwright's closing speech is a plea for this:

> Du atmend Dunkles drunt, des Züge ich nicht scheide,
> Sei mir, für Stunden nun, mein abendliches "Du",
> Vor dem, vertraut, ich sinne, juble, leide—
> Verschliess dich nicht vor mir—tu's nicht—hör zu!
> Aus mir wogt Wort—lass an dein Herz es branden. . . .   (*GW*, 317)

> [You breathing in the darkness there, whose features I distinguish not,
> Be for these evening hours my "thou,"
> Before whom, familiar, I meditate, rejoice, and suffer—
> Do not shut yourselves off from me—don't do it—listen!
> Out of me surges the word—let it break upon your heart. . . .]

Beer-Hofmann also uses the prologue to pay tribute to Paula, having the spectators say: "Tausendmal weiser ist die Frau also du!" "Vornehmer auch!" "Die fühlt, was sich hier schickt—was nicht!" (*GW*, 315) ["A thousand times wiser is the woman than you!" "Also more refined!" "She senses what is proper here, what not!"] He also allows her to express her disapproval of their appearing in the prologue as themselves:

> Sonst bargst du stolz dich hinter deinem Werk—was zieht
> Dich heut hieher? Trittst hin vor alle Welt—
> . . .Beginnen lass!—Ziemt uns noch hier zu stehn?
> Komm—lass zurück uns finden doch in unsere Ruh!   (*GW*, 315)

> [At other times you concealed yourself proudly behind your work—
> What draws you here today? Stepping forth before the world—
> . . . Let the play begin!—Is it seemly for us to stand here still?
> Come—let's find the way back to our quiet peace!]

In view of Beer-Hofmann's practice of extensive revision, it is possible that he added these lines to the prologue after its original completion— after he had witnessed Paula's dismay at the news that he and she were in it. Still, perhaps he gave her these lines from the outset, knowing her well enough to anticipate her displeasure.

Through his wife the playwright also hints at how difficult it is to release the world and the characters he has created. "Gib endlich freie Bahn!" ["Block their path no more!"] she urges him.

Die du geformt, die Welt—lass wirklich sie nun walten!
Herrschsüchtiger Vormund!—da du sie aus dir
Entliessest, waren mündig die Gestalten!
Sie gehn weit weg und wissen nicht von ihrem Herrn,
Sie wenden nicht den Kopf, wenn du sie rufst—
Was willst du noch von ihnen?—
(*leise*) War nicht in dir
Genug des reinsten Glücks, da du sie schufst?!   (*GW,* 314)

[The world that you have formed—let it now really reign!
Domineering guardian!—when you released them
From yourself, these figures were of age!
They travel far and know not of their master,
They do not turn their heads when you call out to them—
What more do you want of them?—
(*softly*) Was not in you
Enough of purest happiness while you created them?!]

Toward the end of the prologue, Beer-Hofmann again takes up the
thread of the David story:

Noch einmal, David, lass von deinen Schultern gleiten
Prunk, Pracht—drin du erstarrst, versteinst—
Kehr heim, mein David, heim aus fremden Weiten,
Noch einmal leb den Schein von deinen Erdentagen,
Sei wieder, du, begnadet, sündig—stirb wie einst! . . .   (*GW,* 317)

[Once more, David, let glide from your shoulders
The pomp and splendor—in which you grow rigid, turn to stone—
Return home, my David, home from afar,
Live once again the sheen of your earthly days,
Be full of grace again, and sinful—die as once before! . . .]

These lines suggest that in *König David* and *Davids Tod* Beer-Hofmann
intended to trace the re-emergence of David the man from the myth
that encompassed him. This is confirmed by the undated Note No. 12
to *Davids Tod*: "David in some respects already mythical during his
lifetime. Perhaps (?) his existence altogether mythically encrusted
already. Moving, then, the breakthrough of the human: the senile,
helpless, desperate, sometimes blasphemous, pitiable human being.
Perhaps: he leaves the splendidly adorned, rigid shell of his own myth
behind him and emerges from it: a sufferer, a great human being (great
because he could suffer so much)."[68]

König David and *Davids Tod,* however, remained unfinished. The
1963 edition of the collected works includes only the beginning of the

first scene of *Davids Tod.* It consists of a song, "Vom guten Hirten" ["About the Good Shepherd"], a free rendering of Psalm 23. The poem is dedicated to the memory of Beer-Hofmann's friend and publisher, S. Fischer.[69] The manuscripts of *Die Historie von König David* (including outlines, scenarios, and the playwright's voluminous notes on the entire cycle) are in the Houghton Library of Harvard University, with the rest of Beer-Hofmann's literary estate.[70]

4

Conclusions

Having been examined individually, Beer-Hofmann's works as a whole now need to be placed into perspective. Several questions arise: How does Beer-Hofmann fit into his own era? Do his works still speak to present-day readers, his plays to present-day audiences? Or are they primarily of historical value and interest, for what they tell us about the values, concerns, and preoccupations of a certain group of writers during a particular period in the history of modern German literature?

Beer-Hofmann and like-minded contemporaries were keenly aware that they stood at the close of an age. While certain about that, they were equally *un*certain about what the new age would bring, what shape it would take, and what ideas, values, and forces would govern it. Rapid industrialization (almost inevitably accompanied by the decline of style, the levelling effects of mass taste, and sharply increasing materialism), the rise of nationalism and militarism, the steady advance of technology, the ascendance of psychology, and the decline of religion—all of these developments were effecting radical and in many respects ominous changes in European life and thought, customs and social conventions, and beliefs and attitudes toward virtually every aspect of life.[1]

Writers who found the changes ominous reacted in somewhat differing ways: Neo-Impressionism, Symbolism, Neo-Romanticism, and *Jugendstil* were simultaneous or overlapping phenomena. What Jost Hermand has said about *Jugendstil*, however, applies in large measure to all of them:

What finds expression here is the dream of a select, stylized zone in which one could withdraw completely from the demands of the everyday world. As so often around 1900, one can observe in this a curious mixture of imperialism and inwardness. . . . Thomas Mann once very aptly called these years the time of "security" or "inwardness protected by power." . . . Finally, it was a period in which one cultivated "personality," a period in which one sought to place himself apart, in order not to be infected by the levelling mass taste of the technical age. In doing so, one depended paradoxically enough on the dividend, which Georg Simmel once called "the gatekeeper of inwardness."[2]

It is clear that these observations apply to some extent to the early Beer-Hofmann. That this phase of his life was one of "inwardness" protected by financial security and the prevailing power structure has been shown by the detailed biography of chapter 1. Still, even with respect to the early Beer-Hofmann, Hermand's observations must be qualified; for Beer-Hofmann recognized early on that "the flight from life" was a cul-de-sac, and it did not take him long to move beyond the dandyism and the postured aestheticism of his young years. He had already done so by 1900, when *Der Tod Georgs* was published. The equanimity with which the elderly Beer-Hofmann bore his exile and the drastic reversal of his financial circumstances and pleasant way of life is further proof that financial security and superficial aestheticism had little to do with the essence of the man.[3]

The subject matter of his works indicates which problems and questions preoccupied him as a young man and which continued to be his prevailing concerns as a writer. These can be categorized as (1) the representation of a just and meaningful universal order, despite acute awareness of human suffering and the existence of evil and injustice in the world; (2) the problem of being an artist and the purpose and process of artistic creation; and (3) the renewal of literary language and the revitalization of the drama.

Beer-Hofmann was already wrestling with the problem of a purposeful universal order when he wrote *Das Kind* (1893). By the time *Der Tod Georgs* was published (1900), he had worked his way to the affirmation of a universal order that was not only purposeful but also just, in some cosmic sense that transcends our perception and understanding. *Der Graf von Charolais* (1904) is not a negation of his earlier position, but certainly an acknowledgment, in profoundly pessimistic terms, of the unfathomable nature of God and the course of events in the world. God is no more understandable in *Jaákobs Traum* (1915) and the rest of the *Historie von König David*; however, the universal order is affirmed nevertheless. The playwright has made his own covenant, accepting the suffering it entails.

At every stage of his development, Beer-Hofmann's works also reflect his preoccupation with the problem of being an artist and with the process of literary creation. The hero of *Der Tod Georgs* has no specific vocation, but he certainly represents Beer-Hofmann's conception of the artist in temperament and aesthetic sensibility; Georg, even more than Paul himself, embodies the young Beer-Hofmann's emerging conception of the artist's role and task. The further development of that conception is seen in *Jaákobs Traum* and *Der junge David*, both allegories of the poet and his calling. Here the artist is not merely sensitive to all things, and especially to those who suffer; his state is viewed as a matter of *Auserwähltsein,* and his primary task is to be the *exculpator dei.* The work of art and the artist's task are also the subject of a number of Beer-Hofmann's lyric poems: "Mit einem kleinen silbernen Spiegel" (1904), "Der einsame Weg" (1905), "Der Beschwörer" (1929), "Erahnte Insel" (1936), and the undated poems, "Herakleitische Paraphrase" and "Der Künstler spricht." Each expresses the same view of the artist that we encounter in the early novel and in the later *David* cycle.

Beer-Hofmann was never drawn to the subjects that preoccupied the Naturalists: poverty, squalor, the exploitation of the working class, and other social ills. When he addressed problems with social and political implications (for example, anti-Semitism), he did so indirectly, in the form of an allegory (*Jaákobs Traum*). This is corroborated by Beer-Hofmann's exchange of letters with the British Broadcasting Company. The BBC had asked him to address the Austrian people; he declined this invitation in a letter written on November 26, 1943: "I have spoken sometimes to my fellow-men from the stage, *i.e.,* through my plays, or through my books, always indirectly. . . ." The BBC urged him to reconsider and he again refused, explaining in a letter written on December 13, 1943: "It is not out of personal shyness that I have to decline. . . . I have repeatedly read over the air writings of mine. What keeps me from accepting is the following: not unlike many others I should not know *what* to say in chaotic and troubled times as ours—what to say without acting against my conscience, what to advise, which assurances to give without saying untrue or frivolous words. . . ."[4]

Beer-Hofmann's protagonists are not the poor and downtrodden or the exploited working class; he takes us into no wretched hovels that smell of cabbage, sweat, and dirt. This does not mean that he was less concerned than the Naturalists about the problems of his day; it does mean that he differed sharply from them in his opinions concerning suitable subject matter for the work of art. Aside from the fact that the artist "must [create] and cannot do otherwise," Beer-Hofmann believed that the artist's only justification for his otherwise questionable activity was that he helped others by providing them with *beauty*.

Beer-Hofmann's works do not ignore the existence of suffering and ugliness; on the contrary, they sometimes depict them in very graphic detail. The description of the aged and infirm evoked by the sight of the hideous masks above the toy shop entrance in *Der Tod Georgs* is a good example. Vivid as the description is, however, it is somehow detached, or once-removed. This is not as paradoxical as it sounds. Because of the perspective the author has used, the major emphasis in this passage is not upon the aged themselves, but upon Paul's *impression* of them. However graphically they are depicted, our perception of them is filtered through the eyes and mind of Paul. The same is true of the scene in which Charolais imagines the deterioration of his father's corpse: though the depiction is painfully exact, the focal point of our attention is still Charolais and the pain and grief his mental images are causing him. Similar examples can be found in *Jaákobs Traum* and *Der junge David.*

Beer-Hofmann's choice of subject matter was also influenced by his view of the dream and fantasy as necessary and valid complements of the waking state. He saw these not as forms of escapism, but as therapeutic activities needed to offset the nature of modern life. As early as *Der Tod Georgs,* he also regarded the dream as the prophetic shaper of life; but it was in *Jaákobs Traum* that his material enabled him to treat this aspect of the dream most fully.

No age is totally static, of course, but an era of extremely rapid and all-encompassing change (such as Beer-Hofmann's) confronts the writer with special problems that relate to the "how" as well as the "what" of artistic creation. Time-honored forms and conventions were rapidly losing their validity; once meaningful, they were now becoming empty habits. The writer must somehow cope with this, if his work is to have meaning and is to secure a lasting place in the history of literature. Thomas Mann dealt with this problem by ironizing the deteriorating forms and conventions, and consequently even his early work has considerable relevance for the modern reader. The life of leisure and the cultivation of aesthetic pleasures depicted in *Der Tod Georgs* is no more remote from the present-day reader than the life of the patrician North German bourgeoisie in *Buddenbrooks* (like Beer-Hofmann's novel, published at the turn of the century); but the "loving irony" with which Thomas Mann treats this life and its increasingly hollow conventions is a successful technique that makes his novel seem less of a "period piece" than *Der Tod Georgs.*

Beer-Hofmann was keenly aware of the growing emptiness of traditional forms and the deterioration of literary language. His efforts to reverse these trends were not entirely successful, despite the talent his work reveals. Probably the greatest single reason for this is that the task he set for himself was impossible. Seen in this light (and as Georg Lukács recognized as early as 1908), his efforts were nothing short of heroic. The view of life and the universal order as organic, abiding, and just was already in its demise at the turn of the century, and any attempt to resuscitate it was doomed from the outset. Breathing fire into cold ash, as Steiner observed, is impossible. Hofmannsthal's well-known remark, "Between today and the time in which we were young lies an abyss, one whose boundaries are not even fixed but which grows larger by the hour," was made in 1927. If World War I had already made the kind of life depicted in *Der Tod Georgs* seem esoterically remote, how much more so it must seem today. If it was already difficult in the early part of this century to accept the contention that things happen as they are meant to, it became virtually impossible to believe this after the holocaust of World War II and the systematic extinction of human beings on a scale that utterly staggers the imagination. This is why *Die Historie von König David* has had a relatively limited audience, and not—as some contend—because its subject matter is of interest only to Jews. The distant past has provided many writers with material, and the segment of human history that Beer-Hofmann selected was in fact enormously rich and colorful. The problem is not the subject matter; the historical events of the twentieth century have made a declining number of readers receptive to Beer-Hofmann's view of life and the universal order. To use the author's own words: "We know of too much suffering."

Those same events also influence the modern reader's reactions to Beer-Hofmann's language and style. Reverence for the word, a characteristic of Beer-Hofmann and contemporaries like Hofmannsthal and Rudolf Borchardt, is virtually unknown today. The brutalization of human life in the modern era has unquestionably had a brutalizing effect upon language as well. Beautiful language is not widely regarded as a value in itself, and literary pathos is more likely to embarrass the modern reader than to move him.

There are, of course, internal as well as external reasons for Beer-Hofmann's relatively limited appeal to present-day readers. He was not, nor ever really cared to be, a master of the art of saying much with few words. He was no more drawn to the language of Naturalism than to its subject matter. In his "perfectomania," his determination to render every facet of a phenomenon or an experience, every nuance of an impression or a sensation, he is often verbose. Adjective is piled upon adjective; the representation of an idea, an impression, an experience is interrupted repeatedly by interjections, by qualifying or modifying elements of one sort or another—all, of course, designed to achieve the most precise expression and the fullest possible reproduction of the subject. The very wordiness of such passages, however, sometimes detracts from their author's purpose. The principal reason for this, as Walter Lennig observed, is that such language inescapably creates the impression of "Manierismus," which, in fact, is one of the most widely noted characteristics of *Jugendstil* literature.[5] Curt Hohoff names Beer-Hofmann, Robert Walser, and Caesar Flaischlen as three primary prose writers of *Jugendstil,* "since they constantly tend to use language in a purely decorative way, as adornment, as ornament."[6] This goes too far—particularly with respect to Beer-Hofmann's development after *Der Tod Georgs*—but it does indicate the impression that his language and style leave upon many readers.

Another internal reason for Beer-Hofmann's relatively limited appeal to the modern reader is his pronounced use of metaphors and symbols.[7] Both his early and his mature works are laden with metaphorical language: "Wie ein Gitter von schwarzen Herzen sah das Laub der Linde vor dem Fenster aus" ["The foliage of the linden tree outside the window looked like a lattice of black hearts"] (*Der Tod Georgs, GW,* 529); "Wie Wurzeln eines absterbenden Baumes verdorrt sich aus der Erde recken, ästelte sich, freiliegend, um ihre magern Arme ein blaues Netz knolliger Adern" ["A blue network of knotted veins branched over their gaunt arms as the roots of a dying tree protrude, withered, from the earth"] (*Der Tod Georgs, GW,* 595); "träumen an der Erde Brüsten" ["dreaming on the breasts of the earth"], "gereift an Eurer Liebe milder Sonne" ["ripened by the mild sun of your love"] (*Der Graf von Charolais, GW,* 382, 449); "Wenn unabwendbar über uns jetzt einer / Die eisigen schweren schwarzen Flügel schlägt" ["If unavoidably above us / Death beats his icy, heavy black wings"] (*Der junge David, GW,* 231). Although this metaphorical language may be graphic, it is not "bold," to use Harald Weinrich's formulation: "We must not allow ourselves to be impressed by hyperbole. . . . 'A mountain of debts,' 'a sea of tears,' 'a man like an oak'—to say these things is hyperbolic, but anything but bold. Boldness lies in the slight span of the image that compels us to the perception of contradictoriness. But the whole context must be considered, a context that is not measured too narrowly. . . . If the little metaphorical riddle is immediately followed by its solution, for this reason alone the metaphor is not bold."[8] The use of particles (such as "wie") also lessens the impact of metaphorical language, as Weinrich shows.[9]

Beer-Hofmann's works are equally laden with symbols, which sometimes are obtrusive. The most obvious example is the erotic symbolism of *Der Tod Georgs*. Along with the countless man-made symbols of the worshippers, the landscape surrounding the temple is itself described in terms of erotic symbolism: "Reichgewässert breitete sich die Wiese bis an die dampfende Kluft"; "Dann quoll die Menge der Betenden aus dem Tempel . . . und überwogte die Wiese, dass unter den Tritten die safttrunkenen Stengel der Blumen knirschend brachen" (*GW,* 546–47). ["Watered richly, the meadow extended to the steaming chasm"; "Then the multitude of worshippers gushed from the temple . . . and surged over the meadow, the sap-laden stalks of the flowers breaking beneath their feet."] Used so insistently, the symbol loses something of its dynamic and productive character; it no longer allows the reader to be a "co-creator."[10] Symbolism at its best "is not dependent upon *a* key, *a* formula, an intricate combination accessible only to the highly sophisticated mind, or perhaps invented by it."[11] That is the one extreme. Neither, however, should the symbol spell itself out: "The symbol is *capable* of linking up the general with the specific, the universal with the temporal, the external with the accidental, the infinite with the finite. . . . A successful, that is poetic, symbol will *intimate* this nexus through context; it will not articulate it, for 'it is the essense of poetry to be ambiguous.' "[12] What is disturbing about Beer-Hofmann's symbolism is that it sometimes lacks this ambiguity.

For reasons both external and internal, then, Beer-Hofmann's efforts to revitalize a dying view of life and the world must be regarded as a cause that failed. Viewed historically, however, his work can scarcely be overrated for its importance and value to the student of literature: no work conveys the atmosphere and tone of the period more richly and completely than does *Der Tod Georgs,* and none is more instructive as an example of literary *Jugendstil* (a period style much more interesting for its peculiarities than for any quality of permanence). *Der Tod Georgs* is also of great historical importance as one of the earliest pieces of stream-of-consciousness writing in world literature. As suggested in chapter 2, Joyce and others were subsequently more daring in their experimentation with this technique, but Beer-Hofmann's novel must occupy a prominent place in any serious discussion of the origins of stream-of-consciousness fiction.

In his acceptance speech to the American Academy of Arts and Letters, Beer-Hofmann observed that a writer's work can never hope to be complete; indeed, he was never entirely satisfied with what he had produced. His "perfectomania" and practice of repeated revision notwithstanding, Beer-Hofmann's dramas were eminently successful, both in terms of the philosophic and artistic aims he had set for himself and in terms of audience reception (though, as Musil noted, success in the latter respect was never the primary consideration for Beer-Hofmann). Keenly aware of the crisis in which the theatre found itself, he contributed significantly to its rejuvenation both as a playwright and a director. Like *Der Tod Georgs* in the realm of prose fiction, *Der Graf von Charolais* and *Die Historie von König David* deserve a prominent place in the history of the twentieth-century drama: in its impassioned intensity, *Charolais* is a prelude to the dramas of Expressionism[13] and— though Beer-Hofmann and Brecht are light-years apart in virtually every respect—Beer-Hofmann's resolute inclusion of epic elements in the *David* cycle (in the face of strong skepticism and criticism) anticipates practices that we have associated for decades with Brecht and the epic theatre.

Like Stefan Zweig's *Die Welt von Gestern* [*The World of Yesterday*], the entire body of Beer-Hofmann's work tells us much about an era we would otherwise be hard pressed to understand.[14] During the writing of *Paula, ein Fragment,* Beer-Hofmann's greatest hope was that he could convey to the modern reader "how things really were then." In a sense not only *Paula,* but all of Beer-Hofmann's literary production can be seen in this light, and perhaps he would have liked nothing better than to be viewed by posterity as that kind of "creative historian."

Notes

Chapter 1 The Life of Richard Beer-Hofmann

1. William M. Johnston, *The Austrian Mind* (Berkeley: University of California Press, 1972), in particular chapter 3. [Austrian edition: *Österreichische Kultur- und Geistesgeschichte* (Wien, Köln, Graz: Hermann Böhlaus Nachf., 1974).]

2. Carl E. Schorske, *Fin-de-Siècle Vienna* (New York: Vintage Books, 1981), pp. 5–6. [Originally published by Alfred A. Knopf, New York, 1980.]

3. Ibid., p. xxvi.

4. Ibid., p. 6.

5. Ibid. See also David S. Luft, *Robert Musil and the Crisis of European Culture* (Berkeley: University of California Press, 1980), pp. 1–13.

6. Frederic Morton, *A Nervous Splendor* (New York: Little, Brown, 1979).

7. Johnston, *The Austrian Mind,* p. 115. See also Allan Janik and Stephen Toulmin, *Wittgenstein's Vienna* (New York: Simon & Schuster, 1973), especially chapter 2 ("Habsburg Vienna").

8. Johnston, *The Austrian Mind,* p. 16.

9. Schorske, *Fin-de-Siècle Vienna,* p. 147.

10. Sigmund Freud, for example, waited seventeen years for his professorship, whereas eight years was the norm in the medical faculty. See Schorske, *Fin-de-Siècle Vienna,* p. 184.

11. Schorske, *Fin-de-Siècle Vienna,* p. 148. See also Amos Elon, *Herzl* (New York: Holt, Rinehart & Winston, 1975), pp. 64–71.

12. Janik and Toulmin, *Wittgenstein's Vienna,* p. 46.

13. Antje Kleinewefers, *Das Problem der Erwählung bei Richard Beer-Hofmann* (Hildesheim, New York: Georg Olms Verlag, 1972), p. 7.

14. Kurt Bergel, ed., *Georg Brandes und Arthur Schnitzler: Ein Briefwechsel* (Berne:Francke Verlag, 1956), p. 48. See also Eugene Weber, "The Correspondence of Arthur Schnitzler and Richard Beer-Hofmann," *Modern Austrian Literature* 6, no. 3/4 (1973): 40–51.

15. Richard Beer-Hofmann, *Gesammelte Werke* (Frankfurt: S. Fischer Verlag, 1963), p. 656. In a facsimile of Beer-Hofmann's handwriting, this poem also appeared in *Corona* 2 (1932): 476–77.

16. Bergel, *Brandes–Schnitzler Briefwechsel*, p. 48.

17. Olga Schnitzler, *Spiegelbild der Freundschaft* (Salzburg: Residenz Verlag, 1962). See also *Arthur Schnitzler. Sein Leben. Sein Werk. Seine Zeit,* Heinrich Schnitzler, Christian Brandstätter and Reinhard Urbach, eds. (Frankfurt: S. Fischer Verlag, 1981).

18. See O. Schnitzler, *Spiegelbild,* especially pp. 124–54; Hermann Bahr, *Liebe der Lebenden: Tagebücher 1921–1923* (Hildesheim: Franz Borgmeyer, 1925); Erich Kahler, *Die Verantwortung des Geistes* (Frankfurt: S. Fischer Verlag, 1952), pp. 131–142. Also Kahler, "Richard Beer-Hofmann," *Die Neue Rundschau* 56–57 (1945/46): 227–37; and the same article in English in *Commentary* 1 (April, 1946): 43–50.

19. Alfred Gold, "Aesthetik des Sterbens," *Die Zeit* (Vienna), no. 282, February 24, 1900, pp. 121–22.

20. *Briefwechsel zwischen George und Hofmannsthal,* 2nd rev. ed. (Berlin: Helmut Küpper vormals Georg Bondi, 1953), p. 37.

21. Letter to Hermann Bahr, undated but written in 1902. Hugo von Hofmannsthal, *Briefe 1900–1909* (Vienna: Bermann-Fischer Verlag, 1937), pp. 97–98.

22. Kahler, "Richard Beer-Hofmann," *Commentary* 1: 45.

23. Quoted in O. Schnitzler, *Spiegelbild,* p. 134.

24. Quoted in O. Schnitzler, *Spiegelbild,* p. 135.

25. Hugo von Hofmannsthal, *Briefe 1890–1901* (Berlin: S. Fischer Verlag, 1935), p. 55. (Letter of July 27, 1892 to Felix Salten.)

26. See Bahr, *Liebe der Lebenden,* p. 15.

27. O. Schnitzler, *Spiegelbild,* pp. 131–32.

28. See, for example, *The Letters of Arthur Schnitzler to Hermann Bahr,* Donald G. Daviau, ed. (Chapel Hill: University of North Carolina Press, 1978). The letters contain numerous references to Beer-Hofmann (see the index on p. 176).

29. Rainer Maria Rilke, "Moderne Lyrik" [lecture given March 5, 1898 in Prague, probably written in February, 1898 in Berlin] in *Sämtliche Werke* (Frankfurt: Insel-Verlag, 1965) 5: 386–87. See also Victor A. Oswald, Jr., "The Old Age of Young Vienna," *Germanic Review* 27 (1952): 188.

30. *Hugo von Hofmannsthal/Richard Beer-Hofmann Briefwechsel,* Eugene Weber, ed. (Frankfurt: S. Fischer Verlag, 1972), p. 69.

31. See also Marcel Reich-Ranicki, "Mitleid mit dem grossen Hofmannsthal," *Die Zeit* (Hamburg), no. 6, February 6, 1973, p. 13.

32. Hugo von Hofmannsthal, *Nachlese der Gedichte* (Berlin: S. Fischer Verlag, 1934), p. 86.

33. I am indebted to the Leo Baeck Institute, New York, for permission to quote from this letter, which is part of the Institute's Beer-Hofmann collection.

34. By permission of the Leo Baeck Institute, New York.

35. *Hugo von Hofmannsthal–Arthur Schnitzler Briefwechsel,* Therese Nickel and Heinrich Schnitzler, eds. (Frankfurt: S. Fischer Verlag, 1964), pp. 23–24, 58, 88, 93, 135, 199. See also Hofmannsthal, *Briefe 1890–1901,* pp. 23–24, and *Briefe 1900–1909,* pp. 51, 86.

36. Also in *Hugo von Hofmannsthal/Richard Beer-Hofmann Briefwechsel,* p. 35.

37. For a discussion of the friendship of Brandes and Beer-Hofmann, see Sol Liptzin, "Georg Brandes und Richard Beer-Hofmann," *Modern Austrian Literature* 12, no. 1 (1979): 19–29; see also Klaus Bohnen, "Richard Beer-Hofmann und Georg Brandes: Briefe einer Lebensbekanntschaft," *Nordisch-deutsche Beiträge* 4 (1979): 39–49.

38. By permission of the Leo Baeck Institute, New York.

39. See *Max Reinhardt and His Theatre,* Oliver M. Sayler, ed. (New York: Brentano's Publishers, 1924), p. 104.

40. See Olga Schnitzler, *Spiegelbild,* p. 146.

41. Otto Oberholzer, *Richard Beer-Hofmann* (Berne: Francke Verlag, 1947), pp. 25–26.

42. Karl Kraus, "Die demolirte Literatur" (Vienna, 1897), quoted in A. Schmidt, *Dichtung und Dichter Österreichs* (Salzburg: Verlag das Bergland Buch, 1964), 1: 235.

43. Werner Vordtriede, "Gespräche mit Beer-Hofmann," *Die Neue Rundschau* 63 (1952): 131. The "first work" Beer-Hofmann refers to here was his first *major* work, *Der Tod Georgs.*

44. Vordtriede, "Gespräche," pp. 139–40. See also Richard M. Sheirich, "*Frevel* and *der erhöhte Augenblick* in Richard Beer-Hofmann: Reflections on a Biographical Problem," *Modern Austrian Literature* 13, no. 2 (1980): 1–16.

45. According to Beer-Hofmann's daughter Mirjam (in a conversation with me on January 3, 1974), the candied fruits he purchased from Paula on this occasion were for Lou Andreas-Salomé, whom he had met earlier that year. Lou Salomé recalls her visit to Vienna and the young writers she met there in *Lebensrückblick* (Zurich: Im Max Niehaus Verlag, 1951), pp. 131–32. The footnote to this passage erroneously states that Richard Beer-Hofmann came from the circle for the *Blätter für die Kunst* (p. 343). Beer-Hofmann admired much of George's work (see the *George–Hofmannsthal Briefwechsel,* p. 148; and *Stefan George–Friedrich Gundolf Briefwechsel,* Berlin, 1962, p. 236), but he was never a member of the George circle and in later years was quite critical of the man. See Vordtriede, "Gespräche," and *Das verlassene Haus. Tagebuch aus dem amerikanischen Exil 1938–1947.* (Munich, Vienna: Hanser Verlag, 1975), p. 136.

46. At this time Beer-Hofmann evidently had not yet told his family about Paula, for he wrote to his aunt, Agnes Beer, from Skodsborg on August 8 that he was there with two friends, Schnitzler and Paul Goldmann. (Unpublished letter in the Beer-Hofmann collection of the Leo Baeck Institute.)

47. See *Hofmannsthal/Beer-Hofmann Briefwechsel,* p. 227. One of the founders and editors of *Pan* was Hugo von Hofmannsthal's close friend, Eberhard von Bodenhausen. An English translation of the "Schlaflied" by Sol Liptzin appeared in the Winter, 1941 issue of *Poet Lore* and is also reprinted in Theodor Reik, *The Secret Self* (New York: Farrar, Straus and Young, 1952).

48. Rainer Maria Rilke, *Briefe aus Muzot,* Ruth Sieber-Rilke and Carl Sieber, eds. (Leipzig: Insel Verlag, 1937), p. 145. For a comprehensive discussion of the relationship between Rilke and Beer-Hofmann, see Klaus W. Jonas, "Richard Beer-Hofmann and Rainer Maria Rilke," *Modern Austrian Literature* 8, no. 3/4 (1975): 43–73; and "Rainer Maria Rilke und Richard Beer-Hofmann," *Philobiblon* 17 (1973): 156–77.

49. This translation is by the poet's younger daughter, the late Naemah Beer-Hofmann. I have amended the punctuation to make it correspond more closely to the original, without, I hope, doing violence to standard English usage. Miss Beer-Hofmann's translation appeared most recently in Klaus W. Jonas, "Richard Beer-Hofmann and Rainer Maria Rilke," p. 63.

50. In his interpretation of the "Schlaflied," for example, Theodor Reik went so far as to contend that the phrase "Mirjam, mein Leben" is a "Yiddish-German expression of intense and intimate affection, and its emotional character knows no parallel. . . . The

poet did not choose the words 'mein Leben'. They fell into his lap. It was not selection, but inner force and necessity. There were no other words, when he thought of the only human relationship that lasts on earth, the relationship between parents and children" (Reik, *The Secret Self,* p. 306). There is no reason to question the assertion that the phrase "mein Leben" has special significance for German-speaking Jews, but Reik (who was not trained in literary criticism) was mistaken about the lack of "selection." On the level at which lyric poetry is constructed (a process described by Gottfried Benn in *Probleme der Lyrik*), "Mirjam, mein Leben" is Beer-Hofmann's conscious and deliberate reinforcement of the preceding line ("Du bist ihr Leben—ihr Leben ist dein"). It is also the poet's deliberate application of the general conclusion expressed in that line to himself and his child. For a very different interpretation see Horst Althaus, *Zwischen Monarchie und Republik* (Munich: Fink Verlag, 1976), p. 20. Althaus regards "das Blut unserer Väter" as a reference to the socio-economic class to which the writers of Young Vienna belonged: the affluent, liberal, upper-middle class.

51. On the early notes to the *Historie* see Richard M. Sheirich, "Beer-Hofmann's 'Die Historie von König David': The Unpublished Manuscripts." Dissertation, Harvard, 1964, pp. 2–3. Most of the notes of 1898–1900 deal with plans for *Scha-ül,* a five-act play which became *Der junge David.* On Beer-Hofmann's plans for two dramas about Ariadne, see Eugene Weber, "Richard Beer-Hofmann. Aufzeichnungen zu 'Ariadne auf Kreta' und 'Ariadne anf Naxos,' " *Hofmannsthal-Blätter* 13–14 (1975): 3–14.

52. Leo Van Jung was a Viennese musician whom Beer-Hofmann met in 1890. They became lifelong friends. The Beer-Hofmann collection at Harvard contains a musical score that Van Jung composed for *Jaákobs Traum.*

53. *Hofmannsthal–Schnitzler Briefwechsel,* pp. 123, 125, 125–26, 126–27.

54. Alfred Kerr, *Die Welt im Drama,* 2nd ed. (Cologne, Berlin: Kiepenheuer & Witsch, 1964), p. 102.

55. *Meister und Meisterbriefe um Hermann Bahr,* Josef Gregor, ed. (Vienna: H. Bauer, 1947), p. 184.

56. "Richard Beer-Hofmann," *Die Neue Rundschau* 56–57: 237.

57. Quoted in Harry Zohn, *Wiener Juden in der deutschen Literatur* (Tel Aviv: Verlag 'Olamenu,' 1964), p. 34.

58. O. Schnitzler, *Spiegelbild,* p. 147.

59. Alfred Kerr gives brief recollections of this trip in *Die Welt im Drama,* pp. 101ff.

60. Vordtriede, "Gespräche," pp. 136–37.

61. Rudolf Kassner, "Im Gespräch," *Die Neue Rundschau* 65 (1954): 506–13.

62. By permission of the Leo Baeck Institute, New York.

63. Saylor, *Max Reinhardt and His Theatre,* p. 67.

64. *Hofmannsthal–Schnitzler Briefwechsel,* p. 208. See also the letter on p. 207 and the footnote to it on p. 370.

65. Saylor, *Max Reinhardt and His Theatre,* p. 105.

66. Quoted by permission of the late Helene Thimig-Reinhardt and the Harvard College Library. The telegram is catalogued as part of Beer-Hofmann's literary estate under the call number, b MS Ger 183.458.

67. Sheirich, "Beer-Hofmann's 'Historie,' " p. 203.

68. See Vordtriede, "Gespräche," p. 126. An English translation of the *Gedenkrede* by Sam Wachtell was published in New York by Bermann-Fischer in 1943.

69. *Hugo von Hofmannsthal–Rudolf Borchardt Briefwechsel,* Marie Luise Borchardt, Herbert Steiner, eds. (Frankfurt: S. Fischer Verlag, 1954), p. 44.

70. Rudolf Borchardt, *Gesammelte Werke in Einzelbänden: Gedichte* (Stuttgart: Ernst Klett Verlag, 1957), p. 36. Another poem dedicated to Beer-Hofmann is Rilke's "Vene-

zianischer Morgen," written in the early summer of 1908. See Rainer Maria Rilke, "Der neuen Gedichte anderer Teil," *Sämtliche Werke* (Wiesbaden: Insel-Verlag, 1955), 1: 609.

71. On May 15, 1912, for example, the friends celebrated Schnitzler's fiftieth birthday in Venice. Rilke encountered the group quite by accident and joined the birthday celebration. See "Rainer Maria Rilke und Arthur Schnitzler: Ihr Briefwechsel," *Wort und Wahrheit* 13 (1958): 283–89 [edited and published by Heinrich Schnitzler]. See also *Rainer Maria Rilke-Marie von Thurn und Taxis-Hohenlohe Briefwechsel* (Zurich: Max Niehans Verlag, 1951), 1: 150.

72. O. Schnitzler, *Spiegelbild,* pp. 151–52.

73. Martin Buber, ed. *Gustav Landauer: Sein Lebensgang in Briefen* (Frankfurt: Rütten & Loening, 1929), 2: 339.

74. Buber, *Gustav Landauer Briefe,* 2: 340.

75. *Brandes–Schnitzler Briefwechsel,* p. 127.

76. This date and that of the Vienna premiere are the ones given in *Daten.* The note in *GW* lists the same date for the Vienna premiere, but *December 7* as the date of the Berlin premiere (p. 881). The chronological table of Reinhardt productions in *Max Reinhardt and His Theatre* names *May* 4 and December 7 as the dates of the Vienna and Berlin premieres, respectively. The discrepancy may stem from the fact that the editor, accustomed to the practice in the English-speaking world of giving first the month and then the day, mistook 5.4.19 for May 4. The discrepancy between the dates in *Daten* and in *GW* for the Berlin premiere has not been accounted for.

77. Quoted in Alfred Werner, *Richard Beer-Hofmann: Sinn und Gestalt* (Vienna: Verlag Hch. Glanz, 1936), p. 8.

78. Rilke, *Briefe aus Muzot,* p. 146. (Letter of April 25, 1922 to Ilse Blumenthal-Weiss.)

79. Vordtriede, "Gespräche," pp. 147–48. The name Vordtriede uses in relating this anecdote is "Gisela," but Mirjam Beer-Hofmann Lens told me in a conversation on January 3, 1974 that the name her father's acquaintance actually suggested was Elsa— which makes the point all the more telling.

80. Kahler, "Richard Beer-Hofmann," *Commentary* 1: 46.

81. *Brandes–Schnitzler Briefwechsel,* p. 133. See also Sol Liptzin, "Georg Brandes and Richard Beer-Hofmann," p. 26.

82. A different opinion is advanced by Sol Liptzin, who maintained that Beer-Hofmann regarded the Jews as "a community of fate rather than a race or a religion," an assertion he seems to contradict when he adds that this community is held together by "the acceptance of certain doctrines enunciated by their prophets . . ." (*Richard Beer-Hofmann,* pp. 90ff.).

83. See Robert F. Arnold, *Das deutsche Drama* (Munich: C.H. Beck'sche Verlagsbuchhandlung, 1925), p. 746; Albert Soergel and Curt Hohoff, *Dichtung und Dichter der Zeit* (Düsseldorf: August Bagel Verlag, 1961), 1: 422; Adalbert Schmidt, *Dichtung und Dichter Österreichs im 19. und 20. Jahrhundert* (Salzburg, Stuttgart: Verlag das Berglandbuch, 1964), 1: 237.

84. O. Schnitzler, *Spiegelbild,* p. 96.

85. Helene Thimig came from a distinguished family of actors. The daughter of the famous character actor, Hugo Thimig, she began her career at the Deutsches Theater in Berlin. In 1932 she married Max Reinhardt; they emigrated in 1938 to the United States, where Reinhardt died in 1943. For a detailed account of their life together see Helene Thimig-Reinhardt, *Wie Max Reinhardt lebte . . . Eine Handbreit über dem Boden* (Percha: Verlag R.S. Schulz, 1973).

86. Quoted by permission of the late Helene Thimig-Reinhardt and the Harvard College Library.

87. Gabriel Beer-Hofmann died in London in 1971. He was the author of numerous film scenarios and several books, written under the pseudonym, G.S. Marlowe.
88. Richard Beer-Hofmann, "Theater 'Habima,' " *Das neue Russland* 9–10 (1926), Heft 40, pp. 41–42.
89. Edited by Hans Böhm, the book is Volume 1 of *Die Kunst der Bühne*, published in Berlin by Eigenbrödler in 1927. Beer-Hofmann's contribution, "Moissi," also appears in *GW*, p. 645.
90. *Sonderausgabe zu Thomas Manns 70. Geburtstag. Die Neue Rundschau* (Stockholm: Bermann-Fischer, 1945).
91. Hermann Kunisch, ed. *Handbuch der deutschen Gegenwartsliteratur* (Munich: Nymphenburger Verlagshandlung, 1965), p. 678. This section of the *Handbuch* was written by Hildegard Brenner.
92. Sheirich, "Beer-Hofmann's *Historie,*" p. 541.
93. Liptzin, *Richard Beer-Hofmann*, p. 104.
94. Sheirich, "Beer-Hofmann's *Historie,*" pp. 525, 532.
95. I am indebted to Mirjam Beer-Hofmann Lens for supplying me with the complete text of this speech. See also Eugene Weber, "Richard Beer-Hofmann: Briefe, Reden, Gedichte aus dem Exil," *Literatur und Kritik* 10 (1975): 469–79.
96. Beer-Hofmann's grave is with Paula's in the Friesenberg Cemetery at Zurich. Naemah Beer-Hofmann, who died in 1972, is also interred there.

Chapter 2 The Prose Works

1. Vordtriede, "Gespräche," pp. 133–34.
2. Cf. Eduard Spranger, "Der psychologische Perspektivismus im Roman," in *Zur Poetik des Romans*, Volker Klotz, ed. (Darmstadt: Wissenschaftliche Buchgesellschaft, 1965), pp. 217–38. This essay first appeared in *Jahrbuch des Freien Deutschen Hochstifts* (Frankfurt: Das Freie Deutsche Hochstift, 1930), pp. 70–90.
3. Wolfdietrich Rasch, "Eine Beobachtung zur Form der Erzählung um 1900," in *Stil- und Formprobleme in der Literatur*, Paul Böckmann, ed. (Heidelberg: Carl Winter, Universitätsverlag, 1959), pp. 451–52. See also Joseph Warren Beach, *The Twentieth Century Novel* (New York: Appleton-Century-Crofts, 1932), pp. 188–89.
4. Richard Beer-Hofmann, *Novellen*, 2. Auflage (Berlin: Verlag von Freund & Jaeckel, 1894), p. 1.
5. Vordtriede, "Gespräche," p. 144. (Conversation of September 20, 1944.)
6. "Gabriele d'Annunzio," in *Loris. Die Prosa des jungen Hugo von Hofmannsthal* (Berlin: S. Fischer Verlag, 1930), p. 87.
7. *Brandes–Schnitzler Briefwechsel*, pp. 67, 179.
8. Cf. Oberholzer, *Richard Beer-Hofmann*, pp. 20, 248, 249, 252.
9. Alfred Werner, "Beer-Hofmann: Double Heritage," *The American Scholar* 16 (1947): 330.
10. In the narrowest sense Paul's nocturnal walk along the river, his train trip to Vienna, etc., constitute "external action," but in the broader sense they serve only to create a setting for the real action, which takes place in Paul's mind.
11. Cf. Oberholzer, *Richard Beer-Hofmann*, p. 46.
12. Arthur Goldschmidt, " 'Der Tod Georgs' von Richard Beer-Hofmann," *Das literarische Echo* 2 (1899/1900): 1370.

13. The scientific correctness of Beer-Hofmann's view of the dreamer is, of course, very much open to debate. It may be argued that man no more controls, manipulates, or sets the boundaries of his dreams than he does the events of his waking hours. Such arguments, however, lie beyond the scope of this study; the purpose here is not to prove Beer-Hofmann right or wrong in terms of the clinical findings of psychology, but simply to establish what his views were.

14. Hofmannsthal experienced this same sense of oneness with things past as well as present, as expressed in the first of the "Terzinen über Vergänglichkeit." See *Gedichte und lyrische Dramen* (Stockholm: Bermann-Fischer Verlag, 1946), p. 17. [*Gesammelte Werke in Einzelausgaben*, Herbert Steiner, ed.]

15. "Richard Beer-Hofmann," *Commentary* 1: 45.

16. One of Beer-Hofmann's notes on *Der junge David* summarizes the following information he had obtained from D.H. Guthe's *Kurzes Bibelwörterbuch* and Ernst Meier's *Abhandlungen für die Kunde des Morgenlandes:* "Astharoth in Basan, place of worship of the ancient Eastern goddess of nature, Astarte, revered in Canaan as aštar, aštoret (from which the Aramaic Aphtoret and the Greek Aphrodite derived). A famous place of worship was Hierapolis in Syria. *Lukian, 'De dea Syriaka.'* She is the mother of the gods, goddess of propagation and fruitfulness. Since the moon was considered the giver of nightly dew and hence the fosterer of all growth, she became the moon goddess and the sickle moon her emblem—traces of the moon cult among the Hebrews. Job 31, 26. Transferred to the sky, the mother of the gods became 'the queen of heaven.' Babylonian theologians establish Ištar planetarily as the star goddess Venus." This note (quoted here from *GW*, 882) is undated, but it is quite probable that Beer-Hofmann used these same sources in writing the Syrian temple episode of *Der Tod Georgs*.

17. For a detailed analysis of the erotic symbolism of the temple episode see Oberholzer, *Richard Beer-Hofmann*, pp. 51ff.

18. Ibid., p. 52.

19. Beer-Hofmann later expressed this idea in the prose fragment, "Die Beschenkten." Asking what sort of image the poet gives back to God, who has favored him, he replies: "One . . . that causes death to be forgotten, that grants to the image of things a permanence beyond the actual life of those things—an image that links death to death in such a way that everything appears to be a chain of life" (*GW*, 629).

20. Vordtriede tells of a conversation a few months before Beer-Hofmann's death, in which the poet said: " 'The remarkable thing about *A Thousand and One Nights* is the multiple linking of fates in it.' This was precisely what he had always sensed so strongly in his own life" ("Gespräche," p. 147). Cf. also Richard M. Sheirich, "Beer-Hofmann and the 'Arabian Nights,' " *Harvard Library Bulletin* 14 (1960): 486–92.

21. This recalls a remark Beer-Hofmann made much later in life: "Every genuine literary work must have . . . its prologue in heaven . . . or else an epilogue in heaven. It must always have a connection with God. With certain writers the danger exists that they don't do this and write only with their knowledge and skill . . ." (Vordtriede, "Gespräche," p. 141). Beer-Hofmann expresses the same idea in the prose fragment, "Vorspiel im Himmel," *GW*, 631.

22. Cf. Hugo von Hofmannsthal, "Der Dichter und diese Zeit," in *Prosa II* (Frankfurt: S. Fischer Verlag, 1959), pp. 229, 257. [*Gesammelte Werke in Einzelausgaben*, Herbert Steiner, ed.] This lecture was first published in *Die Neue Rundschau* in 1907.

23. Posterity or the continuity of life as a possible means of triumph over death is hinted at in *Der Tod Georgs*, but developed more fully in Beer-Hofmann's dramas; it will be discussed in detail in chapter 3.

24. " 'Der Tod Georgs' von Richard Beer-Hofmann," *Das Literarische Echo* 2: 1371.

25. William Eickhorst, *Decadence in German Fiction* (Denver: Alan Swallow, 1953), p. 21.

26. Werner Kraft, "Richard Beer-Hofmann," in *Wort und Gedanke* (Bern: Francke Verlag, 1959), p. 195.

27. See, for example, Dolf Sternberger, "Sinnlichkeit um die Jahrhundertwende"; Wilhelm Emrich, "Zur Genealogie des Jugendstils"; Walter Lennig, "Der literarische Jugendstil"; Robert Schmutzler, "Der Sinn des Art Nouveau"; Dominik Jost, "Zum literarischen Jugendstil." All of these essays are in *Jugendstil*, Jost Hermand, ed. (Darmstadt: Wissenschaftliche Buchgesellschaft, 1971).

28. "Der literarische Jugendstil," in *Jugendstil*, p. 374. This essay first appeared in *Deutsche Universitätszeitung* 13 (1958): 423–28.

29. Jens Malte Fischer, "Richard Beer-Hofmann 'Der Tod Georgs,' " *Sprachkunst* 2 (1971): 211–27; and Jürgen Viering, "Jugendstil und Empfindsamkeit," *Euphorion* 71 (1977): 180–94.

30. "Richard Beer-Hofmann 'Der Tod Georgs,' " p. 227.

31. Cf. Jost Hermand, "Undinen-Zauber: Zum Frauenbild des Jugendstils," in *Jugendstil*, pp. 469–94. See also B. Champigneulle, *Jugendstil Art Nouveau*, Brigitte Kahr, trans. (Paris: Editions Aimery Somogy, n.d.), pp. 90–101.

32. Sternberger, "Sinnlichkeit um die Jahrhundertwende," in *Jugendstil*, p. 104. This essay appeared previously in Sternberger's book, *Über den Jugendstil und andere Essays* (Hamburg: Claassen, 1956).

33. Jost, "Zum literarischen Jugendstil," in *Jugendstil*, p. 464. This essay first appeared in the *Neue Zürcher Zeitung*, February 18, 1968, p. 53.

34. Schmutzler, "Der Sinn des Art Nouveau," in *Jugendstil*, pp. 309–10. This study was originally published in Schmutzler's book, *Art Nouveau – Jugendstil* (Stuttgart: Verlag Gerd Hatje, 1962).

35. Jost, "Zum literarischen Jugendstil," p. 463.

36. Schmutzler, "Der Sinn des Art Nouveau," pp. 298–300.

37. Richard Specht, "Literatur der Gegenwart," in *Ewiges Österreich*, Erwin Rieger, ed. (Vienna: Verlag Manz, 1928), p. 44. See also Viering, "Jugendstil und Empfindsamkeit," pp. 180–83.

38. Lennig, "Der literarische Jugendstil," p. 375.

39. Ibid. See also Ulrike Weinhold, *Künstlichkeit und Kunst in der deutschsprachigen Dekadenz-Literatur* (Frankfurt, Berne: Lang, 1977).

40. See Ludwig Pesch, "Richard Beer-Hofmann," *Wort und Wahrheit* 19 (1964): 617; Erich Kahler, "Richard Beer-Hofmann," *Commentary* 1: 49; Alfred Werner, "Richard Beer-Hofmann: Double Heritage," *The American Scholar* 16: 330. William Rose Benét also expressed this view in his presentation speech during the ceremonies in which the National Institute of Arts and Letters gave Beer-Hofmann its Award for Distinguished Achievements.

41. Rasch, "Zur Frage des epischen Präteritums," *Wirkendes Wort*, 3. Sonderheft (August, 1961), 72–73. See also Matgorzata Pótrola, "Charakteristische Merkmale des indirekten erlebten inneren Monologs in Richard Beer-Hofmanns Erzählung 'Der Tod Georgs,' " *Acta Universitatis Lodziensis* 59 (1979): 99–107.

42. Lawrence E. Bowling, "What is the Stream of Consciousness Technique?" *PMLA* 65 (1950): 342.

43. Ibid., p. 343.

44. Robert Humphrey, *Stream of Consciousness in the Modern Novel* (Berkeley: University of California Press, 1965), p. 7.

45. Ibid., p. 8. Hofmannsthal expresses this idea in the d'Annunzio essay, and Gustav Landauer was later to say the same thing (quoting Oscar Wilde) in a commentary on *Der*

Graf von Charolais: "The decisive thing is not what a man does, but what he is" (*Gustav Landauer: Sein Lebensgang in Briefen,* Martin Buber, ed., 1: 129–30).

46. For comprehensive presentations of all sides of the controversy see Käte Hamburger, *Die Logik der Dichtung* (Stuttgart, 1957); Wolfgang Kayser, *Entstehung und Krise des modernen Romans* (Stuttgart, 1954), and "Wer erzählt den Roman?" in *Die Vortragsreise* (Berne, 1958); Franz Stanzel, "Die typischen Erzählsituationen im Roman," *Wiener Beiträge zur englischen Philologie* 63 (1955), and "Episches Präteritum, erlebte Rede, historisches Präsens," *Deutsche Vierteljahresschrift für Literaturwissenschaft und Geistesgeschichte* 33 (1959): 1–12; Wolfdietrich Rasch, "Zur Frage des epischen Präteritums," *Wirkendes Wort,* 3. Sonderheft (1961), 68–81; Eberhard Lämmert, *Bauformen des Erzahlens* (Stuttgart, 1955).

47. Bowling, "What is the Stream of Consciousness Technique?" p. 336.

48. Cited in Joseph Warren Beach, *The Twentieth Century Novel,* pp. 359–60.

49. The use of cinematic devices, including the flashback, is commonly regarded as a characteristic feature, if not an innovation, of stream-of-consciousness literature (see especially Beach, *The Twentieth Century Novel,* pp. 407ff.), but the flashback, at least, is not really so new. As Robert Humphrey notes, it is equivalent to the epic device of *in medias res,* whose use dates as far back as the *Odyssey* (*Stream of Consciousness in the Modern Novel,* p. 95).

50. Beach, *The Twentieth Century Novel,* p. 524.

51. For an authoritative discussion of the leitmotif as a principle of organization in the work of Joyce, see Stuart Gilbert, *James Joyce's "Ulysses": A Study,* 2nd rev. ed. (New York: Knopf, 1952).

52. Georg Lukács recognized this strict regard for form as early as 1908: "The battle he [Beer-Hofmann], among all present-day writers, wages for form is the most heroic. It is as though a deep wisdom compelled him to contain the overflowing wealth of his insights within strict boundaries. Form is still an obstacle for him with which he wages hard and painful battles; not for the sake of what is said, but rather to escape silence, renunciation." "Der Augenblick und die Formen," [essay written in 1908] in G.L., *Die Seele und die Formen* (Berlin: Egon Fleischel, 1911), p. 264. [A reprint of *Die Seele und die Formen* was published by Luchterhand (Neuwied) in 1971.]

53. Alfred Döblin, "Der Bau des epischen Werks," *Die Neue Rundschau* 40 (1929): 527–51.

54. Vordtriede, "Gespräche," p. 126.

55. Rudolf Kayser, "Der sechzigjährige Richard Beer-Hofmann," *Die Neue Rundschau* 37 (1926): 196.

56. Osmin is the servant of the Turkish pasha in Mozart's opera, *Abduction from the Seraglio,* first performed at the Vienna Burgtheater on July 16, 1782. Don Pizarro is the governor of the Spanish fortress who imprisons his political enemy, Don Florestan, in a deep dungeon in Beethoven's opera, *Fidelio,* first produced in Vienna in 1805.

57. Beethoven composed the Prometheus-ballet music in 1800–1801.

58. Max Lüthi, *Volksmärchen und Volkssage,* 2nd ed. (Bern, Munich: Francke Verlag, 1966), p. 14.

59. Ibid., pp. 14–15, 19–20.

60. Ibid., p. 15.

61. Ibid., pp. 19–20.

62. Some of the material in this section (as well as parts of my discussion of the *Historie von König David* in chapter 3) appeared previously as "Richard Beer-Hofmann: The Poet as *Exculpator Dei,*" in *Protest–Form–Tradition: Essays on German Exile Literature,* Joseph P. Strelka, Robert F. Bell, Eugene Dobson, eds. (University, Alabama: University of Alabama Press, 1979).

63. Cf. Eberhard Lämmert, *Bauformen des Erzählens*. In the section entitled "Andeutung und Auswahl," Lämmert says: "This very lingering, condensing and omitting on the part of the narrator not only gives a special accent to certain stages of the action, but causes the entire narrated material to emerge from the monotony of mere succession as something *newly formed*" (p. 23).

64. Otto Kallir, "Nachwort des Herausgebers," *GW*, 873.

65. See also the prose fragment "Klima" (undated), *GW*, 639.

66. Cf. the prose fragment so entitled, written July 17, 1922 (*GW*, 627), and the fragment "Ur-Zeit des Wortes," written in 1943 (*GW*, 632–33).

67. Vortdriede, "Gespräche," pp. 134–35.

Chapter 3 The Dramatic Works

1. Josef Gregor, ed., *Meister und Meisterbriefe um Hermann Bahr* (Vienna: H. Bauer-Verlag, 1947), p. 179. (Letter of July 23, 1918.)

2. See the editor's note on *Charolais*, *GW*, 895.

3. Translated as "Die unselige Mitgift," "The Fatal Dowry" was included in Wolf von Baudissin's anthology, *Ben Jonson und seine Schule* (Leipzig: Brockhaus, 1836). This was the translation Beer-Hofmann knew.

4. See Eduard Eckhardt, "Deutsche Bearbeitungen älterer englischer Dramen," *Englische Studien* 68 (1933–34): 195–208; Josef Nadler, *Literaturgeschichte der deutschen Stämme und Landschaften* (Regensburg: Verlag von Joseph Habbel, 1932), 4: 916; Paul Goldmann, *Vom Rückgang der deutschen Bühne* (Frankfurt: Literarische Anstalt, 1907), p. 151ff.

5. Cf. Martin Buber, "Geleitwort," *GW*, 8.

6. Alfred Werner, *Richard Beer-Hofmann: Sinn und Gestalt*, p. 23.

7. See Alfred Kerr, "Der Graf von Charolais," *Die Neue Rundschau* 16 (1905): 250–51; Gustav Zieler, "Der Graf von Charolais," *Das literarische Echo* 7 (1905): 655; Julius Bab, *Die Chronik des deutschen Dramas* (Berlin: Osterheld, 1922), 1: 104; Adalbert Schmidt, *Deutsche Dichtung in Österreich* (Vienna, Leipzig: Adolf Luser Verlag, 1935), pp. 23–24, and *Dichtung und Dichter Österreichs*, 1: 236; Robert F. Arnold, *Das deutsche Drama* (Munich: C.H. Beck'sche Verlagsbuchhandlung, 1925), p. 745. In a review first printed in 1922, Robert Musil seems to agree with this criticism, but to a lesser extent: "The critic should be very cautious about exercising his wit on works that deserve to be called literature, but one could probably say that in this play the connection between the first and second parts is not strong enough . . ." (*Theater*, Munich: Rowohlt, 1965, pp. 132–33). Three critics who rejected this criticism of the play were Georg Lukács in *Die Seele und die Formen*, p. 254; Theodor Kappstein in "Berliner Theaterkunst," *Deutschland. Monatsschrift für die gesamte Kultur* (Berlin) 5 (1906): 791; and Heinrich Stümcke in "Von den Berliner Theatern," *Bühne und Welt* 7 (1904–05): 343.

8. Cf. especially "Kirchhofsgedanken," *Andreas Gryphius: Werke in drei Bänden*, Hermann Palm, ed. (Hildesheim: Georg Olms Verlagsbuchhandlung, 1961).

9. Cf. the reference to "den heissen Strom des neuen Lebens" in the Syrian love-death rites in *Der Tod Georgs* (*GW*, 549); see also Theodor Reik, "Lullaby for Mirjam" in *The Secret Self*, pp. 303–04. In this essay Reik deals primarily with the "Schlaflied" (interpreting it as a statement of the seed as an answer to death), but he also discusses the treatment of this theme in *Charolais*, remarking: "Spermatozoa are here considered identical with the life of the individual. . . . Sexual union is seen . . . not only as an

escape from the danger of death, but also as a promise of rescue and immortality" (p. 303).

10. Gustav Landauer was one early critic who sensed other tones than those of profound pessimism in *Charolais*. On December 25, 1904, after having attended the play's premiere in Berlin, he wrote to Beer-Hofmann: "Wilde says what matters is not what a person does, but what he is. You add: but the decisive action of men is always determined by what is done. And you further add: is man, is the world then anything else but this eternal changing of masks? You add it with a good deal of bitterness, in pessimistic tones. The future will decide whether you do not also have other tones for your sense of the world. I believe you do, and hear behind all the bitterness sounds of that ultimate serenity that we can only bear when it is born of the last bitterness and deepest anguish" (*Gustav Landauer: Sein Lebensgang in Briefen*, Martin Buber, ed., 1: 129–30).

11. Cf. Liptzin, *Richard Beer-Hofmann*, p. 46, and Alfred Werner, who tells of a conversation with Beer-Hofmann shortly before his death in which Beer-Hofmann said: "One cannot change one's fate; the road is predestined for each of us. But the way we walk it, the attitude with which we bear our fate, can be of great influence over events" ("Richard Beer-Hofmann: Double Heritage," *The American Scholar* 16: 331).

12. This is very similar to Thomas Mann's view of the God-man relationship and the practice of religion, expressed many times, both publicly and privately. See especially the chapter entitled "Vom Glauben," *Die Betrachtungen eines Unpolitischen* in *Gesammelte Werke in zwölf Bänden* (Frankfurt: S. Fischer Verlag, 1960) 12; "The Coming Humanism," *The Nation* 147 (December 10, 1938): 617–19; *Thomas Mann–Karl Kerényi: Gespräch in Briefen* (Zurich: Rhein-Verlag, 1960), pp. 74–75; and "Fragment über das Religiöse," *Gesammelte Werke*, 11: 425.

13. Robert Musil, "Der Graf von Charolais," *Theater*, p. 132. Marie-Luise Roth, the editor of this volume, also speaks of Musil's high regard for Beer-Hofmann as playwright because he did not write mere "Publikums-und Erfolgsstücke" ("Zum Verständnis der Texte," *Theater*, p. 325); see also Musil's "Wiener Theatermesse" on p. 44 of the same book.

14. Eduard Eckhardt, "Deutsche Bearbeitungen älterer englischer Dramen," p. 207.

15. George Steiner, *The Death of Tragedy* (New York: Alfred A. Knopf, 1961), p. 304–5.

16. Ibid., p. 309.

17. See, for example, the judge's reference to the female menstrual cycle in act II (*GW*, 382); even if the utterance were in character (which in this instance it is not), there is a certain incongruity between the lofty verse form and the subject at hand.

18. Gertrud Prellwitz, "Theater Korrespondenz," *Preussische Jahrbücher* 119 (1905): 357–58.

19. Rudolf Kassner in *Hugo von Hofmannsthal: Die Gestalt des Dichters im Spiegel der Freunde*, Helmut A. Fiechtner, ed. (Vienna: Humboldt Verlag, 1949), p. 240.

20. Karl Frenzel, "Die Berliner Theater," *Die Deutsche Rundschau* 123 (1905): 299.

21. Vordtriede reports a conversation with Beer-Hofmann in which the latter said that the critic, Geneviève Bianquis, had been entirely right to speak of the "tragic innocence" of all the characters in *Der Graf von Charolais*, adding that with this play he had written an end to tragedy, because at the point where no one is any longer responsible for his deeds, tragedy ceases ("Gespräche," p. 144).

22. Steiner, *The Death of Tragedy*, p. 9. [Condensed German version in *Tragik und Tragödie*, Volkmar Sander, ed. (Darmstadt: Wissenschaftliche Buchgesellschaft, 1971), pp. 342–80.]

23. Ibid., p. 222. Cf. Geoffrey Brereton, *Principles of Tragedy* (Coral Gables: University of Miami Press, 1968), pp. 3–17, 39–42.

24. Kraft, "Richard Beer-Hofmann," p. 196. Cf. Brereton, *Principles,* pp. 42–47.

25. Steiner, *The Death of Tragedy,* p. 8. For a discussion of all of the foregoing points concerning tragedy, see also Elder Olson, *Tragedy and the Theory of Drama* (Detroit: Wayne State University Press, 1966), especially pp. 243–60.

26. Alfred Kerr, "Der Graf von Charolais," *Die Neue Rundschau* 16 (1905): 250.

27. Steiner, *The Death of Tragedy,* p. 4.

28. Several excerpts from *Das goldene Pferd* appeared in the Sunday supplement of Vienna's *Neue Freie Presse* in 1930; the complete work, edited by Mirjam Beer-Hofmann Lens and Herbert Steiner, was published posthumously in *Die Neue Rundschau* 66 in 1955.

29. See also the prose fragment, "Was sich nicht ausdrücken lässt," written July 17, 1922, only a few months after the completion of *Das goldene Pferd.*

30. This corresponds very closely to many of the observations about the psychology of dreams in *Der Tod Georgs.* See especially *GW,* 607, 608, 619.

31. This note is already sounded in *Der Tod Georgs,* when Paul reflects on "den segenvollen Frieden eines Lebens, das der Erde sich vermählen durfte" ["the blessed peace of a life wedded to the earth"] (*GW,* 591).

32. In private life Beer-Hofmann was an avid collector of precious gems, *objets d'art,* and other beautiful artifacts; the splendor of his villa in Vienna's Cottage Quarter is described by Olga Schnitzler in *Spiegelbild der Freundschaft.*

33. As detailed as these stage directions are, they represent an editing of the original version. In the foreword to the pantomime Beer-Hofmann says: "In this version the exact instructions concerning gestures . . . mimic and choreographic details, costumes, lighting . . . and musical requirements have been reduced. In their entirety they would be too great a burden on the reader" (*GW,* 467). This represents a concession to the reader that the later Beer-Hofmann was unwilling to make. (Cf. the letter of 1933 to Erich Kahler, *GW,* 877ff.)

34. Tarkah seems patterned after the figure of the Astarte-goddess in *Der Tod Georgs.* Cf. *Finale und Auftakt. Wien 1898–1914,* Otto Breicha and Gerhard Fritsch, eds. (Salzburg: Otto Müller Verlag, 1964), p. 14.

35. There are exceptions. At a few points in the pantomime the lack of restraint seriously undermines the intended effect. In one such scene Halimah is struck in the breast by an arrow—"Bahádur will sie umarmen—der Pfeil in Halimahs Brust hindert ihn" (*GW,* 513)—and however inappropriate, one can scarcely restrain the impulse to laugh.

36. These notes and the manuscripts of the *Historie* are in the Houghton Library of Harvard University. See also Hans-Gerhard Neumann, *Richard Beer-Hofmann. Studien und Materialien zur "Historie von König David"* (Munich: Wilhelm Fink Verlag, 1972), pp. 9–12. [Vol. 9 of *Zur Erkenntnis der Dichtung,* Gerhart Baumann, ed.]

37. Beer-Hofmann used the Kautzsch-Bertholet critical edition of the Bible; five different nineteenth-century translations; the Luther Bible; Dietenberger's translation (1604); the Berleburg Bible (1726) and the Latin Vulgate and Greek Septuagint in the Stier and Theile polyglot of 1854.

38. Richard M. Sheirich, "Beer-Hofmann's *Historie,*" p. 255.

39. Almost inevitably, *Jaákobs Traum,* as the prologue of Beer-Hofmann's "life work," has been compared to Goethe's "Prolog im Himmel" to *Faust*—a comparison which doubtless pleased Beer-Hofmann. Sometimes the comparisons are carried too far; thus Liptzin maintains that "God and Samáel wrestle for the soul of Jaákob even as do God

and Mephistopheles for the soul of Faust" ("Goethe and Beer-Hofmann," *PMLA* 65 [1950]: 642–43). The God of Goethe's *Faust* does not really wrestle; his attitude is one of sovereign detachment throughout.

40. Cf. Paul's reflections (in *Das Kind*) on doubt as a possible means to faith and his conclusion that this is perhaps a more worthy way than that of unquestioning faith, quoted and discussed in chapter 2.

41. This affirmation of suffering and the lack of envy of the angels is not unlike the attitude Rilke displays in the *Duino Elegies*. See especially the seventh, ninth, and tenth elegies.

42. Cf. Deut. 28:23, 29, 33, 34, 65.

43. This is essentially a restatement of Rebekah's answer to Esau's question, "Ist Gott denn nicht gerecht?" ["Is God not just?"]: "Ich weiss nicht, was / Er ist! Wüsst ich's— Er wär mein Gott nicht!" (*GW,* 29). ["I don't know what / He is! If I knew—He would not be my God!"]

44. Cf. Beer-Hofmann's letter to Theodor Herzl, quoted in chapter 1.

45. Cf. the judge's statement on justice and mercy in act II of *Charolais, GW,* 378.

46. This recalls an observation Karl Kerényi made to Thomas Mann when he was working on the Joseph novels: "According to primitive modes of thought, playing a god always meant being one, at least a little" (see Thomas Mann, *Gesammelte Werke in zwölf Bänden,* 11: 634).

47. Cf. Michael's lines, *GW,* 77 with Deut. 28:37; Michael's speech, *GW,* 78 with Isa. 42:6, 7; Isa. 43:10–12, 21; Isa. 45:6–7, 22, 23. Of all the archangels, Michael was chosen to speak these lines presumably because he is designated in Daniel 12:1 as "the great prince which standeth for the children of my people." Beer-Hofmann collected St. Michael's medals and always wore one on his watch chain. (See *GW,* 852–54.)

48. Cf. Samáel's speech, *GW,* 78–79 with Deut. 28:23, 29, 33, 34, 65; Ezek. 25:7; and Isa. 48:10.

49. See *GW,* 63–65, also 43, 82–83. Cf. Paul's sensitivity to all things and his sense of oneness with them in *Der Tod Georgs,* discussed in chapter 2.

50. Cf. Thornton Wilder, "Mythos und Dichtung. Zu 'Jaákobs Traum' von Richard Beer-Hofmann," Herbert E. Herlitschka, trans., *Almanach des S. Fischer Verlags* 77 (1963): 72–73. Wilder greatly admired Beer-Hofmann's work and was one of the members of the American Academy of Arts and Letters who nominated Beer-Hofmann for its Distinguished Achievement Award. See also O. Schnitzler, *Spiegelbild,* p. 125.

51. Liptzin, *Richard Beer-Hofmann,* p. 74.

52. Jacob remained in Haran for twenty years, serving Laban fourteen years for his two daughters, Leah and Rachel, and six years for his cattle (Gen. 31:41); it was during the return to his homeland that he wrestled with God "until the breaking of the day."

53. How serious an offense this was is indicated, first, by the very specific language of the Law pertaining to birthrights (Deut. 21:15–17), and second, by the fact that the Biblical Jacob, twenty years after his theft of the blessing, was still filled with trepidation before his reunion with Esau (Gen. 32:3–11); during their meeting he "bowed himself to the ground seven times" and offered Esau many gifts (Gen. 33:1–15).

54. This episode is related in Gen. 25:29–34; God's resulting judgment on Esau was harsh indeed: "Was not Esau Jacob's brother? saith the Lord: yet I loved Jacob, and I hated Esau, and laid his mountains and his heritage waste for the dragons of the wilderness. Whereas Edom saith, we are impoverished, but we will return and build the desolate places; thus saith the Lord of hosts, They shall build, but I will throw down; and they shall call them, The border of wickedness, and, The people against whom the Lord hath indignation forever" (Mal. 1:2–4).

55. Cf. especially the ninth elegy in Rainer Maria Rilke, *Sämtliche Werke,* Ruth Sieber-Rilke and Ernst Zinn, eds. (Wiesbaden, 1955), 1: 718. Werner Kraft also views Beer-Hofmann's relationship to the word as essentially religious; see *Wort und Gedanke,* p. 203–4.

56. The moment of "confrontation" or "communion" described here is essentially the same as Hofmannsthal's moment of "transformation." Hofmannsthal does not equate the poet with the prophet or priest as a member of an elite caste, but he ascribes to the poet (in "Der Dichter und diese Zeit") the same function that the priest served in past ages.

57. Victor A. Oswald, "The Old Age of Young Vienna," p. 198.

58. The last part of this passage paraphrases the prophecies of Isaiah. See Isa. 61:1–2; 65:17; 66:22; 9:2; 42:6–7.

59. There are obvious parallels between this idea and the "ancestral archetypes" of C.G. Jung. Though there is no evidence that Beer-Hofmann was acquainted with or directly influenced by Jung's theory of archetypes, the theory finds an interesting corroboration in Beer-Hofmann's works. Cf. especially C.G. Jung, *The Structure and Dynamics of the Psyche* (New York: Pantheon Books, 1960). [Vol. 8 of *The Collected Works of C.G. Jung,* Sir Herbert Read et al, eds., R.F.C. Hull, trans.]

60. Cf. Ruth's words to Naomi, *GW,* 89, and Ruth's speech, *GW,* 303.

61. Liptzin, *Richard Beer-Hofmann,* pp. 74–75.

62. See, for example, Clair Haydn Bell's review of Liptzin's *Richard Beer-Hofmann* in *Monatshefte für Deutschen Unterricht* 29 (1937): 176.

63. At Saul's insistence, she called up the specter of the prophet Samuel, who told Saul of his impending death (I Sam. 28:7–19).

64. Cf. also the prose fragment, "Sonnensysteme," written in April or May of 1930, *GW,* 626.

65. See also Hans-Gerhard Neumann, *Richard Beer-Hofmann,* pp. 31–32.

66. Cited in Sheirich, "Beer-Hofmann's *Historie,*" p. 302. See also Beer-Hofmann's remarks to Vordtriede on this subject in connection with *Der Tod Georgs* ("Gespräche," p. 132).

67. Paula's deep distress at being included in the "Vorspiel" and her ultimate deferral to Beer-Hofmann's wishes are described in *Paula, ein Fragment, GW,* 818–20.

68. Cited in Sheirich, "Beer-Hofmann's *Historie,*" p. 352.

69. "Vom guten Hirten" was first published in *Die Neue Rundschau* 45, no. 12 (1934).

70. Beer-Hofmann's literary estate is catalogued in the Houghton Library under call number b MS Ger 131. After Harvard purchased the estate it was discovered that a section of the *Historie* manuscripts was missing; Beer-Hofmann had entrusted this material to Herbert Steiner, who later presented it to the Houghton Library. It is catalogued separately, under call number b MS Ger 131.1. The correspondence is also catalogued separately, under call number b MS Ger 183.

Chapter 4 Conclusions

1. For detailed intellectual, social, and political histories of the period, readers have already been referred to William Johnston, *The Austrian Mind;* Allan Janik and Stephen Toulmin, *Wittgenstein's Vienna;* and Carl Schorske, *Fin-de-Siècle Vienna.* For an additional perspective see Gordon A. Craig, *Germany 1866–1945* (New York: Oxford University Press, 1978), especially chapters 1, 3, 5, and 6. For detailed literary histories see

Klaus Günther Just, *Von der Gründerzeit bis zur Gegenwart* (Bern: Francke Verlag, 1973); *Jahrhundertende-Jahrhundertwende,* Helmut Kreuzer, ed. (Wiesbaden: Akademische Verlagsgesellschaft Athenaion, 1976) [Vol. 18 of the *Neues Handbuch der Literaturwissenschaft,* Klaus von See, ed.]; and Herbert Lehnert, *Geschichte der deutschen Literatur vom Jugendstil zum Expressionismus* (Stuttgart: Reclam, 1978).

2. Jost Hermand, "Jugendstil," *Deutsche Vierteljahresschrift für Literaturwissenschaft und Geistesgeschichte* 38 (1964): 109. See also Horst Althaus, *Zwischen Monarchie und Republik* (Munich: Fink Verlag, 1976), p. 20.

3. Cf. Erich Kahler, "Richard Beer-Hofmann," pp. 43–44.

4. Quoted by permission of the Harvard College Library. The letters are catalogued under the call number b MS Ger 183.668.

5. See Jost Hermand, "Jugendstil," p. 82.

6. Hohoff, *Dichtung und Dichter der Zeit,* p. 127.

7. For a systematic analysis of the individual symbols see O. Oberholzer, *Richard Beer-Hofmann.*

8. Harald Weinrich, "Die Semantik der kühnen Metapher," *Deutsche Vierteljahresschrift für Literaturwissenschaft und Geistesgeschichte* 37 (1963): 341.

9. Ibid., p. 331.

10. Henry H.H. Remak, "Vinegar and Water: Allegory and Symbolism in the German *Novelle* Between Keller and Bergengruen," in *Literary Symbolism,* Helmut Rehder, ed. (Austin: University of Texas Press, 1965), p. 38.

11. Ibid., pp. 53–54.

12. Ibid., p. 37.

13. Lehnert acknowledges this in *Geschichte der deutschen Literatur,* p. 332.

14. A book by Jeffrey B. Berlin, Donald G. Daviau, and Jorun B. Johns on the correspondence of Stefan Zweig with Raoul Auernheimer and Richard Beer-Hofmann is forthcoming.

Selected Bibliography

[For additional materials consult Kathleen Harris and Richard M. Sheirich, "Richard Beer-Hofmann: A Bibliography," *Modern Austrian Literature* 15, no. 1 (1982): 1–60.]

Works by Richard Beer-Hofmann

Daten. Unpublished notebook. Houghton Library, Harvard University, call number 6 MS Ger 131.
Gesammelte Werke. Frankfurt a.M.: S. Fischer, 1963.
Novellen. 2nd ed. Berlin: Freund & Jaeckel, 1894.
"Theater Habima," *Das neue Russland* 9–10 (1926), 40–42.
Der Tod Georgs. Afterword by Hartmut Scheible. Stuttgart (Reclam Universalbibliothek no. 9989), 1980.

Secondary Works

Althaus, Horst. *Zwischen Monarchie und Republik.* Munich: Fink Verlag, 1976.
Andreas-Salomé, Lou. *Lebensrückblick.* Zurich, Wiesbaden: Max Niehaus, 1951.
Arnold, Robert F., ed. *Das deutsche Drama.* Munich: C.H. Beck'sche Verlagsbuchhand-lung, 1925.
Bab, Julius. *Die Chronik des deutschen Dramas.* 4 vols. Berlin: Osterheld, 1922.

Bahr, Hermann. *Liebe der Lebenden: Tagebücher 1921–1923.* Hildesheim: Franz Borg-meyer, 1925.

[———]. *Meister und Meisterbriefe um Hermann Bahr.* Edited by Joseph Gregor. Vienna: H. Bauer, 1947.

Baudissin, Wolf von, ed. *Ben Jonson und seine Schule.* Leipzig: Brockhaus, 1836.

Beach, Joseph Warren. *The Twentieth Century Novel.* New York: Appleton-Century-Crofts, 1932.

Bell, Clair Haydn. Review of *Richard Beer-Hofmann,* by Sol Liptzin. *Monatshefte für deutschen Unterricht* 29 (1937): 175–76.

Berlin, Jeffrey B. "Richard Beer-Hofmann and Theodor Reik: A Letter in Exile." *The Psychoanalytic Review* 64 (1981): 479–86.

Berlin, Jeffrey B., and Elizabeth J. Levy. "On the Letters of Theodor Reik to Arthur Schnitzler [and Richard Beer-Hofmann]." In *Psychoanalysis and Old Vienna: Freud, Reik, Schnitzler, Kraus,* edited by Murray H. Sherman. New York, London: Human Sciences Press, 1978, pp. 109–30.

Böhm, Hans, ed. *Moissi: Der Mensch und der Künstler in Worten und Bildern.* Berlin: Eigenbrödler, 1927.

Bohnen, Klaus. "Richard Beer-Hofmann und Georg Brandes: Briefe einer Lebensbe-kanntschaft." *Nordisch-deutsche Beiträge* 4 (1979): 39–49.

Borchardt, Rudolf. *Gedichte.* Stuttgart: Ernst Klett, 1957. [*Gesammelte Werke in Einzel-bänden.* Edited by Marie Luise Borchardt and Herbert Steiner.]

Bowling, Lawrence E. "What is the Stream of Consciousness Technique?" *PMLA* 65 (1950): 333–45.

Brandes, Georg, and Arthur Schnitzler. *Ein Briefwechsel.* Edited by Kurt Bergel. Berne: Francke, 1956.

Breicha, Otto, and Gerhard Fritsch, eds. *Finale und Auftakt. Wien 1898–1914.* Salzburg: Otto Müller, 1964.

Brereton, Geoffrey. *Principles of Tragedy.* Coral Gables: University of Miami Press, 1968.

Champigneulle, Bernard. *Jugendstil – Art Nouveau.* Translated by Brigitte Kahr. Paris: Somogy, n.d.

Craig, Gordon A. *Germany 1866–1945.* New York: Oxford University Press, 1978.

Döblin, Alfred. "Der Bau des epischen Werks." *Die Neue Rundschau* 40 (1929): 527–51.

Eckhardt, Eduard. "Deutsche Bearbeitungen älterer englischer Dramen." *Englische Studien* 68 (1933–34): 195–208.

Eickhorst, William. *Decadence in German Fiction.* Denver: Alan Swallow, 1953.

Elon, Amos. *Herzl.* New York: Holt, Rinehart & Winston, 1975.

Elstun, Esther N. "The Aesthetics of Richard Beer-Hofmann." Ph.D. dissertation, Rice University, 1969.

———. "Richard Beer-Hofmann: The Poet as *Exculpator Dei.*" In *Protest – Form – Tradition: Essays on German Exile Literature,* edited by Joseph P. Strelka, Robert Bell, and Eugene Dobson. University, Alabama: University of Ala-bama Press, 1979.

Emrich, Wilhelm. "Zur Genealogie des Jugendstils." In *Zeugnisse.* Frankfurt a.M.: Europäische Verlagsanstalt, 1963. [Also in *Jugendstil,* Darmstadt: Wissen-schaftliche Buchgesellschaft, 1971.]

Fiechtner, Helmut, ed. *Hugo von Hofmannsthal. Die Gestalt des Dichters im Spiegel der Freunde.* Vienna: Humboldt, 1949.

Fischer, Jens Malte. "Richard Beer-Hofmann. 'Der Tod Georgs.' " *Sprachkunst* 2 (1971): 211–27.

Frenzel, Karl. "Die Berliner Theater." *Die Deutsche Rundschau* 123 (1905): 296–309.

Gainham, Sarah. *The Habsburg Twilight.* New York: Atheneum, 1979.

George, Stefan, and Friedrich Gundolf. *Briefwechsel.* Edited by Robert Böhringer and Georg Landmann. Munich, Düsseldorf: Helmut Küpper, 1962.

George, Stefan, and Hugo von Hofmannsthal. *Briefwechsel.* 2nd rev. ed. Berlin: Helmut Küpper, 1953.

Gilbert, Stuart. *James Joyce's "Ulysses."* 2nd rev. ed. New York: Knopf, 1952.

Gold, Alfred. "Ästhetik des Sterbens." *Die Zeit* (Vienna), no. 282 (February 24, 1900), 121–22.

Goldmann, Paul. *Vom Rückgang der deutschen Bühne.* Frankfurt a.M.: Literarische Anstalt, 1907.

Goldschmidt, Arthur. "Der Tod Georgs." *Das literarische Echo* 2 (1899–1900): 1370–71.

Gregor, Joseph, ed. *Meister und Meisterbriefe um Hermann Bahr.* Vienna: H. Bauer, 1947. [Museion Veröffentlichungen der österreichischen Nationalbibliothek in Wien, Neue Folge, 1. Reihe, Band 1.]

Gryphius, Andreas. *Werke in drei Bänden.* Edited by Hermann Palm. Hildesheim: Georg Olms, 1961.

Hamburger, Käte. *Die Logik der Dichtung.* 2nd rev. ed. Stuttgart: Ernst Klett, 1968. [American edition: *The Logic of Literature.* Translated by Marilyn J. Rose, Bloomington: Indiana University Press, 1973.]

Harris, Kathleen, and Richard M. Sheirich. "Richard Beer-Hofmann: A Bibliography." *Modern Austrian Literature* 15, no. 1 (1982): 1–60.

Hermand, Jost, ed. *Jugendstil.* Darmstadt: Wissenschaftliche Buchgesellschaft, 1971.

–––. "Jugendstil." *Deutsche Vierteljahresschrift für Literaturwissenschaft und Geistesgeschichte* 38 (1964): 70–110, 273, 315.

–––. "Undinen-Zauber. Zum Frauenbild des Jugendstils." In *Wissenschaft als Dialog,* edited by Renate von Heydebrand and Klaus Günther Just. Stuttgart: J.B. Metzlersche Verlagsbuchhandlung, 1969. [Also in: *Jugendstil,* Darmstadt, 1971.]

Hofmannsthal, Hugo von. *Briefe 1890–1901.* Berlin: S. Fischer, 1935.

–––. *Briefe 1900–1909.* Vienna: Bermann-Fischer, 1937.

–––. *Gedichte und lyrische Dramen.* Stockholm: Bermann-Fischer, 1946. [*Gesammelte Werke in Einzelbänden,* ed. Herbert Steiner.]

–––. *Loris. Die Prosa des jungen Hugo von Hofmannsthal.* Berlin: S. Fischer, 1930.

–––. *Nachlese der Gedichte.* Berlin: S. Fischer, 1934.

–––. *Prosa.* Frankfurt a.M.: S. Fischer, 1959. [*Gesammelte Werke in Einzelbänden,* ed. Herbert Steiner.]

[–––.] *Hugo von Hofmannsthal. Die Gestalt des Dichters im Spiegel der Freunde.* Edited by Helmut Fiechtner. Vienna: Humboldt, 1949.

Hofmannsthal, Hugo von, and Richard Beer-Hofmann. *Briefwechsel.* Edited by Eugene Weber. Frankfurt a.M.: S. Fischer, 1972.

Hofmannsthal, Hugo von, and Rudolf Borchardt. *Briefwechsel.* Edited by Marie Luise and Herbert Steiner. Frankfurt a.M.: S. Fischer, 1954.

Hofmannsthal, Hugo von, and Arthur Schnitzler. *Briefwechsel.* Edited by Therese Nickel and Heinrich Schnitzler. Frankfurt a.M.: S. Fischer, 1964.

Humphrey, Robert. *Stream of Consciousness in the Modern Novel.* Berkeley: University of California Press, 1965.

Janik, Allan, and Stephen Toulmin. *Wittgenstein's Vienna.* New York: Simon & Schuster, 1973.

Johnston, William M. *The Austrian Mind.* Berkeley: University of California Press, 1972. [Austrian edition: *Österreichische Kultur- und Geistesgeschichte.* Vienna, Cologne, Graz: Hermann Böhlaus Nachf., 1974.]

Jonas, Klaus. "Richard Beer-Hofmann and Rainer Maria Rilke." *Modern Austrian Literature* 8, no. 3/4 (1975): 43–73.

———. "Rainer Maria Rilke und Richard Beer-Hofmann." *Philobiblon* 17 (1973): 156–77.

Jost, Dominik. "Zum literarischen Jugendstil." *Neue Zürcher Zeitung,* February 18, 1968, p. 53. [Also in *Jugendstil,* Darmstadt, 1971.]

———. *Literarischer Jugendstil.* Stuttgart: J.B. Metzlersche Verlagsbuchhandlung, 1969. [Sammlung Metzler no. 81.]

Jung, C.G. *The Collected Works.* Edited by Sir Herbert Read, et al. Translated by R.F.C. Hull. 16 vols. New York: Pantheon, 1956–66.

Just, Klaus Günther. *Von der Gründerzeit bis zur Gegenwart.* Berne: Francke, 1973.

Kahler, Erich. "Richard Beer-Hofmann." *Die Neue Rundschau* 56–57 (1945–46): 227–37. [English version in *Commentary* 1 (April, 1946): 43–50.]

———. *Die Verantwortung des Geistes.* Frankfurt a.M.: S. Fischer, 1952.

Kappstein, Theodor. "Berliner Theaterkunst." *Deutschland* 5 (1906): 526–32.

Kassner, Rudolf. "Im Gespräch." *Die Neue Rundschau* 65 (1954): 506–13.

Kayser, Rudolf. "Der sechzigjährige Richard Beer-Hofmann." *Die Neue Rundschau* 37 (1926): 196–97.

Kayser, Wolfgang. *Entstehung und Krise des modernen Romans.* 2nd ed. Stuttgart: J.B. Metzlersche Verlagsbuchhandlung, 1954.

———. *Die Vortragsreise.* Berne: Francke, 1958.

Kerr, Alfred. "Der Graf von Charolais." *Die Neue Rundschau* 16 (1905): 247–52.

———. *Die Welt im Drama.* Edited by Gerhard F. Hering. Cologne, Berlin: Kiepenheuer & Witsch, 1964.

Kleinewefers, Antje. *Das Problem der Erwählung bei Richard Beer-Hofmann.* Hildesheim, New York: George Olms, 1972.

———. "Richard Beer-Hofmann und Hugo von Hofmannsthal: Bemerkungen zu einer schwierigen Freundschaft." *Emuna* 9 (1974): 248–54.

Kraft, Werner. *Wort und Gedanke.* Berne: Francke, 1959.

Kraus, Karl. "An der Schwelle des Goethe-Jahres." *Die Fackel* 33 (March, 1932): 1–5.

———. *Die demolirte Literatur.* Vienna, 1897.

Kreuzer, Helmut, ed. *Jahrhundertende–Jahrhundertwende.* Wiesbaden: Athenaion, 1976. [Vol. 18 of the *Neues Handbuch der Literaturwissenschaft,* Klaus von See, ed.]

Kunisch, Hermann, ed. *Handbuch der deutschen Gegenwartsliteratur.* Munich: Nymphenburger Verlagshandlung, 1965.

Lämmert, Eberhard. *Bauformen des Erzählens.* Stuttgart: J.B. Metzlersche Verlagsbuchhandlung, 1955.

[Landauer, Gustav.] *Gustav Landauer: Sein Lebensgang in Briefen.* Edited by Martin Buber. 2 vols. Frankfurt a.M.: Rütten & Loening, 1929.

Lehnert, Herbert. *Geschichte der deutschen Literatur vom Jugendstil zum Expressionismus.* Stuttgart: Reclam, 1978.

Lennig, Walter. "Der literarische Jugendstil." *Deutsche Universitätszeitung* 13 (1958): 423–28. [Also in *Jugendstil,* Darmstadt, 1971.]

Liptzin, Sol. "Georg Brandes and Richard Beer-Hofmann." *Modern Austrian Literature* 12 (1979): 19–29.

———. "Goethe and Beer-Hofmann." *PMLA* 65 (1950): 641–44.

———. *Richard Beer-Hofmann.* New York: Bloch, 1936.

———. "Richard Beer-Hofmann and Joseph Viktor Widmann." *Modern Austrian Literature* 8, no. 3/4 (1975): 74–80.

Lüthi, Max. *Volksmärchen und Volkssage.* 2nd ed. Berne, Munich: Francke, 1966.

Luft, David S. *Robert Musil and the Crisis of European Culture.* Berkeley: University of California Press, 1980.

Lukács, Georg. *Die Seele und die Formen.* 1911. Reprint. Neuwied: Luchterhand, 1971.

Mann, Thomas. "The Coming Humanism." *The Nation* 147 (December 10, 1938): 617–19.

―――. *Gesammelte Werke in zwölf Bänden.* Frankfurt a.M.: S. Fischer, 1960.

[Mann, Thomas.] *Die Neue Rundschau. Sonderausgabe zum 70. Geburtstag Thomas Manns.* Stockholm: Bermann-Fischer, 1945.

Mann, Thomas, and Karl Kerényi. *Gespräch in Briefen.* Edited by Karl Kerényi. Zurich: Rhein-Verlag, 1960.

Morton, Frederic. *A Nervous Splendor.* New York: Little, Brown, 1979.

Musil, Robert. *Theater.* Edited by Marie Luise Roth. Munich: Rororo, 1965.

Nadler, Josef. *Literaturgeschichte der deutschen Stämme und Landschaften.* 4 vols., 3rd ed. Regensburg: Joseph Habbel, 1932.

Neumann, Hans-Gerhard. *Richard Beer-Hofmann. Studien und Materialien zur "Historie von König David."* Munich: Wilhelhm Fink, 1972. [Vol. 9, Zur Erkenntnis der Dichtung, edited by Gerhart Baumann.]

Oberholzer, Otto. *Richard Beer-Hofmann.* Berne: Francke, 1947.

Olson, Elder. *Tragedy and the Theory of Drama.* Detroit: Wayne State University Press, 1966.

Oswald, Victor A., Jr. "The Old Age of Young Vienna." *Germanic Review* 27 (1952): 188–99.

Pesch, Ludwig. "Richard Beer-Hofmann: Zur Neuausgabe der Werke des im Exil gestorbenen Dichters." *Wort und Wahrheit* 19 (1964): 616–20.

Pótrola, Matgorzata. "Charakteristische Merkmale des indirekten erlebten inneren Monologs in Richard Beer-Hofmanns Erzählung 'Der Tod Georgs,' " *Acta Universitatis Lodziensis* 59 (1979): 99–107.

Prellwitz, Gertrud. "Theater-Korrespondenz." *Preussische Jahrbücher* 119 (1905): 355–59.

Rasch, Wolfdietrich. "Eine Beobachtung zur Form der Erzählung um 1900." In *Stil- und Formprobleme in der Literatur,* edited by Paul Böckmann. Heidelberg: Carl Winter, 1959.

―――. "Zur Frage des epischen Präteritums." *Wirkendes Wort,* 3. Sonderheft (1961), 68–81.

Reich-Ranicki, Marcel. "Mitleid mit dem grossen Hofmannsthal." *Die Zeit* (Hamburg), no. 6, February 6, 1973, p. 13.

Reik, Theodor. *The Secret Self.* New York: Farrar, Straus & Young, 1952.

―――. *Das Werk Richard Beer-Hofmanns.* Vienna: Löwit, 1919.

Remak, Henry H.H. "Vinegar and Water: Allegory and Symbolism in the German *Novelle* Between Keller and Bergengruen." In *Literary Symbolism,* edited by Helmut Rehder. Austin: University of Texas Press, 1965.

Rilke, Rainer Maria. *Briefe aus Muzot.* Edited by Ruth Sieber-Rilke and Carl Sieber. Leipzig: Insel, 1937.

―――. *Sämtliche Werke.* 5 vols. Frankfurt a.M.: Insel, 1965.

Rilke, Rainer Maria, and Arthur Schnitzler. "Ihr Briefwechsel." *Wort und Wahrheit* 13 (1958): 283–98. [Edited and published by Heinrich Schnitzler.]

Rilke, Rainer Maria, and Marie von Thurn und Taxis-Hohenlohe. *Briefwechsel.* 2 vols. Zurich: Max Niehans, 1951.

Sander, Volkmar, ed. *Tragik und Tragödie.* Darmstadt: Wissenschaftliche Buchgesellschaft, 1971.

Saylor, Oliver M., ed. *Max Reinhardt and His Theatre.* New York: Brentano's Publishers, 1924.

Schmidt, Adalbert. *Deutsche Dichtung in Österreich.* 2nd ed. Vienna, Leipzig: Adolf Luser, 1935.

———. *Dichtung und Dichter Österreichs.* 2 vols. Salzburg, Stuttgart: Verlag das Bergland-Buch, 1964.

Schmutzler, Robert. *Art Nouveau – Jugendstil.* Stuttgart: Gerd Hatje, 1962. [Condensed as "Der Sinn des Art Nouveau" in *Jugendstil,* Darmstadt, 1971.]

Schnitzler, Arthur. *The Letters of Arthur Schnitzler to Hermann Bahr.* Edited by Donald G. Daviau. Chapel Hill, N.C.: University of North Carolina Press, 1978.

Schnitzler, Arthur, and Otto Brahm. *Der Briefwechsel.* Edited by Oskar Seidlin. Berlin: Selbstverlag der Gesellschaft für Theatergeschichte, 1953. [Vol. 57, Schriften der Gesellschaft für Theatergeschichte.]

Schnitzler, Heinrich, et al, eds. *Arthur Schnitzler. Sein Leben. Sein Werk. Seine Zeit.* Frankfurt: S. Fischer, 1981.

Schnitzler, Olga. *Spiegelbild der Freundschaft.* Salzburg: Residenz, 1962.

Schorske, Carl E. *Fin-de-Siècle Vienna.* New York: Knopf, 1980.

Sheirich, Richard M. "Beer-Hofmann and the 'Arabian Nights.' " *Harvard Library Bulletin* 14 (1960): 486–92.

———. "Beer-Hofmann's 'Die Historie von König David': The Unpublished Manuscripts." Ph.D. dissertation, Harvard University, 1964.

———. "*Frevel* and *der erhöhte Augenblick* in Richard Beer-Hofmann: Reflections on a Biographical Problem." *Modern Austrian Literature* 13, no. 2 (1980): 1–16.

Soergel, Albert, and Curt Hohoff. *Dichtung und Dichter der Zeit.* 2 vols. Düsseldorf: August Bagel, 1961.

Specht, Richard. "Literatur der Gegenwart." In *Ewiges Österreich,* edited by Erwin Rieger. Vienna: Manz, 1928.

Spranger, Eduard. "Der psychologische Perspektivismus im Roman." In *Zur Poetik des Romans,* edited by Volker Klotz. Darmstadt: Wissenschaftliche Buchgesellschaft, 1965.

Stanzel, Franz. "Episches Präteritum, erlebte Rede, historisches Präsens." *Deutsche Vierteljahrsschrift für Literaturwissenschaft und Geistesgeschichte* 33 (1959): 1–12.

———. *Die typischen Erzählsituationen im Roman.* Vienna, Stuttgart: Wilhelm Braumüller, 1955. [Vol. 63, Wiener Beiträge zur englischen Philologie.]

———. *Typische Formen des Romans.* Göttingen: Vandenhoeck & Ruprecht, 1964.

Steiner, George. *The Death of Tragedy.* New York: Knopf, 1961. [Condensed German version in *Tragik und Tragödie,* edited by Volkmar Sander. Darmstadt: Wissenschaftliche Buchgesellschaft. 1971.]

Sternberger, Dolf. "Sinnlichkeit um die Jahrhundertwende." In *Über den Jugendstil und andere Essays.* Hamburg: Claassen, 1956. [Also in *Jugendstil,* Darmstadt: Wissenschaftliche Buchgesellschaft, 1971.]

Sterner, Gabriele. *Jugendstil. Kunstformen zwischen Individualismus und Massengesellschaft.* Cologne: M. DuMont Schauberg, 1975.

Stümcke, Heinrich. "Von den Berliner Theatern 1904–1905." *Bühne und Welt* 7 (1904–1905): 340–45.

Thimig-Reinhardt, Helene. *Wie Max Reinhardt lebte.* Percha: R.S. Schulz, 1973.

Viering, Jürgen. "Jugendstil und Empfindsamkeit. Zu Richard Beer-Hofmanns *Der Tod Georgs.*" *Euphorion* 71 (1977): 180–94.

Vordtriede, Werner. "Gespräche mit Beer-Hofmann." *Die Neue Rundschau* 63 (1952): 122–51.

———. *Das verlassene Haus. Tagebuch aus dem amerikanischen Exil 1938–1947.* Munich, Vienna: Hanser, 1975.

Webb, Karl Eugene. *Rainer Maria Rilke and Jugendstil.* Chapel Hill, N.C.: University of North Carolina Press, 1978.

Weber, Eugene. "The Correspondence of Arthur Schnitzler and Richard Beer-Hofmann." *Modern Austrian Literature* 6, no. 3/4 (1973): 40–51.

———. "Richard Beer-Hofmann: Aufzeichungen zu *Ariadne auf Kreta* und *Ariadne auf Naxos.*" *Hofmannsthal-Blätter* 13–14 (1975): 3–14.

———. "Richard Beer-Hofmann: Briefe, Reden, Gedichte aus dem Exil." *Literatur und Kritik* 10 (1975): 469–79.

Weinhold, Ulrike. *Künstlichkeit und Kunst in der deutschsprachigen Dekadenz-Literatur.* Frankfurt, Berne: Lang, 1977.

Weinrich, Harald. "Die Semantik der kühnen Metapher." *Deutsche Vierteljahresschrift für Literaturwissenschaft und Geistesgeschichte* 37 (1963): 325–44.

Werner, Alfred. "Richard Beer-Hofmann: Double Heritage." *The American Scholar* 16 (1947): 325–34.

———. *Richard Beer-Hofmann. Sinn und Gestalt.* Vienna: H. Glanz, 1936.

Wilder, Thornton. "Mythos und Dichtung. Zu 'Jaakobs Traum' von Richard Beer-Hofmann." Translated by Herberth E. Herlitschka. *Almanach des S. Fischer Verlags* 77 (1963): 66–73.

Wildgans, Anton. *Ein Leben in Briefen.* Edited by Lilly Wildgans. 3 vols. Vienna: Wilhelm Frick, 1947.

Wunberg, Gotthard, ed. *Das junge Wien. Österreichische Literatur- und Kunstkritik 1887–1902.* 2 vols. Tübingen: Niemeyer, 1976.

Zieler, Gustav. "Der Graf von Charolais." *Das literarische Echo* 7 (1905): 655–57.

Zohn, Harry. *Wiener Juden in der deutschen Literatur.* Tel Aviv: Olamenu, 1964.

Index of Names and Titles